Martin E. P. Seligman, Ph.D.

Learned Optimism

Martin E. P. Seligman, Ph.D., professor of psychology at the University of Pennsylvania and
a past president of the American Psychological Association is a leading motivational
expert and an authority on learned helplessness. He is the director of the Positive Psychology Center at the University of Pennsylvania.
His many books include *Authentic Happiness*
and *The Optimistic Child*. Dr. Seligman's
research has been supported by the National
Institute on Mental Health, the National Institute on Aging, the National Science Foundation, the Department of Education, the
MacArthur Foundation, the Templeton Foundation, and the Guggenheim Foundation.

Learned Optimism

How to Change Your Mind and Your Life

Martin E. P. Seligman, Ph.D.

VINTAGE BOOKS
A Division of Random House, Inc.
New York

This book is dedicated with optimism about our future
to my newborn, Lara Catrina Seligman

FIRST VINTAGE BOOKS EDITION, JANUARY 2006

Vintage ISBN-10: 1-4000-7839-3
Vintage ISBN-13: 978-1-4000-7839-4

Author photograph © Kyle Cassidy ASC/Pandemon
Book design by Georgia Küng

www.vintagebooks.com

Printed in the United States of America
20 19 18 17 16 15 14 13 12

Contents

Preface to the Vintage Edition

When I first began to work on learned optimism, I thought I was working on pessimism. Like almost all researchers with a background in clinical psychology, I was accustomed to focusing on what was wrong with individuals and then on how to fix it. Looking closely at what was already right and how to make it even better did not enter my mind.

The turning point was a meeting in 1988 with Richard Pine, the person who was destined to become my literary agent, intellectual advisor, and friend. I described my work on pessimism and Richard said, "Your work is not about pessimism; it's about optimism." No one had said this to me before. As I left his office, somewhat shaken, he called out, "I pray you'll write a book about this. They make religions out of this stuff!"

I did. No religions sprouted up, but the book has sold steadily for fifteen years. And something did happen: Positive Psychology. In 1996, I was elected president of the American Psychological Association by what they tell me was the largest vote in history, thanks in part to the popularity of this book and the field of research that it spawned.

The president of the American Psychological Association is supposed to have an initiative, a theme of office, and as I looked over the modern history of psychology, I saw that Richard had given me my theme. Psychology now seemed half-baked to me. The half that was fully-baked was devoted to suffering, victims, mental illness, and trauma. Psychology had worked steadily and with considerable success for fifty years on the pathologies that disable the good life, which make life not worth living. By my count fourteen of the major mental illnesses are now treatable by psychotherapy or by medications, with two of them (panic disorder and blood and injury phobia) virtually curable. But clinical psychologists also began to find something disconcerting emerging from therapy: even on that rare occasion when therapy goes superbly and unusually well, and you help the client rid herself of depression, anxiety, and anger, happiness is not guaranteed. Emptiness is not an uncommon result. How can this be?

Curing the negatives does not produce the positives. In jargon, the correlation between sadness and happiness is not anything close to

−1.00; it is more like −0.40. Strangely one can both be happy and sad (although not in the same instant). Women, in fact, being more emotionally labile, are both happier and sadder than men. The skills of becoming happy turn out to be almost entirely different from the skills of not being sad, not being anxious, or not being angry. Psychology had told us a great deal about pathology, about suffering, about victims, and how to acquire the skills to combat sadness and anxiety. But discovering the skills of becoming happier had been relegated to amusement parks, Hollywood, and beer commercials. Science had played no role.

When you lie in bed at night and contemplate your life and the lives of the people you love, you are usually thinking about how to go from +2 to +6, not how to go from −5 to −2. But at its best, psychology had only told us how to relieve misery, not how to find what is best in life and live it accordingly. This was the unbaked half that would become Positive Psychology.

Learned Optimism is the foundation of my thinking about Positive Psychology, and it is the first of the triptych that leads there. In 1996, I published *The Optimistic Child,* which applies the knowledge and the skills you will read about in this volume to teenagers and schoolchildren. In 2002, I published the third book of the series: *Authentic Happiness.* This book sets forward a larger theory about the positive side of life: "happiness" is a scientifically unwieldy notion, but there are three different forms of it you can pursue. For the "Pleasant Life," you aim to have as much positive emotion as possible and learn the skills to amplify positive emotion. For the "Engaged Life," you identify your highest strengths and talents and recraft your life to use them as much as you can in work, love, friendship, parenting, and leisure. For the "Meaningful Life," you use your highest strengths and talents to belong to and serve something you believe is larger than the self.

Learned Optimism can set you on the path to any or all three forms of happiness. The skills you will read about here can increase the duration and intensity of your positive emotions. These skills can enable you to use your highest strengths and talents more effectively. Finally, optimism is invaluable for the meaningful life. With a firm belief in a positive future you can throw yourself into the service of that which is larger than you are.

Wynnewood, Pennsylvania
July 15, 2005

Introduction to the Second Edition

by Martin E. P. Seligman

I have spent my entire professional life working on helplessness and ways to enlarge personal control. *Learned Optimism* was the first of a quartet of books to explore this theme for the general reader.[1] Six years have passed since the first paperback edition of this book was published, so I wanted to bring my new readers up to date with news about a crucial development since the first edition—the prevention of depression by programs of learned optimism.

As you will see in Chapters 4 and 5, our nation, and most of the developed world, is experiencing an unprecedented epidemic of depression—particularly among young people. Why is it that in a nation that has more money, more power, more records, more books, and more education, that depression should be so much more prevalent than it was when the nation was less prosperous and less powerful?

Three forces have now converged, and I want to emphasize the third because it is the most surprising and least congenial. The first two forces

---

[1] The members of the quartet are: a) Seligman, M. E. P. (1991). *Learned Optimism* (paperback edition): Pocket Books (Simon & Schuster, Inc.); b) Peterson, C., Maier, S., and Seligman, M. E. P. (1993). *Learned Helplessness: A Theory for the Age of Personal Control.* New York: Oxford University Press; c) Seligman, M. E. P. (1994). *What You Can Change and What You Can't.* New York: Alfred A. Knopf; and d) Seligman, M. E. P., Reivich, K., Jaycox, L., and Gillham, J. (1995). *The Optimistic Child.* New York: Houghton Mifflin.

are discussed in the concluding chapter of this book: briefly, the first is that, in general, depression is a disorder of the "I," failing in your own eyes relative to your goals. In a society in which individualism is becoming rampant, people more and more believe that they are the center of the world. Such a belief system makes individual failure almost inconsolable.

Individual failure used to be buffered by the second force, the large "we." When our grandparents failed, they had comfortable spiritual furniture to rest in. They had, for the most part, their relationship to God, their relationship to a nation they loved, their relationship to a community and a large extended family. Faith in God, community, nation, and the large extended family have all eroded in the last forty years, and the spiritual furniture that we used to sit in has become threadbare.

But it is the third force, the self-esteem movement, that I want to emphasize. I have five children who range in age from four to twenty-eight. So I have had the privilege of reading children's books every night for a whole generation, and I have seen a sea change in children's books over the last twenty-five years. Twenty-five years ago (as it was during the time of the Great Depression), the emblematic children's book was *The Little Engine That Could*. It is about doing well in the world, about persisting and therefore overcoming obstacles. Now many children's books are about feeling good, having high self-esteem, and exuding confidence.

This is a manifestation of the self-esteem movement, a movement which started, not surprisingly, in California in the 1960s. In 1990, the California legislature sponsored a report that suggested that self-esteem be taught in every classroom as a "vaccine" against social ills, such as drug addiction, suicide, welfare dependency, teenage pregnancy, and depression (Toward a State of Esteem, 1990).[2] The self-esteem movement is a movement with teeth; this is the movement underlying the demise of IQ testing, lest children who score low feel badly about themselves. This is the movement underlying the end of tracking in our public schools, lest kids of lower tracks feel badly about themselves. This is the movement that has made *competition* a dirty word. This is a movement that has led to less plain old hard work. Shirley McLaine suggested to President Clinton that he create a cabinet-level Secretary of Self-Esteem.

I am not against self-esteem, but I believe that self-esteem is just a meter that reads out the state of the system. It is not an end in itself. When you are doing well in school or work, when you are doing well with the people you love, when you are doing well in play, the meter will

[2]Sacramento: California Department of Education

register high. When you are doing badly, it will register low. I have scoured the self-esteem literature looking for the causality as opposed to correlation, looking for any evidence that high self-esteem among youngsters *causes* better grades, more popularity, less teenage pregnancy, less dependence on welfare, as the California report contends. There is a simple experimental design which perfectly separates cause from correlation: Take a group of children in September, all the B students, for instance; measure their self-esteem and then come back in June. If self-esteem *causes* grades to change, the B students with high self-esteem will tend to go up toward A's, and the B students with low self-esteem will go down toward C's. There is nothing of this sort to be found in the literature. Self-esteem seems only to be a symptom, a correlate, of how well a person is doing in the world.

Until January 1996, I believed that self-esteem was merely a meter with little, if any, causal efficacy. The lead article in the *Psychological Review* convinced me that I was wrong, and that self-esteem is causal: Roy Baumeister and his colleagues (1996)[3] reviewed the literature on genocidal killers, on hit men, on gang leaders, and on violent criminals. They argued that these perpetrators have high self-esteem, and that their unwarranted self-esteem causes violence. Baumeister's work suggests that if you teach unwarrantedly high self-esteem to children, problems will ensue. A sub-group of these children will also have a mean streak in them. When these children confront the real world, and it tells them they are not as great as they have been taught, they will lash out with violence. So it is possible that the twin epidemics among young people in the United States today, depression and violence, both come from this misbegotten concern: valuing how our young people feel about themselves more highly than how we value how well they are doing in the world.

If boosting self-esteem is not the answer to curbing the epidemic of depression, what can be done? Since the first edition of *Learned Optimism* was published, my colleagues[4] and I have been doing two sets of projects at the University of Pennsylvania: one with young adults, Penn freshman; and the second with children right before puberty.

[3]Baumeister, Roy F., Smart, Laura, Boden, Joseph M. (1996). "Relation of Threatened Egotism to Violence and Aggression: The Dark Side of High Self-Esteem." *Psychological Review. 103,* pp. 5–33.

[4]My colleagues doing the project with Penn undergraduates are Mr. Peter Shulman, and Drs. Rob DeRubeis, Steve Hollon, Art Freeman, and Karen Reivich. This work has been supported by the Prevention Research Branch of the National Institute of Mental Health.

Our logic is to take young people at risk for depression, teach them the skills of learned optimism that you will read about in Chapters 11–13 of this book, and ask if we can thereby prevent depressive and anxiety disorders. Starting in the spring of 1991, when students accepted their admissions to the University of Pennsylvania, they then got a letter from me by return mail. It asked them to take a questionnaire, a version of which is included in Chapter 3. Most of them sent the questionnaire back filled out. We scored it, and then students in the bottom quarter of pessimism got another letter from me saying that when they arrived in September, we were going to be running workshops about how to cope with this unfamiliar new environment; if they were willing, they would be randomized either into a control group or into one of these workshops. So for the last several years, the most pessimistic quarter of Penn's freshman class has been in these workshops, or has been in our assessment-only control group.

We teach two sets of skills in the workshop, conducted in groups of ten by Penn's talented clinical psychology graduate students: We teach people the skills detailed in Chapters 11–13, and an additional set of behavioral skills, including assertive training, graded task assignment, and stress management.

After eighteen months of follow-up, I can report our first results with 119 people in the control group, and 106 who took the 16-hour learned-optimism workshop. Every six months each person had a complete diagnostic interview, and we looked at moderate and severe episodes of depression and anxiety. Thirty-two percent of the students in the control group had a moderate to severe episode of depression, in contrast to 22 percent of the group that was in the preventive workshop. Similar results were obtained for generalized anxiety disorder: 15 percent of the controls had an episode of generalized anxiety disorder, versus only 7 percent of people who took the workshop. We also found that it was the change from pessimism to optimism that caused the prevention of depression and anxiety.

My colleagues and I have recently launched the parallel learned-optimism program with schoolchildren of various ages.[5] Five studies teach ten- to twelve-year-old children the cognitive and behavioral anti-depression skills from Chapters 11–13 in this book. In these studies we select children for two risk factors: one is mild symptoms of depression, and the

[5]My colleagues on these projects are Drs Karen Reivich, Jane Gillham, Rob De-Rubeis, Lisa Jaycox, Steve Hollon, Andrew Shatte, and Mr. Peter Schulman. We are supported by the NIMH Prevention Research Branch.

other is their parents' fighting a lot. Each of these factors predicts depression in young children. If a child scores high on either of these, the child is then eligible for our training program. Anti-depression skills are taught to groups of ten children after school, using skits, cartoons, role playing, and lots of refreshments. (You will find the methods outlined in Chapter 13, and detailed in *The Optimistic Child.*)

I will tell you about only one study here, the one with longest follow-up. It was done in Abington Township, near Philadelphia (Jaycox, Reivich, Gillham and Seligman, 1994; Gillham, Reivich, Jaycox, and Seligman, 1996).[6] The findings of the Abington study revealed the following:

1. Over the two-year follow-up, the overall percentage of children who show symptoms in the moderate to severe range of depression is shockingly high (between 20 percent and 45 percent).

2. The children who took the optimism workshop had only about half the rate of moderate or severe depressive symptoms as the control group.

3. Immediately after the workshop, the untreated group had significantly more depressive symptoms than the group that took the optimism workshop.

4. The benefits of learned optimism grow over time. As the children in the control group went through puberty, got their first social and sexual rejections, and moved from top dog in middle school to the bottom of the heap in high school, they got more and more depressed when compared to children in the optimism group. At twenty-four months forty-four percent of them had moderate to severe depressive symptoms, whereas only twenty two percent of the optimism group have moderate or severe symptoms.

Teaching children learned optimism before puberty, but late enough in childhood so that they are metacognitive (capable of thinking about thinking), is a fruitful strategy. When the immunized children use these skills to cope with the first rejections of puberty, they get better and better at using these skills. Our analysis shows that the change from pessimism to optimism is at least partly responsible for the prevention of depressive symptoms.

[6]Gillham, J., Reivich, K., Jaycox, L., Seligman, M. E. P. (1995). Prevention of depressive symptoms in schoolchildren: Two-year follow-up. *Psychological Science, 6*(6), pp. 343–51. Jaycox, L., Reivich, K., Gillham, J., & Seligman, M. E. P. (1994). "Prevention of Depressive Symptoms in Schoolchildren." *Behavior Research and Therapy, 32,* pp. 801–16.

As you read this book, you will see that there is an epidemic of depression among adults and among children in the United States today. As Chapters 6–10 document, depression is not just about mental suffering; it is also about lowered productivity and worsened physical health. If this epidemic continues, I believe that America's place in the world will be in jeopardy. America will lose its economic place to less pessimistic nations than ours, and this pessimism will sap our will to bring about social justice in our own country.

This problem will not be ended by Prozac. We are not going to give anti-depressant drugs to an entire generation. Anti-depressant drugs are ineffective before puberty, and there are grave moral dangers to making an entire generation dependent on drugs for their mood and their productivity. We are also not going to do therapy with an entire generation, because there are simply not enough good therapists to go around.

What we can do is to take the skills that you will learn in this book and translate them into an educative mode. In the schools and homes of America, we can teach them to all young people at risk for depression, thereby overcoming depression in our own lives, and in the lives of our children.

July 31, 1997
Wynnewood, Pennsylvania

yes is a world

& in this world of

yes live

(skilfully curled)

all worlds

e. e. cummings
"love is a place"
No Thanks (1935)

Part One

The Quest

1

Two Ways of Looking at Life

THE FATHER is looking down into the crib at his sleeping newborn daughter, just home from the hospital. His heart is overflowing with awe and gratitude for the beauty of her, the perfection.

The baby opens her eyes and stares straight up.

The father calls her name, expecting that she will turn her head and look at him. Her eyes don't move.

He picks up a furry little toy attached to the rail of the bassinet and shakes it, ringing the bell it contains. The baby's eyes don't move.

His heart has begun to beat rapidly. He finds his wife in their bedroom and tells her what just happened. "She doesn't seem to respond to noise at all," he says. "It's as if she can't hear."

"I'm sure she's all right," the wife says, pulling her dressing gown around her. Together they go into the nursery.

She calls the baby's name, jingles the bell, claps her hands. Then she picks up the baby, who immediately perks up, wiggling and cooing.

"My God," the father says. "She's deaf."

"No she's not," the mother says. "I mean, it's too soon to say a thing like that. Look, she's brand-new. Her eyes don't even focus yet."

"But there wasn't the slightest movement, even when you clapped as hard as you could."

The mother takes a book from the shelf. "Let's read what's in the baby book," she says. She looks up "hearing" and reads out loud: " 'Don't be alarmed if your newborn fails to startle at loud noises or fails to orient toward sound. The startle reflex and attention to sound often take some time to develop. Your pediatrician can test your child's hearing neuro-logically.'

"There," the mother says. "Doesn't that make you feel better?"

"Not much," the father says. "It doesn't even mention the other pos-sibility, that the baby is deaf. And all I know is that my baby doesn't hear a thing. I've got the worst feeling about this. Maybe it's because my grand-father was deaf. If that beautiful baby is deaf and it's my fault, I'll never forgive myself."

"Hey, wait a minute," says the wife. "You're going off the deep end. We'll call the pediatrician first thing Monday. In the meantime, cheer up. Here, hold the baby while I fix her blanket. It's all pulled out."

The father takes the baby but gives her back to his wife as soon as he can. All weekend he finds himself unable to open his briefcase and prepare for next week's work. He follows his wife around the house, ruminating about the baby's hearing and about the way deafness would ruin her life. He imagines only the worst: no hearing, no development of language, his beautiful child cut off from the social world, locked in soundless isolation. By Sunday night he has sunk into despair.

The mother leaves a message with the pediatrician's answering service asking for an early appointment Monday. She spends the weekend doing her exercises, reading, and trying to calm her husband.

The pediatrician's tests are reassuring, but the father's spirits remain low. Not until a week later, when the baby shows her first startle, to the backfire of a passing truck, does he begin to recover and enjoy his new daughter again.

THIS FATHER and mother have two different ways of looking at the world. Whenever something bad happens to him—a tax audit, a marital squabble, even a frown from his employer—he imagines the worst: bankruptcy and jail, divorce, dismissal. He is prone to depression; he has long bouts of listlessness; his health suffers. She, on the other hand, sees bad events in their least threatening light. To her, they are temporary and surmountable, challenges to be overcome. After a reversal, she comes back quickly, soon regaining her energy. Her health is excellent.

The optimists and the pessimists: I have been studying them for the past twenty-five years. The defining characteristic of pessimists is that they tend to believe bad events will last a long time, will undermine everything they do, and are their own fault. The optimists, who are confronted with the same hard knocks of this world, think about misfortune in the opposite way. They tend to believe defeat is just a temporary setback, that its causes are confined to this one case. The optimists believe defeat is not their fault: Circumstances, bad luck, or other people brought it about. Such people are unfazed by defeat. Confronted by a bad situation, they perceive it as a challenge and try harder.

These two habits of thinking about causes have consequences. Literally hundreds of studies show that pessimists give up more easily and get depressed more often. These experiments also show that optimists do much better in school and college, at work and on the playing field. They regularly exceed the predictions of aptitude tests. When optimists run for office, they are more apt to be elected than pessimists are. Their health is unusually good. They age well, much freer than most of us from the usual physical ills of middle age. Evidence suggests they may even live longer.

I have seen that, in tests of hundreds of thousands of people, a surprisingly large number will be found to be deep-dyed pessimists and another large portion will have serious, debilitating tendencies toward pessimism. I have learned that it is not always easy to know if you are a pessimist, and that far more people than realize it are living in this shadow. Tests reveal traces of pessimism in the speech of people who would never think of themselves as pessimists; they also show that these traces are sensed by others, who react negatively to the speakers.

A pessimistic attitude may seem so deeply rooted as to be permanent. I have found, however, that pessimism is escapable. Pessimists can in fact learn to be optimists, and not through mindless devices like whistling a happy tune or mouthing platitudes ("Every day, in every way, I'm getting better and better"), but by learning a new set of cognitive skills. Far from being the creations of boosters or of the popular media, these skills were discovered in the laboratories and clinics of leading psychologists and psychiatrists and then rigorously validated.

This book will help you discover your own pessimistic tendencies, if you have them, or those of people you care for. It will also introduce you to the techniques that have helped thousands of people undo lifelong habits of pessimism and its extension, depression. It will give you the choice of looking at your setbacks in a new light.

The Unclaimed Territory

AT THE CORE of the phenomenon of pessimism is another phenomenon—that of helplessness. Helplessness is the state of affairs in which nothing you choose to do affects what happens to you. For example, if I promise you one thousand dollars to turn to page 104, you will probably choose to do so, and you will succeed. If, however, I promise you one thousand dollars to contract the pupil of your eye, using only willpower, you may choose to do it, but that won't matter. You are helpless to contract your pupil. Page turning is under your voluntary control; the muscles that change your pupillary size are not.

Life begins in utter helplessness. The newborn infant cannot help himself, for he* is almost entirely a creature of reflex. When he cries, his mother comes, although this does not mean that he *controls* his mother's coming. His crying is a mere reflex reaction to pain and discomfort. He has no choice about whether he cries. Only one set of muscles in the newborn seems to be under even the barest voluntary control: the set involved in sucking. The last years of a normal life are sometimes ones of sinking back into helplessness. We may lose the ability to walk. Sadly, we may lose the mastery over our bowels and bladder that we won in our second year of life. We may lose our ability to find the word we want. Then we may lose speech itself, and even the ability to direct our thoughts.

The long period between infancy and our last years is a process of emerging from helplessness and gaining personal control. Personal control means the ability to change things by one's voluntary actions; it is the opposite of helplessness. In the first three or four months of an infant's life some rudimentary arm and leg motions come under voluntary control. The flailing of his arms refines into reaching. Then, to his parents' dismay, crying becomes voluntary: The infant can now bawl whenever he wants his mother. He badly overuses this new power, until it stops working. The first year ends with two miracles of voluntary control: the first steps and the first words. If all goes well, if the growing child's mental and physical needs are at least minimally met, the years that follow are ones of diminishing helplessness and of growing personal control.

Many things in life are beyond our control—our eye color, our race, the drought in the Midwest. But there is a vast, unclaimed territory of actions over which we can take control—or cede control to others or to fate. These actions involve the way we lead our lives, how we deal with other people, how we earn our living—all the aspects of existence in which we normally have some degree of choice.

The way we think about this realm of life can actually diminish or enlarge

---

* Throughout this book, when the pronoun "he" is used, as it is in this sentence, simply to mean a human being, the reader is asked to read it as "he or she." To use "he or she" in every instance would be awkward and distracting, and at the moment there seems to be no workable alternative, although in due time the ever-vigorous English language will doubtless evolve one.

the control we have over it. Our thoughts are not merely reactions to events; they change what ensues. For example, if we think we are helpless to make a difference in what our children become, we will be paralyzed when dealing with this facet of our lives. The very thought "Nothing I do matters" prevents us from acting. And so we cede control to our children's peers and teachers, and to circumstance. When we overestimate our helplessness, other forces will take control and shape our children's future.

Later in this book we will see that judiciously employed, mild pessimism has its uses. But twenty-five years of study has convinced me that if we *habitually* believe, as does the pessimist, that misfortune is our fault, is enduring, and will undermine everything we do, more of it will befall us than if we believe otherwise. I am also convinced that if we are in the grip of this view, we will get depressed easily, we will accomplish less than our potential, and we will even get physically sick more often. Pessimistic prophecies are self-fulfilling.

A poignant example is the case of a young woman I knew, a student at a university where I once taught. For three years her advisor, a professor of English literature, had been extremely helpful, almost affectionate. His backing, along with her high grades, had won her a scholarship to study at Oxford for her junior year. When she returned from England, her main interest had shifted from Dickens, her advisor's specialty, to earlier British novelists, particularly Jane Austen, the specialty of one of his colleagues. Her advisor tried to persuade her to do her senior paper on Dickens, but seemed to accept without resentment her decision to work on Austen and agreed to continue as her co-advisor.

Three days before her oral examination, the original advisor sent a note to the examining committee accusing the young woman of plagiarism in her senior thesis. Her crime, he said, was failing to give credit to two scholarly sources for her statements about Jane Austen's adolescence, in effect taking credit for those perceptions herself. Plagiarism is the gravest of academic sins, and the young woman's whole future—her fellowship to graduate school, even graduation itself—was threatened.

When she looked at the passages the professor said she had failed to credit, she found that both had come from the same source—the professor himself. She had gotten them during a casual conversation with him, in which he had spoken of the perceptions as just his own thoughts on the matter; he had never mentioned the published sources from which he had obtained them. The young woman had been sandbagged by a mentor jealous of losing her.

Many people would have reacted with fury at the professor. Not Elizabeth. Her habit of pessimistic thinking took over. To the committee, she was certain, she would appear guilty. And, she told herself, there was no way she could prove otherwise. It would be her word against his, and he was a professor. Instead of defending herself, she collapsed inwardly, looking at every aspect of the situation in the worst possible light. It was all her own fault, she told herself. It really didn't matter that the professor had gotten the ideas from someone else. The main thing was that she had "stolen" the ideas, since she had failed to credit the professor. She had cheated, she believed; she *was* a cheat, and she probably always had been.

It may seem incredible that she could blame herself when she was so obviously innocent. But careful research shows that people with pessimistic habits of thinking can transform mere setbacks into disasters. One way they do this is by converting their own innocence into guilt. Elizabeth dredged up memories that seemed to her to confirm her extreme verdict: the time in seventh grade when she had copied test answers from another girl's paper; the time in England when she had failed to correct the misimpression of some English friends that she came from a wealthy family. And now this act of "cheating" in the writing of her thesis. She stood silent at her hearing before the examining committee and was denied her degree.

This story does not have a happy ending. With the washout of her plans, her life was ruined. For the past ten years she has worked as a salesgirl. She has few aspirations. She no longer writes, or even reads literature. She is still paying for what she considered her crime.

There was no crime, only a common human frailty: a pessimistic habit of thinking. If she had said to herself, "I was robbed. The jealous bastard set me up," she would have risen to her own defense and told her story. The professor's dismissal from an earlier teaching job for doing the same thing might have emerged. She would have graduated with high honors— if only she had had different habits of thinking about the bad events in her life.

Habits of thinking need not be forever. One of the most significant findings in psychology in the last twenty years is that individuals can choose the way they think.

The science of psychology has not always cared about individual styles of thinking, or about individual human action or the individual at all. Quite the opposite. When I was a graduate student in psychology, twenty-five years ago, dilemmas such as the one I've just described were not explained the way they are today. At that time people were assumed to be products of their environment. The prevailing explanation of human action was that people were "pushed" by their internal drives or "pulled" by external events. Though the details of the pushing and pulling depended on the particular theory you happened to hold, in outline all the fashionable theories agreed on this proposition. The Freudians held that unresolved childhood conflicts drove adult behavior. The followers of B. F. Skinner held that behavior was repeated only when reinforced externally. The ethologists held that behavior resulted from fixed action patterns determined by our genes, and the behaviorist followers of Clark Hull held that we were goaded into action by the need to reduce drives and satisfy biological needs.

Starting around 1965, the favored explanations began to change radically. A person's environment was considered less and less important in causing his behavior. Four different lines of thought converged on the proposition that self-direction, rather than outside forces, could explain human action.

- In 1959, Noam Chomsky wrote a devastating critique of B. F. Skinner's seminal book *Verbal Behavior*. Chomsky argued that language in particular and human action in general were not the result of strengthening past verbal habits by reinforcement. The essence of language, he said, is that it is generative: Sentences never said or heard before (such as "There's a purple Gila monster sitting on your lap") could nevertheless be understood immediately.
- Jean Piaget, the great Swiss investigator of how children develop, had persuaded most of the world—the Americans last—that the unfolding mind of the individual child could be scientifically studied.
- In 1967, with the publication of Ulric Neisser's *Cognitive Psychology*, a new field captured the imagination of the young experimental psychologists fleeing the dogmas of behaviorism. Cognitive psychology argued that the workings of the human mind could be measured and their consequences studied by using the information-processing activities of computers as a model.
- Behavioral psychologists found that animal and human behavior was inadequately explained by drives and needs and began to invoke the cognitions—the thoughts—of the individual to explain complex behavior.

So the dominant theories in psychology shifted focus in the late 1960s from the power of the environment to individual expectation, preference, choice, decision, control, and helplessness.

This fundamental change in the field of psychology is intimately related to a fundamental change in our own psychology. For the first time in history—because of technology and mass production and distribution, and for other reasons—large numbers of people are able to have a significant measure of choice and therefore of personal control over their lives. Not the least of these choices concerns our own habits of thinking. By and large, people have welcomed that control. We belong to a society that grants to its individual members powers they have never had before, a society that takes individuals' pleasures and pains very seriously, that exalts the self and deems personal fulfillment a legitimate goal, an almost sacred right.

Depression

WITH THESE FREEDOMS have come perils. For the age of the self is also the age of that phenomenon so closely linked to pessimism: depression, the ultimate expression of pessimism. We are in the middle of an epidemic of depression, one with consequences that, through suicide, takes as many lives as the AIDS epidemic and is more widespread. Severe depression is ten times more prevalent today than it was fifty years ago. It assaults women twice as often as men, and it now strikes a full decade earlier in life on average than it did a generation ago.

Until recently there were only two accepted ways of thinking about depression: the psychoanalytic and the biomedical. The psychoanalytic view is based on a paper that Sigmund Freud wrote almost seventy-five years ago. Freud's speculations were built on very little observation and a very free use of imagination. He claimed that depression was anger turned against the self: The depressive disparages himself as worthless and wants to kill himself. The depressive, said Freud, learns to hate himself at his mother's knee. One day early in the child's life, the mother inevitably abandons the child, at least as the child sees it. (She goes off on vacation or stays out too late or has another child.) In some children this produces rage, but because the mother is too beloved to be the target of rage, the child turns it upon a more acceptable target—himself (or, more precisely, that part of himself that identifies with his mother). This becomes a destructive habit. Now, whenever abandonment strikes again, he rages against himself rather than against the real perpetrator of the current loss. Self-loathing, depression as a reaction to loss, suicide—all follow neatly.

In Freud's view, you do not get rid of depression easily. Depression is a product of childhood conflicts that remain unresolved beneath frozen layers of defense. Only by breaking through those layers, Freud believed, and eventually resolving the ancient conflicts, can the tendency to depression wane. Year after year of psychoanalysis—the therapist-guided struggle

to gain insight into the childhood origins of turning rage upon the self—
is Freud's prescription for depression.

For all its hold over the American (particularly the Manhattan) imagination, I have to say that this view is preposterous. It dooms its victim to
years of one-way conversation about the murky, distant past in order to
overcome a problem that usually would have gone away by itself in a matter
of months. In more than 90 percent of cases, depression is episodic: It
comes and then it goes. The episodes last between three and twelve months.
Although many thousands of patients have had hundreds of thousands of
sessions, psychoanalytic therapy has not been demonstrated to work for
depression.

Worse, it blames the victim. Psychoanalytic theory argues that because
of character flaws, the victim brings depression upon himself. He *wants* to
be depressed. He is motivated by the drive for self-punishment to spend
endless days in misery, and to do away with himself if he can.

I do not mean this critique as a general indictment of Freudian thinking.
Freud was a great liberator. In his early work on hysteria—physical losses
like paralysis with no physical cause—he dared to examine human sexuality
and confront its darker aspects. However, his success in using the underside
of sexuality to explain hysteria gave rise to a formula he used for the rest
of his life. All mental suffering became a transmutation of some vile part
of us, and to Freud the vile parts were us at our most basic and universal.
This implausible premise, insulting as it is to human nature, began an
epoch in which anything can be said:

You want to have sex with your mother.
You want to kill your father.
You harbor fantasies that your newborn baby might die—because you
    want him to die.
You want to spend your days in endless misery.
Your most loathsome, inner secrets are what is most basic to you.

Used in this manner, words lose their connection with reality; they become detached from emotion and from the common, recognized experience
of mankind. Try saying any of these things to an armed Sicilian.

The other, more acceptable view of depression is biomedical. Depression, say the biological psychiatrists, is an illness of the body. It comes
from an inherited biochemical defect—sited, perhaps, on an arm of chro-
mosome number 11—that produces an imbalance of brain chemicals. Biological psychiatrists treat depression with drugs or electroconvulsive

therapy ("shock treatment"). These are quick, inexpensive, and moderately effective remedies.

The biomedical view, unlike the psychoanalytic, is partly right. Some depressions seem to be the result of a poorly functioning brain, and to some extent they are inherited. Many depressions will respond (sluggishly) to antidepressant drugs and (briskly) to electroconvulsive therapy. But these victories are only partial and are a mixed blessing. Antidepressant drugs and high electrical current passing through the brain can have nasty side effects, which a large minority of depressed people cannot tolerate. Further, the biomedical view glibly generalizes from the small number of hard-core, inherited depressions that usually respond to drugs to the much more common, everyday depressions that afflict so many lives. A very considerable proportion of depressed people have not inherited depression from their parents, and there is no evidence that milder depression can be relieved by taking drugs.

Worst of all, the biomedical approach makes patients out of essentially normal people and makes them dependent on outside forces—pills dispensed by a benevolent physician. Antidepressant drugs are not addicting in the usual sense; the patient does not crave them when they are withdrawn. Rather, when the successfully treated patient stops taking his drugs, the depression often returns. The effectively drugged patient cannot credit himself for carving out his happiness and his ability to function with a semblance of normality; he must credit the pills. The antidepressant drugs are as good an example of our overmedicated society as the use of tranquilizers to bring peace of mind or hallucinogens to see beauty. In each case, emotional problems that could be solved by one's own skills and actions are turned over to an outside agent for solution.

WHAT IF the great majority of depressions are much simpler than the biological psychiatrists and the psychoanalysts believe?

- What if depression is not something you are motivated to bring upon yourself but something that just descends upon you?
- What if depression is not an illness but a severe low mood?
- What if you are not a prisoner of past conflicts in the way you react? What if depression is in fact set off by present troubles?
- What if you are not a prisoner of your genes or your brain chemistry, either?
- What if depression arises from mistaken inferences we make from

the tragedies and setbacks we all experience over the course of a life?

- What if depression occurs merely when we harbor pessimistic beliefs about the causes of our setbacks?
- What if we can unlearn pessimism and acquire the skills of looking at setbacks optimistically?

Achievement

THE TRADITIONAL VIEW of achievement, like the traditional view of depression, needs overhauling. Our workplaces and our schools operate on the conventional assumption that success results from a combination of talent and desire. When failure occurs, it is because either talent or desire is missing. But failure also can occur when talent and desire are present in abundance but optimism is missing.

From nursery school on, there are frequent tests of talent—IQ tests, SATs, MCATs, and so on—tests that many parents consider so important to their child's future that they pay to have the child instructed in the art of taking them. At every stage in life, these tests allegedly separate the competent from the less competent. While talent has proved to be roughly measurable, it has turned out to be depressingly hard to increase. Cram courses for SATs can raise pupils' scores somewhat; they leave untouched the true level of talent.

Desire is another matter; it can be boosted all too easily. Preachers inflame desire for salvation to white-hot in an hour or two. Clever advertising creates desire in a moment where none existed before. Seminars can hike motivation and leave employees pumped-up and exuberant. Yet all these ardors are ephemeral. Burning desire for salvation wanes without constant fanning; the fancy for one product is forgotten in minutes or is replaced by a new fancy. Pumping-up seminars work for a few days or weeks, then more pumping up is needed.

BUT WHAT IF the traditional view of the components of success is wrong?

- What if there is a third factor—optimism or pessimism—that matters as much as talent or desire?
- What if you can have all the talent and desire necessary—yet, if you are a pessimist, still fail?

- What if optimists do better at school, at work, and on the playing field?
- What if optimism is a learned skill, one that can be *permanently* acquired?
- What if we can instill this skill in our children?

Health

THE TRADITIONAL VIEW of health turns out to be as flawed as the traditional view of talent. Optimism and pessimism affect health itself, almost as clearly as do physical factors.

Most people assume that physical health is a wholly physical matter and that it is determined by constitution, health habits, and how completely you avoid germs. They believe that for the most part your constitution is the result of your genes, although you can enhance it with the right eating habits, with vigorous exercise, by avoiding cholesterol of the bad sort, by having regular checkups, by wearing seat belts. You can avoid illness by inoculation, rigorous hygiene, safe sex, staying away from people with colds, brushing your teeth three times a day, and the like. When someone's health fails, therefore, it must be because he had a weak constitution, had poor health habits, or came across too many germs.

This conventional view omits a major determinant of health—our own cognitions. Our physical health is something over which we can have far greater personal control than we probably suspect. For example:

- The way we think, especially about health, changes our health.
- Optimists catch fewer infectious diseases than pessimists do.
- Optimists have better health habits than pessimists do.
- Our immune system may work better when we are optimistic.
- Evidence suggests that optimists live longer than pessimists.

DEPRESSION, achievement, and physical health are three of the most obvious applications of learned optimism. But there is also the potential for a new understanding of yourself.

By the end of this book, you will know how pessimistic or optimistic you are, and you will be able to measure your spouse's and children's optimism, if you wish. You will even be able to measure how pessimistic you used to be. You will know much more about why you get depressed—

suffer from the blues or fall into really serious despair—and what maintains your depression. You will understand more about the times you have failed although you had the talent and desired the goal very much. You will also have learned a new set of skills to stop depression and prevent its return. You can choose to use these skills when you need them to help in your daily life. Evidence is now accumulating that they will improve your health. Further, you'll be able to share these skills with people you care about.

Most significantly, you will also gain an understanding of the new science of personal control.

Learned optimism is not a rediscovery of the "power of positive thinking." The skills of optimism do not emerge from the pink Sunday-school world of happy events. They do not consist in learning to say positive things to yourself. We have found over the years that positive statements you make to yourself have little if any effect. What *is* crucial is what you think when you fail, using the power of "non-negative thinking." Changing the destructive things you say to yourself when you experience the setbacks that life deals all of us is the central skill of optimism.

MOST PSYCHOLOGISTS spend their lives working within traditional categories of problems: depression, achievement, health, political upsets, parenting, business organizations, and the like. I have spent my life trying to create a new category, which cuts across many of the traditional ones. I see events as successes or failures of personal control.

Viewing things this way makes the world look quite different. Take an apparently unrelated collection of events: depression and suicide becoming commonplace; a society elevating personal fulfillment to a right; the race going not to the swift but to the self-confident; people suffering chronic illness frighteningly early in life and dying before their time; intelligent, devoted parents producing fragile, spoiled children; a therapy curing depression just by changing conscious thinking. Where others would see this mélange of success and failure, suffering and triumph, as absurd and puzzling, I see it as all of a piece. This book, for better or worse, follows my lines of sight.

We begin with the theory of personal control. I will introduce to you two principal concepts: learned helplessness and explanatory style. They are intimately related.

Learned helplessness is the giving-up reaction, the quitting response that follows from the belief that whatever you do doesn't matter. *Explanatory style* is the manner in which you habitually explain to yourself why events happen. It is the great modulator of learned helplessness. An optimistic explanatory style stops helplessness, whereas a pessimistic explanatory style spreads helplessness. Your way of explaining events to yourself determines how helpless you can become, or how energized, when you encounter the everyday setbacks as well as momentous defeats. I think of your explanatory style as reflecting "the word in your heart."

Each of us carries a word in his heart, a "no" or a "yes." You probably don't know intuitively which word lives there, but you can learn, with a fair degree of accuracy, which it is. Soon you will test yourself and discover your own level of optimism or pessimism.

Optimism has an important place in some, though not all, realms of your life. It is not a panacea. But it can protect you against depression; it can raise your level of achievement; it can enhance your physical well-being; it is a far more pleasant mental state to be in. Pessimism, on the other hand, also has its proper place, and you will find out more about its redeeming aspect later in the book.

If the tests indicate that you are a pessimist, that's not the end of the matter. Unlike many personal qualities, basic pessimism is not fixed and unchangeable. You can learn a set of skills that free you from the tyranny of pessimism and allow you to use optimism when you choose. These skills are not mindlessly simple to acquire, but they can be mastered. The first step is to discover the word in your heart. Not coincidentally, that is also the initial step toward a new understanding of the human mind, one that has unfolded over the past quarter-century—an understanding of how an individual's sense of personal control determines his fate.

2

Learning to Be Helpless

BY THE TIME I was thirteen, I had figured something out: Whenever my parents sent me to sleep over at my best friend Jeffrey's house, that meant there was real trouble at home. The last time it had happened, I found out later that my mother had had a hysterectomy. This time I sensed my father was in trouble. Lately he had been acting strange. Usually he was calm and steady, just what I thought a father should be. Now he was often emotional, sometimes angry, sometimes weepy.

Driving me over to Jeffrey's that evening, through the darkening streets of residential Albany, New York, he suddenly drew a sharp breath, then pulled the car over to the curb. We sat there together silently, and finally he told me that for a minute or two he had lost all feeling on the left side of his body. I could detect the fear in his voice and I was terrified.

He was only forty-nine, at the height of his powers. A product of the Great Depression, he had gone from outstanding achievement in law school to a secure civil-service job rather than risk trying for something that might pay better. Recently, he had decided to make the first bold move of his life: He was going to run for high office in the State of New York. I was enormously proud of him.

I was also going through a crisis, the first of my young life. That fall my father had taken me out of public school, where I'd been content, and put me in a private military academy, because it was the only school in Albany that sent bright youngsters to good colleges. I soon realized I was the only middle-class boy in a school made up of rich boys, many of whom came from families that had been in Albany for 250 years or more. I felt rejected and alone.

My father stopped the car at Jeffrey's front walk, and I said good-bye to him, my heart in my throat. At dawn the next morning, I woke in a panic. Somehow I knew I had to get home, knew something was happening. I stole out of the house and ran the six blocks home. I got there in time to see a stretcher being carried down the front stairs. My father was on it. Watching from behind a tree, I saw that he was trying to be brave, but I could hear him gasping that he couldn't move. He didn't see me and never knew that I had witnessed his most awful moment. Three strokes followed, which left him permanently paralyzed and at the mercy of bouts of sadness and, bizarrely, euphoria. He was physically and emotionally helpless.

I was not taken to visit him at the hospital or, for some time, at the Guilderland Nursing Home. Finally the day came. When I entered his room, I could tell he was as afraid as I was of my seeing him in his helpless state.

My mother talked to him about God and the hereafter.

"Irene," he whispered, "I don't believe in God. I don't believe in anything after this. All I believe in is you and the children, and I don't want to die."

This was my introduction to the suffering that helplessness engenders. Seeing my father in this state, as I did again and again until his death years later, set the direction of my quest. His desperation fueled my vigor.

A year afterward, urged by my older sister, who regularly brought home her college reading to her precocious brother, I first read Sigmund Freud. I was lying in a hammock reading his *Introductory Lectures*. When I came to the section in which he speaks of people who frequently dream that their teeth are falling out, I felt a rush of recognition. I had had those dreams too! And I was stunned by his interpretation. For Freud, dreams of teeth falling out symbolize castration and express guilt over masturbation. The dreamer fears that the father will punish the sin of masturbation by castrating him. I wondered how he knew me so well. Little did I know then that, to produce this flash of recognition in the reader, Freud took advantage of the coincidence between the common occurrence of toothy dreams in adolescence and the even more common occurrence of masturbation. His explanation combined just enough spellbinding plausibility with tantalizing hints of more revelations to come. I determined in that moment that I wanted to spend my life asking questions like Freud's.

Some years later, when I went off to Princeton determined to become a psychologist or psychiatrist, I found out that Princeton's psychology department was undistinguished, while its philosophy department was world-class. Philosophy of mind and philosophy of science seemed allied. By the time I finished an undergraduate major in modern philosophy, I was still convinced that Freud's questions were right. His answers, however, were no longer plausible to me, and his method—making giant leaps from a few cases—seemed dreadful. I had come to believe that only by experiment could science unravel the causes and effects involved in emotional problems such as helplessness—and then learn how to cure them.

I went to graduate school to study experimental psychology. In the fall of 1964, an eager twenty-one-year-old with only a brand-new bachelor's degree under my arm, I arrived in the laboratory of Richard L. Solomon at the University of Pennsylvania. I had desperately wanted to study under Solomon. Not only was he one of the world's great learning theorists, he was also engaged in the very kind of work I wanted to do: He was trying to understand the fundamentals of mental illness by extrapolating from well-controlled experiments on animals.

Solomon's lab was in the Hare building, the oldest and grimiest building on the campus, and when I opened the rickety door I half expected it to fall off its hinges. I could see Solomon across the room, tall and thin, almost totally bald, immersed in what seemed to be his own private aura of intellectual intensity. But if Solomon was absorbed, everyone else in the lab was frantically distracted.

His most senior graduate student, a friendly, almost solicitous Midwesterner named Bruce Overmier, immediately volunteered an explanation.

"It's the dogs," said Bruce. "The dogs won't do anything. Something's wrong with them. So nobody can do any experiments." He went on to say that over the past several weeks the laboratory dogs—being used in what he unilluminatingly called the "transfer" experiments—had had Pavlovian conditioning. Day after day they had been exposed to two kinds of stimulation—high-pitched tones and brief shocks. The tones and the shocks had been given to the dogs in pairs—first a tone and then a shock. The shocks weren't too painful, the sort of minor jolt you feel when you touch a doorknob on a dry winter day. The idea was to get the dogs to associate the neutral tone and the noxious shock—to "pair" them—so that later, when they heard the tone, they would react to it as if it were a shock—with fear. That was all.

After that, the main part of the experiment had begun. The dogs had been taken to a "two-compartment shuttlebox," which is a large box with (as you might expect) two compartments in it, separated by a low wall. The investigators wanted to see if the dogs, now in the shuttlebox, would react to the tones the same way they had learned to react to shock—by jumping the barrier to get away. If they had, this would have shown that emotional learning could transfer across widely different situations.

The dogs first had to learn to jump over the barrier to escape the shock; once they'd learned that, they could then be tested to see if tones alone evoked the same reaction. It should have been a cinch for them. To escape the shock, all they'd have to do was jump over the low barrier that divided the shuttlebox. Dogs usually learn this easily.

These dogs, said Overmier, had just lain down whimpering. They hadn't even tried to get away from the shocks. And that, of course, meant that nobody could proceed with what they really wanted to do—test the dogs with the tones.

As I listened to Overmier and then looked at the whimpering dogs, I realized that something much more significant had already occurred than any result the transfer experiment might produce: Accidentally, during the early part of the experiment, the dogs must have been taught to be helpless. That's why they had given up. The tones had nothing to do with it. During Pavlovian conditioning they felt the shocks go on and off regardless of whether they struggled or jumped or barked or did nothing at all. They had concluded, or "learned," that nothing they did mattered. So why try?

I was stunned by the implications. If dogs could learn something as complex as the futility of their actions, here was an analogy to human helplessness, one that could be studied in the laboratory. Helplessness was all around us—from the urban poor to the newborn child to the despondent patient with his face to the wall. My father had his life destroyed by it. But no scientific study of helplessness existed. My mind raced on: Was this a laboratory model of human helplessness, one that could be used to understand how it comes about, how to cure it, how to prevent it, what drugs worked on it, and who was particularly vulnerable to it?

Although it was the first time I had seen learned helplessness in the laboratory, I knew what it was. Others had seen it before, but thought of it as an annoyance, not as a phenomenon worthy of study in its own right. Somehow my life and experience—perhaps the impact that my father's paralysis had had on me—had prepared me to see what it was. It would take the next ten years of my life to prove to the scientific community that what afflicted those dogs was helplessness, and that helplessness could be learned, and therefore unlearned.

As excited as I was by the possibilities of this discovery, I was dejected about something else. The graduate students here gave shocks that were in some degree painful to perfectly innocent dogs. Could I work in this laboratory? I asked myself. I had always been an animal lover, particularly a dog lover, so the prospect of causing pain—if only minor pain—was very distasteful. I took a weekend off and went to share my doubts with one of my philosophy teachers. Though he was only a few years older than I, I regarded him as wise. He and his wife had always made time for me and helped me sort out the puzzles and contradictions that filled undergraduate life in the Sixties.

"I've seen something in the lab that might be the beginning of understanding helplessness," I said. "No one has ever investigated helplessness before, yet I'm not sure I can pursue it, because I don't think it's right to give shock to dogs. Even if it's not wrong, it's repulsive." I described my observations, where I thought they might lead, and, mostly, my misgivings.

My professor was a student of ethics and of the history of science, and his line of questioning was informed by what he worked on. "Marty, do you have any other way of cracking the problem of helplessness? How about case studies of helpless people?"

It was clear to both of us that case histories were a scientific dead end. A case study is an anecdote about the life of only one person. It provides no way of finding out what caused what; usually there isn't even a way of finding out what really happened, except through the eyes of the narrator, who always has his own point of view and so distorts the narration. It was equally clear that only well-controlled experiments could isolate cause and discover cure. Further, there was no way I could ethically give trauma to other human beings. This seemed to leave only experiments with animals.

"Is it ever justified," I asked, "to inflict pain on any creature?"

My professor reminded me that most human beings, as well as household pets, are alive today because animal experiments were carried out. Without them, he asserted, polio would still be rampant and smallpox widespread. "On the other hand," he went on, "you know that the history of science is littered with unpaid promissory notes from basic research—assurances for techniques that were supposed to alleviate human misery but somehow never did.

"Let me ask you two things about what you propose to do. First, is there a reasonable chance that you will eliminate much more pain in the long run than the pain you cause in the short run? Second, can scientists ever generalize from animals to people?"

My answer to both these queries was yes. First, I believed I had a model that might unravel the mystery of human helplessness. If that could be done, the potential alleviation of pain would be substantial. And second, I knew that science had already developed a set of clear tests designed to tell when the generalization from animals is likely to work and when it is likely to fail. I resolved to do these tests.

My professor warned me that scientists often get caught up in their own ambitions and conveniently forget the ideals they had when they started out. He asked me to make two resolutions: The day it became clear to me that I had found out the fundamentals of what I needed to know, I would stop working with dogs. The day I found the answers to the major questions that needed animals to answer them, I would stop working with animals altogether.

I returned to the lab with high hopes for creating an animal model of helplessness. Only one other student, Steven Maier, believed that this goal made any sense at all. A shy, studious young man from the heart of the Bronx, Maier quickly became absorbed in the project. He had grown up in poverty and had stood out at the Bronx High School of Science. He knew what real-world helplessness was about, and he had a taste for struggle. He also had a keen sense that finding an animal model of helplessness was something worth devoting a career to. We thought of an experiment to show that animals could learn helplessness. We called it the "triadic" experiment, because it involved three groups yoked together.

We would give the first group escapable shock: By pushing a panel with its nose, a dog in that group could turn off the shock. That dog would thus have control, because one of its responses mattered.

The shock-giving device for the second group would be "yoked" to that for the first dogs: They would get exactly the same shocks as the first, but no response they made would have any effect. The shock a dog in the second group experienced would cease only when the "yoked" dog in the first group pushed its panel.

A third group would get no shocks at all.

Once the dogs went through that experience, each according to its category, all three would be taken to the shuttlebox. They should easily learn to jump over the barrier to escape from shock. We hypothesized, however, that if the dogs in the second group had learned that nothing they did mattered, they would just lie down in the shock and do nothing.

Professor Solomon was openly skeptical. There was no room among psychology's fashionable theories for the notion that animals—or people—could learn to be helpless. "Organisms," said Solomon, when we went to him to discuss our project, "can learn responses only when the responses produce reward or punishment. In the experiments you propose, responses would be unrelated to reward or punishment. These would come regardless of what the animal did. This is not a condition that produces learning in any existing theory of learning." Bruce Overmier joined in. "How can animals learn that nothing they do matters?" he asked. "Animals don't have mental life of this high order; they probably don't have any cognitions at all."

Both, though skeptical, remained supportive. They also urged us not to leap to any conclusions. It could be that the animals would fail to escape from shock for some other reason and not because they'd learned that responding is futile. The stress of the shock itself might make those dogs appear to give up.

Steve and I felt the triadic experiment would test these possibilities also, since the groups that got escapable and inescapable shock would undergo identical amounts of physical stress. If we were right and helplessness was the crucial ingredient, only the dogs who got inescapable shock would give up.

In early January of 1965, we exposed the first dog to shocks from which it could escape and the second dog to identical shocks from which it could not escape. The third dog was left alone. The next day, we took the dogs to the shuttlebox and gave all three shocks they could easily escape by hopping over the low barrier dividing one side of the box from the other.

Within seconds the dog that had been taught to control shocks discovered that he could jump over the barrier and escape. The dog that earlier had received no shocks discovered the same thing, also in a matter of seconds. But the dog that had found that nothing it did mattered made no effort to escape, even though it could easily see over the low barrier to the shockless zone of the shuttlebox. Pathetically, it soon gave up and lay down, though it was regularly shocked by the box. It never found out that the shock could be escaped merely by jumping to the other side.

We repeated this experiment on eight triads. Six of the eight dogs in the helpless group just sat in the shuttlebox and gave up, whereas none of the eight dogs in the group that had learned they could control shock gave up.

Steve and I were now convinced that only inescapable events produced giving up, because the identical pattern of shock, if it was under the animal's control, did not produce giving up. Clearly, animals can learn their actions are futile, and when they do, they no longer initiate action; they become passive. We had taken the central premise of learning theory—that learning occurs only when a response produces a reward or a punishment—and proved it wrong.

Steve and I wrote up our finding, and to our surprise the editor of the *Journal of Experimental Psychology*, usually the most conservative of journals, saw fit to make it the lead article. The gauntlet was thrown down to learning theorists the world over. Here were two callow graduate students telling the great B. F. Skinner, guru of behaviorism, and all his disciples that they were wrong in their most basic premise.

The behaviorists did not blithely surrender. At our home department in the university, the most venerable professor—he himself had edited the *Journal of Experimental Psychology* for twenty years—wrote me a note saying that a draft of our article made him "physically sick." At an international meeting I was accosted by Skinner's leading disciple—in a men's room of all places—and informed that the animals "don't learn *that* anything, they only learn responses."

There haven't been many experiments in the history of psychology that can be called crucial, but Steve Maier, then only twenty-four years old, now constructed one. It was a courageous act, because Steve's experiment frontally attacked a powerfully entrenched orthodoxy, behaviorism. For sixty years behaviorism had dominated American psychology. All the great figures in the field of learning were behaviorists, and for two generations almost every good academic job in psychology had gone to a behaviorist. All this although behaviorism was clearly farfetched. (Science often gets a lot of mileage out of the farfetched.)

Just as with Freudianism, behaviorism's main idea was counterintuitive (that is, it ran against common sense). The behaviorists insisted that *all* of a person's behavior was determined *only* by his lifelong history of rewards and punishments. Actions that had been rewarded (a smile, for example, that had brought a caress) were likely to be repeated, and actions that had been punished were likely to be suppressed. And that was it.

Consciousness—thinking, planning, expecting, remembering—has no effect on actions. It's like the speedometer on a car: It doesn't make the car go, it just reflects what's happening. The human being, said the behaviorists, is entirely shaped by his external environment—by rewards and punishments—rather than by his internal thoughts.

It is hard to believe that intelligent people could have long subscribed to such an idea, but since the end of World War I, American psychology had been ruled by the dogmas of behaviorism. The appeal of this notion, so implausible on its face, is basically ideological. Behaviorism takes an enormously optimistic view of the human organism, one that makes progress appealingly simple: All you have to do to change the person is to change the environment. People commit crimes because they are poor, and so if poverty is eliminated, crime will disappear. If you catch a thief, you can rehabilitate him by changing the contingencies in his life: Punish him for stealing and reward him for whatever constructive behavior he might display. Prejudice is caused by ignorance about the people you are prejudiced against and can be overcome by getting to know them. Stupidity is caused by deprivation of education and can be overcome by universal schooling.

While the Europeans were taking a genetic approach to behavior—speaking in terms of character traits, genes, instincts, and so on—the Americans embraced the notion that behavior was wholly determined by environment. It is more than happenstance that the two countries in which behaviorism flourished—the United States and the Soviet Union—are at least in theory the cradles of egalitarianism. "All men are created equal" and "From each according to his abilities, to each according to his needs" were the ideological underpinnings of behaviorism as well as of the American and Soviet political systems respectively.

That is where things stood in 1965 when we prepared our counterattack against the behaviorists. We thought the behaviorist notion that it all comes down to rewards and punishments that strengthen associations was utter nonsense. Consider the behaviorists' explanation of a rat bar-pressing for food: When a rat that had gotten food by pressing a bar proceeds to press the bar again, it's because the association between bar-pressing and food has previously been strengthened by reward. Or the behaviorist explanation of human labor: A human being goes to work merely because the response of going to work has already been strengthened by reward, not because of any expectation of reward. The mental life of the person or the rat either does not exist or plays no causal role in the behaviorist worldview. In contrast, we believed that mental events are causal: The rat *expects* that pressing the bar will bring food; the human being *expects* that going to work will result in getting paid. We felt that most voluntary behavior is motivated by what you expect the behavior will result in.

With regard to learned helplessness, Steve and I believed the dogs were just lying there because they had learned that nothing they did mattered—and they therefore expected that no actions of theirs would matter in the future. Once they formed this expectation, they would no longer engage in action.

"Being passive can have two sources," Steve pointed out in his incongruously soft Bronx accent to the increasingly critical members of our weekly research seminar. "Like old people in nursing homes, you can learn to become passive if it pays off. The staff is much nicer to you if you appear docile than if you are demanding. Or, you can become passive if you give up completely, if you believe that nothing at all you do—docile or demanding—matters. The dogs are not passive because they've learned that passivity turns off the shock; rather, the dogs give up because they expect that nothing they do will matter."

The behaviorists couldn't possibly say that the "helpless" dogs had learned an expectation that nothing they did would matter: Behaviorism, after all, maintained that the only thing an animal—or a human being—could ever learn was an action (or, in the jargon of the profession, a motor response); it could never learn a thought or an expectation. So the behaviorists stretched for an explanation, arguing that something had happened to the dogs to reward them for lying there; somehow the dogs must have been rewarded for just sitting still.

The dogs were getting inescapable shock. There were moments, the behaviorists argued, when the dogs happened to be sitting as the shock ceased. The behaviorists said the cessation of pain at those moments was a reinforcer and strengthened sitting. The dogs now would sit even more, the behaviorists continued, and the shock would stop again, and this further reinforced sitting.

This argument was the last refuge of a seriously considered (although, in my judgment, misguided) view. It could have been argued as easily that the dogs had not been rewarded for just sitting there, but punished—by the fact that the shock sometimes *went on* when the dogs were sitting; that should have punished sitting and suppressed it. The behaviorists ignored this logical hole in their argument and insisted the only thing the dogs had learned was a strong response of sitting still. We replied that it was clear the dogs, faced with shock they had no control over, were capable of processing information, with the result that they could learn that nothing they did mattered.

It was at this point that Steve Maier created his brilliant test. "Let's put the dogs through the very process that the behaviorists say will make them super-helpless," Steve said. "They say the dogs are rewarded for staying still? Okay, we'll reward them for staying still. Whenever they stay still for five seconds, we'll turn off the shock." Which is to say, the test would deliberately do exactly what the behaviorists had said was being done accidentally.

Behaviorists would predict that a reward for staying still would produce motionless dogs. Steve disagreed. "You and I know," he said, "that the dogs will learn that simply staying still makes the shock stop. They'll learn that they can stop the shock by staying motionless for five seconds. They'll say to themselves, 'Hey, I've really got plenty of control.' And according to our theory, once dogs learn control, they'll never become helpless."

Steve set up a two-part experiment. First, the dogs Steve called the Sitting-Still Group were to experience shock that would cease only if they stayed motionless for five seconds. They could control the shock by remaining still. The second group, the so-called Yoked Group, would be shocked whenever the Sitting-Still Group was, but nothing the dogs in the Yoked Group did could affect their shock. It ceased only when the dogs in the Sitting-Still Group sat still. A third group was called the No-Shock Group.

The second part of the experiment involved taking all the dogs to the shuttlebox to learn to jump away from shock. Behaviorists would predict that when shock came on, the dogs in both the Sitting-Still Group and the Yoked Group would stand still and appear to be helpless—because both groups had previously been rewarded by experiencing relief from shock while staying still. Of those two groups, behaviorists predicted, the Sitting-Still Group would become the more intently still, because they'd been consistently rewarded for stillness, while the dogs of the Yoked Group only occasionally had been. Behaviorists would also say that the No-Shock Group would be unaffected.

We cognitivists disagreed. We predicted that the Sitting-Still Group, learning they had control over when shock ceased, would not become helpless. When they had a chance to jump over the barrier in the shuttlebox, they would readily do so. We also predicted that most of the Yoked Group would become helpless, and that, of course, the No-Shock Group would be unaffected and escape shock nimbly in the shuttlebox.

So we took the dogs through the first part of the experiment and then took them to the shuttlebox. Here's what happened:

The majority of the Yoked-Group dogs just lay there, as both factions would have predicted. The No-Shock-Group dogs were unaffected. As for the Sitting-Still-Group dogs, when they got in the shuttlebox they stood motionless for a few seconds, waiting for the shock to stop. When it didn't, they danced around a bit, trying to find some other passive way to turn off the shock. They soon concluded there was none and promptly jumped over the barrier.

When worldviews clash, as the views of the behaviorists and the cognitivists had clashed over learned helplessness, it is very hard to construct an experiment that leaves the other side without an answer. That is what twenty-four-year-old Steve Maier had managed to do.

The behaviorists' acrobatic attempts reminded me of the matter of the epicycles. Renaissance astronomers had been perplexed by Tycho Brahe's careful observations of the heavens. Every so often the planets seemed to retreat along the paths they had just taken. Astronomers who believed the sun traveled around the earth explained these retreats by means of "epicycles"—small circles within the great circle, onto which, they theorized, heavenly bodies would periodically detour. As more observations were recorded, the traditional astronomers had to postulate ever more epicycles. Eventually, those who believed the earth traveled in a circle around the sun (it actually has an elliptical course) vanquished the earth-centrists, simply because their view required fewer epicycles and was therefore tidier. The phrase "adding epicycles" came to be applied to scientists in any field who, having trouble defending a tottering thesis, desperately postulate unlikely subtheses in hopes of buttressing it.

Our findings, along with those of thinkers like Noam Chomsky, Jean Piaget, and the information-processing psychologists, served to expand the field of inquiry to the mind and to drive the behaviorists into full retreat.

By 1975 the scientific study of mental processes in people and animals displaced the behavior of rats as the favorite subject of doctoral dissertations.

STEVE MAIER and I had now found out how to produce learned helplessness. But, having caused it, could we cure it?

We took a group of dogs that had been taught to be helpless, and we dragged those poor, reluctant animals back and forth across the shuttlebox, over the barrier and back again, until they began to move under their own steam and came to see that their own actions worked. Once they did, the cure was one hundred percent reliable and permanent.

We worked on prevention and discovered a phenomenon we called "immunization": Learning beforehand that responding matters actually prevents learned helplessness. We even found that dogs taught this mastery as puppies were immunized to learned helplessness all their lives. The implications of that, for human beings, were thrilling.

We had now established the basics of the theory, and, as I'd resolved that day at Princeton when my professor and I had discussed the ethics of animal experimentation, Steve Maier and I stopped our dog experiments.

Vulnerability and Invulnerability

OUR PAPERS now appeared regularly. Learning theorists reacted predictably: with incredulity, not a little anger, and heated criticism. That controversy, a rather technical and tedious one, has gone on for twenty years, and somehow we seem to have won it. Even obdurate behaviorists eventually began to teach their students about learned helplessness and to do research on it.

The most constructive reactions came from scientists interested in applying learned helplessness to problems of human suffering. One of the most intriguing came from Donald Hiroto, a thirty-year-old Japanese-American graduate student at Oregon State University. Hiroto was looking for a dissertation project and asked for the details of what we had done. "I want to try it with people, rather than dogs or rats," he wrote, "and see if it really applies to the human condition. My professors are very skeptical."

Hiroto set out to do with people experiments parallel to those we had done with dogs. He first took one group of people to a room, turned on loud noise, and gave them the task of learning how to turn it off. They tried every combination on the panel of buttons at their fingertips, but the noise was unstoppable. No pattern of button pressing would turn it off. Another group of people could turn off the noise by pushing the right pattern of buttons. Still another group was subjected to no noise at all.

Later Hiroto took the people to a room in which there was a shuttlebox. You put your hand on one side, and there is an annoying whooshing sound; move your hand to the other side, and the noise stops.

One afternoon in 1971, Hiroto called me.

"Marty," he said, "I think we've got some results that mean something . . . maybe a lot. The people we gave inescapable noise to back at the beginning, when they put their hand in the 'shuttlebox,' would you believe it, most of them just sat there!" I could tell Hiroto was excited, though he was trying to maintain professional composure. "It was as if they'd learned they were helpless to turn off noise, so they didn't even try, even though everything else—the time and place, all that—had changed. They carried that noise-helplessness right through to the new experiment. But get this: All the other people—the ones who first got escapable noise or no noise—they learned to turn the noise off quite easily!"

I felt this might well be the culmination of years of inquiry, years of work. If people could be taught to be helpless in the face of a trivial irritation such as noise, then perhaps it was true that people out in the world, experiencing instances when their actions are futile, experiencing serious shocks, were being taught helplessness too. Perhaps human reaction to loss in general—rejection by those we have loved, failure at work, death of a spouse—could be understood through the learned helplessness model.*

According to Hiroto's findings, one out of every three people whom he had tried to make helpless did not succumb. That was powerfully significant. One out of three of our animals, too, did not become helpless following inescapable shock. Subsequent tests, using Bill Cosby records that went on and off regardless of what the people did, or nickels that unpredictably dropped out of slot machines, supported Hiroto's findings.

Hiroto's test produced another fascinating result: About one in ten of the people who received no shock just sat in the "shuttlebox" from the outset, not moving, doing nothing about the aggravating noise. This again

* I hasten to note that the people in these and all other helplessness experiments involving human beings didn't leave the lab in a state of depression. At the end of the session the subject would be shown that the noise was rigged or the problem unsolvable. His symptoms would disappear.

was a strong parallel to our animal tests. One in ten of our animals also was helpless from the start.

Our satisfaction was quickly replaced by fierce curiosity. Who gives up easily and who never gives up? Who survives when his work comes to nothing or when he is rejected by someone he has loved long and deeply? And *why*? Clearly, some people don't prevail; like helpless dogs, they crumple up. And some do prevail; like the indomitable experimental subjects, they pick themselves up and, with life somewhat poorer, manage to go on and rebuild. Sentimentalists call this "a triumph of the human will" or "the courage to be"—as if such labels explained it.

Now, after seven years of experiments, it was clear to us that the remarkable attribute of resilience in the face of defeat need not remain a mystery. It was not an inborn trait; it could be acquired. Exploring the colossal implications of that discovery is what I have worked on for the last decade and a half.

3

Explaining Misfortune

OXFORD UNIVERSITY is an intimidating place to give a lecture. It's not so much the spires and gargoyles, or even the knowledge that for over seven hundred years this place has led the intellectual world. It's Oxford's dons. They had turned out in force that day in April 1975 to hear the upstart American psychologist who was on sabbatical at Maudsley Hospital's Institute of Psychiatry in London and who had traveled to Oxford to talk about his research. As I arranged my speech on the rostrum and looked nervously out into the hall, I could see the ethologist Niko Tinbergen, a 1973 Nobel laureate. I could see Jerome Bruner, a celebrated academic who had recently come to Oxford from Harvard to take the Regius professorship in child development. There too was Donald Broadbent, the founder of modern cognitive psychology and the foremost "applied" social scientist in the world, and Michael Gelder, the dean of British psychiatry. And there was Jeffrey Gray, the renowned expert on anxiety and the brain. These were the greats of my profession. I felt like an actor who has been pushed out onto a stage to do a soliloquy before Guinness, Gielgud, and Olivier.

I launched into my speech about learned helplessness, and I was relieved to find the dons reasonably responsive, some of them nodding at my conclusions, most of them chuckling at my jokes. But in the middle of the front row was an intimidating stranger. He was not laughing at my jokes, and at several crucial points he conspicuously shook his head no. He seemed to be keeping a running total of mistakes I had unknowingly made.

At last the speech was finished. The applause was appreciative, and I was relieved, for the occasion was now over except for the polite platitudes traditionally offered by the professor assigned to be the "discussant." The discussant, however, turned out to be the naysayer from the front row. His name was given as John Teasdale. I had heard the name before but knew almost nothing about him. Teasdale, it proved, was a new lecturer in the psychiatry department, fresh up from the psychology department at Maudsley Hospital in London.

"You really shouldn't be carried away by this enchanting story," he told the audience. "The theory is wholly inadequate. Seligman has glossed over the fact that one-third of his human subjects never become helpless. Why not? And of the ones who did, some bounced back right away; others never recovered. Some were helpless only in the very situation they learned to be helpless about; they no longer tried to escape from noise. Yet others gave up in brand-new situations. Let us ask ourselves why. Some lost self-esteem and blamed themselves for failing to escape the noise, while others blamed the experimenter for giving them unsolvable problems. Why?"

Baffled looks appeared on many of the dons' faces. Teasdale's piercing critique had thrown everything into doubt. Ten years of research, which had looked definitive to me when I began the talk, now seemed full of loose ends.

I was almost dumbstruck. I thought Teasdale was right, and I was embarrassed I hadn't thought of these objections myself. I mumbled something about this being the way science progresses and by way of rejoinder asked if Teasdale himself could solve the paradox he had set before me.

"Yes, I think I can," he said. "But this is neither the time nor the place."

I won't yet reveal Teasdale's solution, for I am going to ask you first to take a short test, one that will help you discover whether you are an optimist or a pessimist. Knowing Teasdale's answer to the question of why some people never become helpless might distort the way you take that test.

Test Your Own Optimism

Take as much time as you need to answer each of the questions. On average the test takes about fifteen minutes. There are no right or wrong answers. It is important that you take the test *before* you read the analysis which follows it, in order to assure that your answers will not be biased.

Read the description of each situation and vividly imagine it happening to you. You have probably not experienced some of the situations, but that doesn't matter. Perhaps neither response will seem to fit; go ahead anyway and circle either A or B, choosing the cause likelier to apply to you. You may not like the way some of the responses sound, but don't choose what you think you *should* say or what would sound right to other people; choose the response you'd be likelier to have.

Circle only one response for each question. Ignore the letter and number codes for now.

1. The project you are in charge of is a great success.

		PsG
(A.)	*I kept a close watch over everyone's work.*	(1)
B.	*Everyone devoted a lot of time and energy to it.*	0

2. You and your spouse (boyfriend/girlfriend) make up after a fight.

		PmG
(A.)	*I forgave him/her.*	0
B.	*I'm usually forgiving.*	✗

3. You get lost driving to a friend's house.

		PsB
A.	*I missed a turn.*	✗
(B.)	*My friend gave me bad directions.*	0

4. Your spouse (boyfriend/girlfriend) surprises you with a gift.

		PsG
A.	*He/she just got a raise at work.*	0
(B.)	*I took him/her out to a special dinner the night before.*	(1)

5. You forget your spouse's (boyfriend's/girlfriend's) birthday.

		PmB
(A.)	*I'm not good at remembering birthdays.*	(1)
B.	*I was preoccupied with other things.*	0

6. You get a flower from a secret admirer.

		PvG
(A.)	*I am attractive to him/her.*	0
B.	*I am a popular person.*	✗

7. You run for a community office position and you win.

                                                                                              PvG

    (A.) *I devote a lot of time and energy to campaigning.*   0
    B. *I work very hard at everything I do.*   X

8. You miss an important engagement.

                                                                                               PvB

    (A.) *Sometimes my memory fails me.*   (1)
    B. *I sometimes forget to check my appointment book.*   0

9. You run for a community office position and you lose.

                                                                                            PsB

    A. *I didn't campaign hard enough.*   X
    (B.) *The person who won knew more people.*   0

10. You host a successful dinner.

                                                                                            PmG

    (A.) *I was particularly charming that night.*   0
    B. *I am a good host.*   X

11. You stop a crime by calling the police.

                                                                                            PsG

    (A) *A strange noise caught my attention.*   0
    B. *I was alert that day.*   X

12. You were extremely healthy all year.

                                                                                             PsG

    (A) *Few people around me were sick, so I wasn't exposed.*   0
    B. *I made sure I ate well and got enough rest.*   X

13. You owe the library ten dollars for an overdue book.

                                                                                            PmB

    (A.) *When I am really involved in what I am reading, I often forget when it's due.*   (1)
    B. *I was so involved in writing the report that I forgot to return the book.*   0

14. Your stocks make you a lot of money.

                                                                                            PmG

    (A) *My broker decided to take on something new.*   0
    B. *My broker is a top-notch investor.*   X

15. You win an athletic contest.

	PmG
(A.) *I was feeling unbeatable.*	0
B. *I train hard.*	X

16. You fail an important examination.

	PvB
A. *I wasn't as smart as the other people taking the exam.*	X
(B.) *I didn't prepare for it well.*	0

17. You prepared a special meal for a friend and he/she barely touched the food.

	PvB
A. *I wasn't a good cook.*	X
(B.) *I made the meal in a rush.*	0

18. You lose a sporting event for which you have been training for a long time.

	PvB
A. *I'm not very athletic.*	X
(B.) *I'm not good at that sport.*	0

19. Your car runs out of gas on a dark street late at night.

	PsB
(A.) *I didn't check to see how much gas was in the tank.*	(1)
B. *The gas gauge was broken.*	0

20. You lose your temper with a friend.

	PmB
A. *He/she is always nagging me.*	X
(B.) *He/she was in a hostile mood.*	0

21. You are penalized for not returning your income-tax forms on time.

	PmB
A. *I always put off doing my taxes.*	X
(B.) *I was lazy about getting my taxes done this year.*	0

22. You ask a person out on a date and he/she says no.

PvB

    A. *I was a wreck that day.*   1

    (B.) *I got tongue-tied when I asked him/her on the date.*   0

23. A game-show host picks you out of the audience to participate in the show.

PsG

    (A.) *I was sitting in the right seat.*   0

    B. *I looked the most enthusiastic.*   1

24. You are frequently asked to dance at a party.

PmG

    A. *I am outgoing at parties.*   1

    (B.) *I was in perfect form that night.*   0

25. You buy your spouse (boyfriend/girlfriend) a gift and he/she doesn't like it.

PsB

    (A.) *I don't put enough thought into things like that.*   (1)

    B. *He/she has very picky tastes.*   0

26. You do exceptionally well in a job interview.

PmG

    (A) *I felt extremely confident during the interview.*   0

    B. *I interview well.*   1

27. You tell a joke and everyone laughs.

PsG

    (A) *The joke was funny.*   0

    B. *My timing was perfect.*   1

28. Your boss gives you too little time in which to finish a project, but you get it finished anyway.

PvG

    A. *I am good at my job.*   0

    (B.) *I am an efficient person.*   (1)

29. You've been feeling run-down lately.

                                                        PmB

    A. *I never get a chance to relax.*   ✗
    (B.) *I was exceptionally busy this week.*   0

30. You ask someone to dance and he/she says no.

                                                        PsB

    (A.) *I am not a good enough dancer.*   (1)
    B. *He/she doesn't like to dance.*   0

31. You save a person from choking to death.

                                                        PvG

    (A.) *I know a technique to stop someone from choking.*   0
    B. *I know what to do in crisis situations.*   ✗

32. Your romantic partner wants to cool things off for a while.

                                                        PvB

    A. *I'm too self-centered.*   ✗
    (B.) *I don't spend enough time with him/her.*   0

33. A friend says something that hurts your feelings.

                                                        PmB

    A. *She always blurts things out without thinking of others.*   ✗
    (B.) *My friend was in a bad mood and took it out on me.*   0

34. Your employer comes to you for advice.

                                                        PvG

    A. *I am an expert in the area about which I was asked.*   0
    (B.) *I am good at giving useful advice.*   (1)

35. A friend thanks you for helping him/her get through a bad time.

                                                        PvG

    (A.) *I enjoy helping him/her through tough times.*   0
    (B.) *I care about people.*   ✗

36. You have a wonderful time at a party.

                                                        PsG

    (A.) *Everyone was friendly.*   0
    B. *I was friendly.*   ✗

37. Your doctor tells you that you are in good physical shape.

                                                                    PvG
    - A. *I make sure I exercise frequently.*   0
    - B. *I am very health-conscious.*   (I)

38. Your spouse (boyfriend/girlfriend) takes you away for a romantic weekend.

                                                                     PmG
    - A. *He/she needed to get away for a few days.*   0
    - B. *He/she likes to explore new areas.*   1

39. Your doctor tells you that you eat too much sugar.

                                                                     PsB
    - A. *I don't pay much attention to my diet.*   1
    - B. *You can't avoid sugar, it's in everything.*   0

40. You are asked to head an important project.

                                                                     PmG
    - A. *I just successfully completed a similar project.*   0
    - B. *I am a good supervisor.*   1

41. You and your spouse (boyfriend/girlfriend) have been fighting a great deal.

                                                                     PsB
    - A. *I have been feeling cranky and pressured lately.*   (I)
    - B. *He/she has been hostile lately.*   0

42. You fall down a great deal while skiing.

                                                                     PmB
    - A. *Skiing is difficult.*   1
    - B. *The trails were icy.*   0

43. You win a prestigious award.

                                                                     PvG
    - A. *I solved an important problem.*   0
    - B. *I was the best employee.*   1

44. Your stocks are at an all-time low.

                                                                     PvB
    - A. *I didn't know much about the business climate at the time.* (I)
    - B. *I made a poor choice of stocks.*   0

45. You win the lottery.

PsG

    (A) *It was pure chance.*   0

    B. *I picked the right numbers.*   x̸

46. You gain weight over the holidays and you can't lose it.

PmB

    (A) *Diets don't work in the long run.*   ①

    B. *The diet I tried didn't work.*   0

47. You are in the hospital and few people come to visit.

PsB

    (A.) *I'm irritable when I am sick.*   ①

    B. *My friends are negligent about things like that.*   0

48. They won't honor your credit card at a store.

PvB

    Ä. *I sometimes overestimate how much money I have.*   x̸

    (B.) *I sometimes forget to pay my credit-card bill.*   0

SCORING KEY

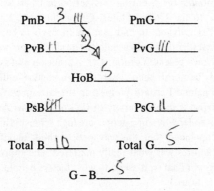

PmB __3__ ||| PmG_____

PvB __||__   PvG __|||__

HoB __5__

PsB __|||||__   PsG __||__

Total B __10__   Total G __5__

G – B __-5__

Put the test aside for the moment. You will score it later, as we go along through the rest of this chapter.

Explanatory Style

WHEN JOHN TEASDALE raised his objections after my speech at Oxford, I felt for a moment as if years of work might have been for nothing. I had no way of knowing at the time that the Teasdale challenge would result in the thing I wanted most of all—using our findings to help needful and suffering human beings.

Yes, Teasdale had granted in his rebuttal, two out of three people became helpless. But, he'd stressed, one out of three resisted: No matter what happened to them to make them helpless, they would not give up. It was a paradox, and until it was resolved, my theory could not be taken seriously.

Leaving the hall with Teasdale after the address, I asked him if he'd be willing to work with me to see if we could construct an adequate theory. He agreed, and we began meeting regularly. I'd come down from London and we'd take long walks through the manicured Oxford grounds and the tree-lined meadows called The Backs, talking out his objections. I asked for his solution to the problem he had posed, about who is vulnerable to helplessness and who is not. I learned that for Teasdale the solution came down to this: how people explain to themselves the bad things that happen to them. People who made certain kinds of explanations, he believed, are prey to helplessness. Teaching them to change these explanations might prove an effective way to treat their depression.

Every two months or so during this period in England, I made week-long trips back to the United States. On my first trip I returned to the University of Pennsylvania to find that my theory was being assaulted by challenges almost identical to Teasdale's. The challengers were two fearless students in my own research group, Lyn Abramson and Judy Garber.

Lyn and Judy had both been caught up in a vogue—enthusiasm for the work of a man named Bernard Weiner. In the late 1960s Weiner, a young social psychologist at the University of California's Los Angeles campus, had started to wonder why some people are high achievers and other people are not. He concluded that the way people think about the causes of successes and failures was what really mattered. His approach was called attribution theory. (That is, it asked to what factors people attributed their successes and failures.)

This view ran against the existing belief about achievement, the classic demonstration of which was called PREE—the partial reinforcement extinction effect. PREE is an old chestnut of learning theory. If you give a rat a food pellet every time he presses a bar, this is called "continuous reinforcement"; the ratio of reward to effort is one-to-one, one pellet for one bar-press. If you then stop giving him food for pressing the bar ("extinction"), he'll press the bar three or four times and then quit completely, because he can see he's never getting fed anymore, since the contrast is so great. If, on the other hand, instead of one-for-one reinforcement, you give the rat "partial" reinforcement—say, an average of only one pellet for every five or ten times he presses—and then start extinction, he'll press the bar a hundred times before he gives up.

PREE had been demonstrated in the 1930s. It was the kind of experiment that made the reputation of B. F. Skinner and established him as the panjandrum of the behaviorists. The PREE principle, however, though it worked with rats and pigeons, didn't work very well with people. Some would give up as soon as extinction began; others would keep going.

Weiner had an idea why it didn't work with people: Those people who thought the cause of extinction was permanent (who concluded, for example, "The experimenter has decided not to reward me anymore") would give up right away, while those who thought the cause was temporary ("There's a short circuit in this damned equipment") would keep on going, because they thought the situation might change and the reward would resume. When Weiner performed this experiment, he found just the results he predicted. It was the explanations people made, and not the schedule of reinforcement they'd been on, which determined their susceptibility to PREE. Attribution theory went on to postulate that human behavior is controlled not just by the "schedule of reinforcement" in the environment but by an internal mental state, the explanations people make for why the environment has scheduled their reinforcements in this way.

This work had great impact in the field, especially upon younger scholars like Lyn Abramson and Judy Garber. It had shaped their whole outlook, and it was the lens through which they examined the theory of learned helplessness. When, during my first trip home from England, I told my colleagues what John Teasdale had said, Lyn and Judy replied that he was right and I was wrong, and the theory would have to be reformulated.

Lyn Abramson had shown up at Penn only the year before, as a first-year graduate student. She was immediately recognized as one of the best young psychology scholars anyone had seen in years. Outward signs to the contrary notwithstanding—her unworldly appearance, her patched jeans, her torn cotton shirts—she had a first-class mind. She first set out to discover which drugs produced learned helplessness in animals and which made helplessness less likely. She was trying to show that depression and helplessness were the same by showing they had the same brain-chemical mechanisms.

Judy Garber had dropped out of a clinical psychology program at a southern university during a time of personal crisis. Putting her life back together, she had volunteered to work in my lab unpaid for several years. She'd told me she wanted to show the world she could make a real contribution to psychology there, so she could eventually apply to a first-rate graduate program. The people in the lab always did a double take when they saw this fashionably dressed young woman with long, painted fingernails feeding white rats their daily chow. But Judy's ability, like Lyn's, soon became manifest, and before long she was involved in more advanced matters. That spring of 1975 Judy too was working on helplessness in animals. When the challenge from Teasdale came along, both Lyn and Judy dropped their own projects and began to work with us on reformulating the theory so it would apply better to people.

Throughout my career, I've never had much use for the tendency among psychologists to shun criticism. It's a longstanding tradition acquired from the field of psychiatry, with its medical authoritarianism and its reluctance to admit error. Going back at least to Freud, the world of the research psychiatrists has been dominated by a handful of despots who treat dissenters like invading barbarians usurping their domain. One critical word from a young disciple and he was banished.

I've preferred the humanistic tradition. To the scientists of the Renaissance, your critic was really your ally, helping you advance upon reality. Critics in science are not like drama critics, determining flops and successes. Criticism to scientists is just another means of finding out whether they're wrong, like running another experiment to see if it confirms or refutes a theory. Along with the advocacy principle of the courtroom, it is one of the best ways human beings have evolved to get closer to the truth.

I had always stressed to my students the importance of welcoming criticism. "I want to be told," I had always said. "In this lab, the payoff is for originality, not toadyism." Now Abramson and Garber, not to mention Teasdale, had told me, and I was not about to bristle with hostility. I promptly enlisted the three of them as allies in making the theory better. I argued with my two brilliant students, sometimes for twelve hours without a break, working to make my theory incorporate their objections.

I launched into two sets of conversations. The first, in Oxford, was with Teasdale. John's commitment was to therapy, and so, as we discussed how to change the theory, we explored the possibility of treating depression by changing the ways depressive people explained to themselves the causes of bad events. The second, with Abramson and Garber back in Philadelphia, took its character from Lyn's strong interest in the etiology—the causes—of mental illness.

Teasdale and I started writing a manuscript together, on how therapy for helplessness and depression should be based on changing people's explanations. Concurrently, Abramson and I started one on how people's explanatory style could cause helplessness and depression.

At that moment, as it happened, the editor-in-chief of the *Journal of Abnormal Psychology* contacted me. The learned-helplessness controversy, he said, had generated a great many submissions to the journal, many of them attacks of just the sort John and Lyn and Judy had made. The editor was planning to devote a whole issue of the journal to the battle, and he asked if I would write one of the articles. I agreed and then persuaded Lyn and John to let me merge the two articles we had been working on separately. I felt it important that when the new theory got this very prominent airing, it would already contain our responses to the attacks.

Our approach drew on Bernard Weiner's attribution theory, but it differed from Weiner in three ways. First, we were interested in *habits* of explanation, not just the single explanation a person makes for a single failure. We claimed there was such a thing as a *style* of explanation: We all had a style of seeing causes, and if given a chance we'd impose this habit on our world. Second, where Weiner had talked about two dimensions of explanation—permanence and personalization—we introduced another—pervasiveness—to make three. (I'll soon explain these concepts.) Third, while Weiner was interested in achievement, we were focused on mental illness and therapy.

The special issue of the *Journal of Abnormal Psychology* was published in February 1978. It contained the article by Lyn, John, and me, answering in advance the main objections to the original learned-helplessness theory. It was well received and itself generated even more research than the original helplessness theory had. We went on to devise the questionnaire you took earlier in this chapter. With the creation of the questionnaire, explanatory style could be easily measured and our approach applied, out in the real world beyond the lab, to actual human problems.

Each year the American Psychological Association gives the Early Career Award to a psychologist who attains "distinguished scientific achievement" within the first ten years of his career. I had won it in 1976 for the theory of helplessness. Lyn Abramson won it in 1982 for the reformulation of the theory of helplessness.

Who Never Gives Up?

HOW DO *you* think about the causes of the misfortunes, small and large, that befall you? Some people, the ones who give up easily, habitually say

of their misfortunes: "It's me, it's going to last forever, it's going to undermine everything I do." Others, those who resist giving in to misfortune,
say: "It was just circumstances, it's going away quickly anyway, and, besides, there's much more in life."

Your habitual way of explaining bad events, your explanatory style, is
more than just the words you mouth when you fail. It is a habit of thought,
learned in childhood and adolescence. Your explanatory style stems directly from your view of your place in the world—whether you think you
are valuable and deserving, or worthless and hopeless. It is the hallmark
of whether you are an optimist or a pessimist.

The test you took earlier in this chapter is designed to reveal your
explanatory style.

THERE ARE three crucial dimensions to your explanatory style: permanence, pervasiveness, and personalization.

Permanence:

PEOPLE WHO give up easily believe the causes of the bad events that
happen to them are permanent: The bad events will persist, will always be
there to affect their lives. People who resist helplessness believe the causes
of bad events are temporary.

PERMANENT (Pessimistic):	TEMPORARY (Optimistic):
"I'm all washed up."	"I'm exhausted."
"Diets never work."	"Diets don't work when you eat out."
"You always nag."	"You nag when I don't clean my room."
"The boss is a bastard."	"The boss is in a bad mood."
"You never talk to me."	"You haven't talked to me lately."

If you think about bad things in *always's* and *never's* and abiding traits,
you have a permanent, pessimistic style. If you think in *sometimes's* and
lately's, if you use qualifiers and blame bad events on transient conditions,
you have an optimistic style.

Now turn back to your test. Look at the eight items marked "PmB"
(which stands for *Permanent Bad*), the questions numbered 5, 13, 20, 21,
29, 33, 42, and 46.

These tested how permanent you tend to think the causes of bad events are. Each one with a *o* after it is optimistic. Each one followed by a *1* is pessimistic. So, for example, if you chose "I'm not good at remembering birthdays" (question 5) rather than "I was preoccupied with other things" to explain why you forgot your spouse's birthday, you chose a more permanent, and therefore pessimistic, cause.

Total the numbers at the right-hand margin of the PmB questions. Write your total on the PmB line in the scoring key on page 39.

If you totaled 0 or 1, you are very optimistic on this dimension;

2 or 3 is a moderately optimistic score;

4 is average;

5 or 6 is quite pessimistic; and

if you scored 7 or 8, you will find Part Three of this book, "Changing: From Pessimism to Optimism," very helpful.

Here's why the permanence dimension matters so much—and here is our answer to John Teasdale's challenge about why some people stay helpless forever while others bounce back right away.

Failure makes everyone at least *momentarily* helpless. It's like a punch in the stomach. It hurts, but the hurt goes away—for some people almost instantly. These are the people whose score totals 0 or 1. For others, the hurt lasts; it seethes, it roils, it congeals into a grudge. These people score 7 or 8. They remain helpless for days or perhaps months, even after only small setbacks. After major defeats they may never come back.

THE OPTIMISTIC STYLE of explaining good events is just the opposite of the optimistic style of explaining bad events. People who believe good events have permanent causes are more optimistic than people who believe they have temporary causes.

TEMPORARY *(Pessimistic):*	PERMANENT *(Optimistic):*
"It's my lucky day."	"I'm always lucky."
"I try hard."	"I'm talented."
"My rival got tired."	"My rival is no good."

Optimistic people explain good events to themselves in terms of permanent causes: traits, abilities, *always's*. Pessimists name transient causes: moods, effort, *sometimes's*.

You probably noticed that some of the questions on the test (exactly half of them, in fact) were about good events; for example, "Your stocks

make you a lot of money." Score those marked "PmG" (*Permanent Good*):
2, 10, 14, 15, 24, 26, 38, and 40.

The ones with a *1* following them are the permanent, optimistic answers.
Total the numbers on the right-hand side. Write the total on the line in
the scoring key marked "PmG" (page 39).

> If your total is 7 or 8, you are very optimistic about the likelihood of
>   good events continuing;
> 6 is a moderately optimistic score;
> 4 or 5 is average;
> 3 is moderately pessimistic; and
> 0, 1, or 2 is very pessimistic.

People who believe good events have permanent causes try even harder
after they succeed. People who see temporary reasons for good events may
give up even when they succeed, believing success was a fluke.

Pervasiveness: Specific vs. Universal

PERMANENCE is about time. Pervasiveness is about space.

Consider this example: In a large retailing firm, half the accounting
department was fired. Two of the fired accountants, Nora and Kevin, both
became depressed. Neither could bear to look for another job for several
months, and both avoided doing their income tax or anything else that
reminded them of accounting. Nora, however, remained a loving and active
wife. Her social life went on normally, her health stayed robust, and she
continued to work out three times a week. Kevin, in contrast, fell apart.
He ignored his wife and baby son, spending all his evenings in sullen
brooding. He refused to go to parties, saying he couldn't bear to see people.
He never laughed at jokes. He caught a cold that lasted all winter, and he
gave up jogging.

Some people can put their troubles neatly into a box and go about their
lives even when one important aspect of it—their job, for example, or
their love life—is suffering. Others bleed all over everything. They catastrophize. When one thread of their lives snaps, the whole fabric unravels.

It comes down to this: People who make *universal* explanations for their
failures give up on everything when a failure strikes in one area. People
who make *specific* explanations may become helpless in that one part of
their lives yet march stalwartly on in the others.

Here are some universal and some specific explanations of bad events:

UNIVERSAL *(Pessimistic)*	SPECIFIC *(Optimistic)*
"All teachers are unfair."	"Professor Seligman is unfair."
"I'm repulsive."	"I'm repulsive to him."
"Books are useless."	"This book is useless."

Nora and Kevin had the same high score on the permanence dimension of the test. They were both pessimists in this respect. When they were fired, they both remained depressed for a long time. But they had opposite scores on the pervasiveness dimension. Kevin believed the firing would undermine everything he tried; he thought he was no good at anything. Nora believed bad events have very specific causes. When she was fired, she thought she was no good at accounting.

On those long Oxford walks with John Teasdale, we took the paradox he cited—about who gives up and who doesn't—broke it into three parts, and made three predictions about who gives up and who doesn't:

The first was that the *permanence* dimension determines how long a person gives up for. Permanent explanations for bad events produce long-lasting helplessness and temporary explanations produce resilience.

The second prediction was about *pervasiveness*. Universal explanations produce helplessness across many situations and specific explanations produce helplessness only in the troubled area. Kevin was a victim of the pervasiveness dimension. Once fired he believed the cause was universal, and he behaved as though disaster had struck all aspects of his life. Kevin's pervasiveness score revealed he was a catastrophizer. The third prediction concerned *personalization* and you will read about it shortly.

Do you catastrophize? Did you catastrophize in this test? For example, in answering question 18, did you label the cause of losing as your not being very athletic (universal) or your not being good at that sport (specific)? Take each question marked "PvB" (*Pervasiveness Bad*): 8, 16, 17, 18, 22, 32, 44, and 48.

Add the numbers at the right-hand margin and write the total on the scoring-key line marked "PvB" (page 39).

A total of 0 or 1 is very optimistic;
2 or 3 is a moderately optimistic score;
4 is average;
5 or 6 is moderately pessimistic; and
7 or 8 is very pessimistic.

Now for the converse. *The optimistic explanatory style for good events is opposite that for bad events.* The optimist believes that bad events have specific causes, while good events will enhance everything he does; the pessimist believes that bad events have universal causes and that good events are caused by specific factors. When Nora was offered temporary work back at the company, she thought: "They finally realized they can't get along without me." When Kevin got the same offer he thought: "They must really be shorthanded."

SPECIFIC (Pessimistic)	UNIVERSAL (Optimistic)
"I'm smart at math."	"I'm smart."
"My broker knows oil stocks."	"My broker knows Wall Street."
"I was charming to her."	"I was charming."

Score your optimism for pervasiveness of good events. Look at each item marked "PvG": 6, 7, 28, 31, 34, 35, 37, and 43.

Each answer followed by a 0 is pessimistic (specific). When asked in question 35 for your reaction to a friend's thanks for helping him, did you answer, "I enjoy helping him through tough times" (specific and pessimistic) or "I care about people" (universal and optimistic)?

Total your score and write it on the line labeled "PvG."

A score of 7 or 8 is very optimistic;
6 is a moderately optimistic score;
4 or 5 is average;
3 is moderately pessimistic; and
0, 1, or 2 is very pessimistic.

The Stuff of Hope

HOPE HAS largely been the province of preachers, of politicians, and of hucksters. The concept of explanatory style brings hope into the laboratory, where scientists can dissect it in order to understand how it works.

Whether or not we have hope depends on two dimensions of our explanatory style: pervasiveness and permanence. Finding temporary and specific causes for misfortune is the art of hope: Temporary causes limit helplessness in time, and specific causes limit helplessness to the original situation. On the other hand, permanent causes produce helplessness far into the future, and universal causes spread helplessness through all your endeavors. Finding permanent and universal causes for misfortune is the practice of despair.

HOPELESS	HOPEFUL
"I'm stupid."	"I'm hung over."
"Men are tyrants."	"My husband was in a bad mood."
"It's five in ten this lump is cancer."	"It's five in ten this lump is nothing."

Perhaps the single most important score from your test is your hope (HoB) score. Take your "PvB" total and add it to your "PmB" total. This is your hope score for bad events.

If it is 0, 1, or 2, you are extraordinarily hopeful;
3, 4, 5, or 6 is a moderately hopeful score;
7 or 8 is average;
9, 10, or 11 is moderately hopeless; and
12, 13, 14, 15, or 16 is severely hopeless.

People who make permanent *and* universal explanations for their troubles tend to collapse under pressure, both for a long time and across situations.

No other single score is as important as your hope score.

Personalization: Internal vs. External

THERE IS ONE final aspect of explanatory style: *personalization.*

I once lived with a woman who blamed everything on me. Bad restaurant meals, late flights, even imperfect creases in her dry-cleaned trousers. "Sweetheart," I said one day, in exasperation after being bawled out because her hair dryer didn't work, "you are the most external person for bad events I've ever met."

"Yes," she shouted, "and it's all your fault!"

When bad things happen, we can blame ourselves (internalize) or we can blame other people or circumstances (externalize). People who blame themselves when they fail have low self-esteem as a consequence. They think they are worthless, talentless, and unlovable. People who blame external events do not lose self-esteem when bad events strike. On the whole, they like themselves better than people who blame themselves do.

Low self-esteem usually comes from an internal style for bad events.

INTERNAL *(Low self-esteem)*	EXTERNAL *(High self-esteem)*
"I'm stupid."	"You're stupid."
"I have no talent at poker."	"I have no luck at poker."
"I'm insecure."	"I grew up in poverty."

Take a look at your PsB (*Personalization Bad*) scores; the questions are 3, 9, 19, 25, 30, 39, 41, and 47.

The items followed by a 1 are pessimistic (internal, or personal). Total your score and write it in the PsB box in the scoring key on page 39.

A score of 0 or 1 indicates very high self-esteem;

2 or 3 indicates moderate self-esteem;

4 is average;

5 or 6 indicates moderately low self-esteem; and

7 or 8 indicates very low self-esteem.

Of the three dimensions of explanatory style, personalization is the easiest to understand. After all, one of the first things a child learns to say is "He did it, not me!" Personalization is also the easiest dimension to overrate. It controls only how you *feel* about yourself, but pervasiveness and permanence—the more important dimensions—control what you *do*: how long you are helpless and across how many situations.

Personalization is the only dimension simple to fake. If I tell you to talk about your troubles in an external way now, you will be able to do it—even if you are a chronic internalizer. You can chatter along, pretending to blame your troubles on others. However, if you are a pessimist and I tell you to talk about your troubles as having temporary and specific causes, you will not be able to do it (unless you have mastered the techniques of Part Three, "Changing: From Pessimism to Optimism").

Here's one last piece of information for you, before you get your totals: *The optimistic style of explaining good events is the opposite of that used for bad events: It's internal rather than external.* People who believe they cause good things tend to like themselves better than people who believe good things come from other people or circumstances.

EXTERNAL *(Pessimistic)*	INTERNAL *(Optimistic)*
"A stroke of luck. . . ."	"I can take advantage of luck."
"My teammates' skill. . . ."	"My skill. . . ."

Your last score is PsG, *Personalization Good*. The relevant questions are 1, 4, 11, 12, 23, 27, 36, and 45.

The items followed by a *0* are external and pessimistic. Those followed by a *1* are internal and optimistic.

Write your total score on the line marked "PsG" in the scoring key on page 39.

A score of 7 or 8 is very optimistic;
6 is a moderately optimistic score;
4 or 5 is average;
3 is moderately pessimistic; and
0, 1, or 2 is very pessimistic.

You can now compute your overall scores.

First, add the three *B*'s (PmB + PvB + PsB). This is your Total B (bad event) score.

Next, add your three G scores (PmG + PvG + PsG). This is your Total G (good event) score.

Subtract B from G. This is your overall score (G − B).

Here is what your totals mean:

If your B score is from 3 to 6, you are marvelously optimistic and you
    won't be needing the "Changing" chapters;
If it's in the 6 to 9 range, you're moderately optimistic;
10 or 11 is about average;
12 to 14 is moderately pessimistic; and
anything above 14 cries out for change.

If your G score is 19 or above, you think about good events very
    optimistically;
if it's from 17 to 19 your thinking is moderately optimistic;
14 to 16 is about average;
11 to 13 indicates that you think quite pessimistically; and
a score of 10 or less indicates great pessimism.

Finally, if your G − B score is above 8, you are very optimistic across
    the board;
if it's from 6 to 8 you're moderately optimistic;
3 to 5 is average;
1 or 2 is a moderately pessimistic score; and
a score of 0 or below is very pessimistic.

Caveat about Responsibility

ALTHOUGH there are clear benefits to learning optimism—there are also dangers. Temporary? Local? That's fine. I want my depressions to be short and limited. I want to bounce back quickly. But external? Is it right that I should blame others for my failures?

Most assuredly we want people to own up to the messes they make, to be responsible for their actions. Certain psychological doctrines have damaged our society by helping to erode personal responsibility: Evil is mislabeled insanity; bad manners are shucked off as neurosis; "successfully treated" patients evade their duty to their families because it does not bring them personal fulfillment. The question is whether or not changing beliefs about failure from internal to external ("It's not my fault . . . it's bad luck") will undermine responsibility.

I am unwilling to advocate any strategy that further erodes responsibility. I don't believe people should change their beliefs from internal to external wholesale. Nevertheless, there is one condition under which this usually should be done: depression. As we will see in the next chapter, depressed people often take much more responsibility for bad events than is warranted.

There is a deeper matter to deal with here: the question of why people should own up to their failures in the first place. The answer, I believe, is that we want people to change, and we know they will not change if they do not assume responsibility. If we want people to change, internality is not as crucial as the permanence dimension is. If you believe the cause of your mess is permanent—stupidity, lack of talent, ugliness—you will not act to change it. You will not act to improve yourself. If, however, you believe the cause is temporary—a bad mood, too little effort, overweight— you can act to change it. If we want people to be responsible for what they do, then yes, we want them to have an internal style. More important, people must have a temporary style for bad events—they must believe that whatever the cause of the bad event, it can be changed.

What If You Are a Pessimist?

IT MATTERS a great deal if your explanatory style is pessimistic. If you scored poorly, there are four areas where you will encounter (and probably already have encountered) trouble. First, as we will see in the next chapter, you are likely to get depressed easily. Second, you are probably achieving less at work than your talents warrant. Third, your physical health—and your immune function—are probably not what they should be, and this may get even worse as you get older. Finally, life is not as pleasurable as it should be. Pessimistic explanatory style is a misery.

If your pessimism score is in the average range, it will not be a problem in ordinary times. But in crisis, in the hard times life deals us all, you will likely pay an unnecessary price. When these events strike, you may find yourself getting more depressed than you should. How are you likely to react when your stocks go down, when you are rejected by someone you love, when you don't get the job you want? As the next chapter shows, you will become very sad. The zest will go out of living. It will be very hard for you to get started on anything challenging. The future will look bleak to you. And you will be likely to feel this way for weeks or even months. You have probably felt this way several times already; most people have. This is so common that textbooks call it a normal reaction.

The commonness of being knocked flat by troubles, however, does not mean it is acceptable or that life has to be this way. If you use a different explanatory style, you'll be better equipped to cope with troubled times and keep them from propelling you toward depression.

That hardly exhausts the prospective benefits of a new explanatory style. If you have an average degree of pessimism, you are going through life at a level somewhat lower than your talents would otherwise permit you. As you will see in chapters six, eight, and nine, even an average degree of pessimism drags down your performance in school, on the job, and in sports. This is true of physical health as well. Chapter ten illustrates how even if you are just ordinarily pessimistic, your health may not be up to par. You will likely suffer the chronic diseases of aging earlier and more severely than necessary. Your immune system may not work as well as it should; you will probably suffer more infectious diseases and recuperate more slowly.

If you use the techniques of chapter twelve, you will be able to choose to raise your everyday level of optimism. You should find yourself reacting to the normal setbacks of life much more positively and bouncing back from life's large defeats much more briskly than you did before. You should achieve more on the job, in school, and on the playing field. And in the long run, even your body should serve you better.

4

Ultimate Pessimism

WHEN IN A pessimistic, melancholy state, we are going through a mild version of a major mental disorder: depression. Depression is pessimism writ large, and to understand pessimism, a subtle phenomenon, it helps to look at the expanded, exaggerated form. This is the technique used by author and illustrator David Macaulay to show us how small everyday devices work. In one of his best-selling books, for example, he shows us how a wristwatch functions by drawing the mechanisms of an immense, vastly expanded watch, all of whose parts are big and easily distinguishable, and walking us through the insides. A study of depression similarly illuminates pessimism. Depression is worth studying in its own right, but it also has a great deal to reveal to people who are concerned merely with the mindset we call pessimism.

Almost all of us have gone through depression and know how it poisons daily life. For some it is a rare experience, descending on us only when several of our best hopes all collapse at once. For many of us, it is more familiar, a state that afflicts us every time we are defeated. For still others, it is a constant companion, draining the joy from even our best times and darkening the grayer times to an unrelieved black.

Until recently, depression was a mystery. Who was most at risk, where it came from, how to make it lift—all were enigmas. Today, thanks to twenty-five years of intensive scientific research on the part of hundreds of psychologists and psychiatrists around the world, the shape of the answers to these questions is known.

Depression comes in three kinds. The first is called normal depression, and it is the type each of us knows well. It springs from the pain and loss that are inevitable parts of being members of a sapient species, creatures who think about the future. We don't get the jobs we want. Our stocks go down. We get rejected by people we love; our spouses die. We give bad lectures and write bad books. We age. When such losses occur, what happens next is regular and predictable: We feel sad and helpless. We become passive and lethargic. We absolutely believe that our prospects are bleak and that we lack the talent to make them brighter. We don't do our work well, and we may be absent from it frequently. The zest goes out of activities we used to enjoy, and we lose our interest in food, company, sex. We can't sleep.

But after a while, by one of nature's benevolent mysteries, we start to get better. Normal depression is extremely common—it's the common cold of mental illness. I have repeatedly found that at any moment approximately 25 percent of us are going through an episode of normal depression, at least in mild form.

The two other kinds of depression are called depressive disorders: unipolar and bipolar depression. These provide everyday work for clinical psychologists and psychiatrists. What determines the difference between them is whether or not mania is involved. Mania is a psychological condition with a set of symptoms that look like the opposite of depression: unwarranted euphoria, grandiosity, frenetic talk and action, and inflated self-esteem.

Bipolar depression always involves manic episodes; it is also called manic-depression (with mania as one pole and depression as the other). Unipolar depressives never have manic episodes. Another difference between the two is that bipolar depression is much more heritable. If one of two identical twins has bipolar depression, there is a 72 percent chance the other also has it. (This is true of only 14 percent of fraternal twins. Fraternal twins are no more closely related than any other full siblings, but they are born at the same time and raised together by the same parents, so a comparison between the two types of twins helps us separate what is learned from what is genetically inherited.) Bipolar depression is exquisitely responsive to a "wonder drug," lithium carbonate. In more than 80 percent of cases of bipolar depression, lithium will relieve the mania to a marked extent and, to a lesser extent, the depression. Unlike normal and unipolar depression, manic-depression is an illness, appropriately viewed as a disorder of the body and treated medically.

The question arises whether unipolar depression, also a certified disorder, and normal depression are related. I believe they are the same thing, differing only in the number of symptoms and their severity. One person may be diagnosed as having unipolar depression and be labeled a patient, while another, held to be suffering from acute symptoms of normal depression, may not be considered a patient. The distinction between these two is shallow. It may be a distinction in how readily two people will seek therapy, or in whether their insurance policies cover unipolar depression, or in how comfortably they can bear the stigma of being labeled a patient.

My view radically differs from the prevailing medical opinion, which holds that unipolar depression is an illness and normal depression just a passing demoralization of no clinical interest. This view is the dominant one in spite of a complete absence of evidence that unipolar depression is anything more than just severe normal depression. No one has established the kind of distinction between them that has been established between dwarfs, for instance, and short normal people—a qualitative distinction.

The clincher, I feel, is that normal depression and unipolar depression are recognized in exactly the same way. Both involve the same four types of negative change: in thought, mood, behavior, and physical responses.

I remember a certain student of mine, whom I'll call Sophie. She'd entered the University of Pennsylvania with a superb high school record. She had been president of her class, its salutatorian, and a popular, pretty cheerleader. Everything she wanted fell into her lap. Good grades came with no effort and boys competed for her affections. She was an only child, doted on by her parents, both of them professionals; her successes were their triumphs, her failures their agonies. Her friends nicknamed her "Golden Girl."

When I first met her, in therapy in her junior year, she was no longer a golden girl. Her romantic life and her academic life were a mess, and she was calamitously depressed. Like most depressives, she had sought therapy not after one traumatic event but after a series of discontents that had been accumulating over several months. She said she felt "empty." She felt there was no hope for her because she was "unlovable" and "untalented," and "a washout." Her classes were boring, the whole academic system a "conspiracy to stifle" her creativity, and her feminist activity a "pointless fraud." In her last semester, she'd gotten two F's. She couldn't get started on any of her projects. When she sat down at her desk to start her homework, she couldn't decide which of the growing piles to tackle first. She would stare at the piles for about fifteen minutes, then give up in despair and switch on the TV. She was currently living with a dropout. She felt exploited and worthless whenever they had sex, and the sexual activity that used to bring her ecstasy was little better than disgusting to her now.

Her major was philosophy, and she'd become particularly attracted to existentialism. She accepted the doctrine that life was absurd, and this too filled her with despair.

I reminded her she was a talented student and an attractive woman, and she burst into tears. "I fooled you too!" she cried.

AS I HAVE SAID, one of the four criteria of depression is a negative change in thought. The way you think when you are depressed differs from the way you think when you are not depressed. When you are depressed you have a dour picture of yourself, the world, and the future. Sophie's future looked hopeless to her, and she attributed this to her lack of talent.

When you're depressed, small obstacles seem like insurmountable barriers. You believe everything you touch turns to ashes. You have an endless supply of reasons why each of your successes is really a failure. The stack of papers on Sophie's desk looked like a mountain to her.

Aaron Beck, one of the world's leading therapists, had a patient who, in the middle of a deep depression, had managed to wallpaper a kitchen. The patient saw this achievement as a failure:

Therapist: Why didn't you rate wallpapering the kitchen as a mastery experience?
Patient: Because the flowers didn't line up.
Therapist: You did in fact complete the job?
Patient: Yes.
Therapist: Your kitchen?
Patient: No, I helped a neighbor do his kitchen.
Therapist: Did he do most of the work?
Patient: No, I really did almost all of it. He hadn't wallpapered before.
Therapist: Did anything else go wrong? Did you spill paste all over? Ruin a lot of wallpaper? Leave a big mess?
Patient: No, the only problem was that the flowers didn't line up.
Therapist: Just how far off was the alignment of the flowers?
Patient (holding his fingers about an eighth of an inch apart): About this much.
Therapist: On each strip of paper?
Patient: No . . . on two or three pieces.
Therapist: Out of how many?
Patient: About twenty or twenty-five.
Therapist: Did anyone else notice it?
Patient: No. In fact my neighbor thought it was great.
Therapist: Could you see the defect when you stood back and looked at the whole wall?
Patient: Well, not really.

The patient considered the well-done job a failure because in his view, he just couldn't get anything right.

A pessimistic explanatory style is at the core of depressed thinking. A negative concept of the future, the self, and the world stems from seeing the causes of bad events as permanent, pervasive, and personal, and seeing the causes of good events in the opposite way. My depressed student Sophie, for example, blamed her troubles on her lack of talent, her un-attractiveness, and the purposelessness of existence. The wallpaperer saw the minor alignment problem as an indication of his whole being.

The second way we recognize both unipolar and normal depression is a negative change in mood. When you are depressed, you feel awful: sad, discouraged, sunk in a pit of despair. You may cry a lot, or you may be beyond tears; on her worst days Sophie would stay in bed sobbing until lunchtime. Life goes sour. Formerly enjoyable activities become savorless mockeries. Jokes are no longer funny but unbearably ironic.

A depressed mood is not usually unbroken. It changes with time of day. Typically it is near its worst just when you wake up. Thoughts of your past defeats and of the losses the new day is sure to bring may overwhelm you while you are lying in bed. If you stay in bed, your mood will lie upon you like a clammy sheet. Getting up and beginning the day lightens the mood, which usually improves as the day goes on, although it will worsen again a bit during the low time of your basic rest and activity cycle (BRAC), usually from three to six P.M. Evening is likely to be the least depressed time of day. Three to five A.M., if you are awake, is the worst.

Sadness is not the only mood of depression; anxiety and irritability are often present. But when depression gets very intense, anxiety and hostility drop away and the sufferer becomes numb and blank.

The third symptom of depression concerns behavior. The depressive shows three behavioral symptoms: passivity, indecisiveness, and suicidal action.

Depressed people often cannot get started on any but the most routine tasks, and they give up easily when impeded. A novelist can't get the first word written. When he finally does manage to get going, he quits writing when the screen on his word processor flickers, and he doesn't go back for a month.

Depressed people cannot decide among alternatives. A depressed stu-dent phones for a pizza and, when asked if he wants it plain or with a topping, stares paralyzed at the receiver. After fifteen seconds of silence, he hangs up. Sophie couldn't get started on her homework; she couldn't even decide what subject to study first.

Many depressed people think about and attempt suicide. They generally have one or both of two motives. The first is surcease: The prospect of going on as they are is intolerable, and they want to end it all. The other is manipulation: They want to get love back, or get revenge, or have the last word in an argument.

The final symptom of depression has to do with the physical self. Depression is often accompanied by undesirable physical symptoms; the more severe the depression, the more symptoms. The appetites diminish. You can't eat. You can't make love. Sophie found sex, formerly the high point of her relationship with the young man she lived with, repugnant. Even sleep is affected: You wake up too early and toss and turn, trying unsuccessfully to get back to sleep. Finally the alarm clock goes off, and you begin the new day not just depressed but exhausted.

These four symptoms—negative changes in thought, mood, behavior, and physical response—diagnose depression, whether unipolar or normal. To be considered depressed, you don't need to have all four symptoms, and it's not necessary that any particular symptom be present. The more symptoms you have, however, and the more intense each is, the more certain you can be the problem is depression.

Test Your Depression

How depressed are you right now?

I want you now to take a widely used test for depression, developed by Lenore Radloff at the Center for Epidemiological Studies of the National Institute of Mental Health. This test, called the CES–D (Center for Epidemiological Studies–Depression), covers all the symptoms of depression. Circle the answer which best describes how you have felt *over the past week*.

During the past week

1. I was bothered by things that usually don't bother me.
    0 *Rarely or none of the time (less than 1 day).*
    1 *Some or a little of the time (1–2 days).*
    ②*Occasionally or a moderate amount of the time (3–4 days).*
    3 *Most or all of the time (5–7 days).*

2. I did not feel like eating; my appetite was poor.
    (0) *Rarely or none of the time (less than 1 day).*
    1 *Some or a little of the time (1–2 days).*
    2 *Occasionally or a moderate amount of the time (3–4 days).*
    3 *Most or all of the time (5–7 days).*

3. I felt that I could not shake off the blues even with help from my family and friends.
    0 *Rarely or none of the time (less than 1 day).*
    (1) *Some or a little of the time (1–2 days).*
    2 *Occasionally or a moderate amount of the time (3–4 days).*
    3 *Most or all of the time (5–7 days).*

4. I felt that I was not as good as other people.
    0 *Rarely or none of the time (less than 1 day).*
    (1) *Some or a little of the time (1–2 days).*
    2 *Occasionally or a moderate amount of the time (3–4 days).*
    3 *Most or all of the time (5–7 days).*

5. I had trouble keeping my mind on what I was doing.
    0 *Rarely or none of the time (less than 1 day).*
    1 *Some or a little of the time (1–2 days).*
    2 *Occasionally or a moderate amount of the time (3–4 days).*
    (3) *Most or all of the time (5–7 days).*

6. I felt depressed.
    0 *Rarely or none of the time (less than 1 day).*
    (1) *Some or a little of the time (1–2 days).*
    2 *Occasionally or a moderate amount of the time (3–4 days).*
    3 *Most or all of the time (5–7 days).*

7. I felt that everything I did was an effort.
    0 *Rarely or none of the time (less than 1 day).*
    (1) *Some or a little of the time (1–2 days).*
    2 *Occasionally or a moderate amount of the time (3–4 days).*
    3 *Most or all of the time (5–7 days).*

8. I felt hopeless about the future.
    0 *Rarely or none of the time (less than 1 day).*
    1 *Some or a little of the time (1–2 days).*

②*Occasionally or a moderate amount of the time (3–4 days).*
3 *Most or all of the time (5–7 days).*

9. I thought my life had been a failure.
0 *Rarely or none of the time (less than 1 day).*
①*Some or a little of the time (1–2 days).*
2 *Occasionally or a moderate amount of the time (3–4 days).*
3 *Most or all of the time (5–7 days).*

10. I felt fearful.
0 *Rarely or none of the time (less than 1 day).*
①*Some or a little of the time (1–2 days).*
2 *Occasionally or a moderate amount of the time (3–4 days).*
3 *Most or all of the time (5–7 days).*

11. My sleep was restless.
0 *Rarely or none of the time (less than 1 day).*
①*Some or a little of the time (1–2 days).*
2 *Occasionally or a moderate amount of the time (3–4 days).*
3 *Most or all of the time (5–7 days).*

12. I was unhappy.
0 *Rarely or none of the time (less than 1 day).*
①*Some or a little of the time (1–2 days).*
2 *Occasionally or a moderate amount of the time (3–4 days).*
3 *Most or all of the time (5–7 days).*

13. I talked less than usual.
0 *Rarely or none of the time (less than 1 day).*
①*Some or a little of the time (1–2 days).*
2 *Occasionally or a moderate amount of the time (3–4 days).*
3 *Most or all of the time (5–7 days).*

14. I felt lonely.
0 *Rarely or none of the time (less than 1 day).*
1 *Some or a little of the time (1–2 days).*
②*Occasionally or a moderate amount of the time (3–4 days).*
3 *Most or all of the time (5–7 days).*

15. People were unfriendly.
0 *Rarely or none of the time (less than 1 day).*

(1) *Some or a little of the time (1–2 days).*
2 *Occasionally or a moderate amount of the time (3–4 days).*
3 *Most or all of the time (5–7 days).*

16. I did not enjoy life.
    0 *Rarely or none of the time (less than 1 day).*
    (1) *Some or a little of the time (1–2 days).*
    2 *Occasionally or a moderate amount of the time (3–4 days).*
    3 *Most or all of the time (5–7 days).*

17. I had crying spells.
    (0) *Rarely or none of the time (less than 1 day).*
    1 *Some or a little of the time (1–2 days).*
    2 *Occasionally or a moderate amount of the time (3–4 days).*
    3 *Most or all of the time (5–7 days).*

18. I felt sad.
    0 *Rarely or none of the time (less than 1 day).*
    (1) *Some or a little of the time (1–2 days).*
    2 *Occasionally or a moderate amount of the time (3–4 days).*
    3 *Most or all of the time (5–7 days).*

19. I felt that people disliked me.
    0 *Rarely or none of the time (less than 1 day).*
    1 *Some or a little of the time (1–2 days).*
    (2) *Occasionally or a moderate amount of the time (3–4 days).*
    3 *Most or all of the time (5–7 days).*

20. I could not get "going."
    0 *Rarely or none of the time (less than 1 day).*
    1 *Some or a little of the time (1–2 days).*
    (2) *Occasionally or a moderate amount of the time (3–4 days).*
    3 *Most or all of the time (5–7 days).*

(25)

This test is easy to score. Add up the numbers you circled for the questions. If you couldn't decide and circled two numbers for the same question, count only the higher of the two. Your score will be between 0 and 60.

Before interpreting your score, you should know that getting a high score is not equivalent to a diagnosis of depression. A diagnosis depends on other factors, such as how long your symptoms have lasted, and it can be made only after a thorough interview with a qualified psychologist or psychiatrist. Rather, this test gives an accurate indication of your level of depressive symptoms right now.

If you scored from 0 to 9, you are in the nondepressed range, below the mean of American adults. A score of 10 to 15 puts you in the mildly depressed range; and 16 to 24 in the moderately depressed range. If you scored over 24, you may be severely depressed.

If you scored in the severely depressed range or, whatever the range you scored in, and in addition you believe that you would kill yourself if you had a chance, I urge you to see a mental-health professional right away. If you scored in the moderately depressed range *and* in addition you would like to kill yourself, you should see a professional right away. If you scored in the moderate range, take the test again in two weeks. If you still score in that range, make an appointment with a mental-health professional.

As you took the test you probably realized you or someone you love suffers recurrently from this all-too-common malady. It is by no means surprising that almost everyone, even if he is not depressed, knows someone who is, for the United States is experiencing an unparalleled epidemic of depression. Dr. Gerald Klerman, when he was the director of the U.S. government's Alcohol, Drug Abuse and Mental Health Agency, coined the apt term "The Age of Melancholy" to describe our era.

In the late 1970s, Klerman sponsored two major studies of the rate of mental illness in America, and the findings were startling. The first, called the ECA (epidemiological catchment area) Study, was designed to find out how much mental illness, of every kind, there is in the United States. Researchers visited and interviewed 9,500 people who were randomly picked to be a cross section of adult Americans. They were all given the same diagnostic interview that a troubled patient who walks into a knowledgeable psychologist's or psychiatrist's office would get.

Because such an unusually large number or adults of different ages were interviewed, and asked *if* and *when* they had experienced major symptoms, the study gave an unprecedented picture of mental illness over many years and made it possible to trace the changes that had taken place over the course of the twentieth century. One of the most striking changes was in the so-called lifetime prevalence of depression—that is, in the percentage of the population that has been depressed at least once in their lifetime. (Obviously, the older you are the more chance you have had to get any given disorder. The lifetime prevalence of broken legs, for instance, goes up with age, since the older you are, the more opportunities you have had to break a leg.)

What everyone who was interested in depression expected was that the earlier in the century a person was born, the higher would be the person's lifetime prevalence of depression—that is, the more episodes of depression he would have had. If you'd been born in 1920, you'd have had more chances to suffer depression than if you'd been born in 1960. Before they saw the findings, medical statisticians would have stated that if you were twenty-five years old at the time you were interviewed for the study—if, that is, you were born around 1955—there was about a 6 percent chance you'd had at least one instance of severe depression, and if you were between twenty-five and forty-four years old, your risk of acute depression would have climbed—say, to about 9 percent—as any sensible cumulative statistic should.

When the statisticians looked at the findings, they saw something very odd. The people born around 1925—who, since they were older, had had more chance to get the disorder—hadn't suffered much depression at all. Not 9 percent but only 4 percent of them had had an episode. And when the statisticians looked at the findings for people born even earlier—before World War I—they found something even more astounding. Again, the lifetime prevalence had not climbed, as one would have thought; it nosedived to a mere 1 percent.

These findings were probably not artifacts of forgetting or reporting biases. So this suggests that people born in the middle third of the century are ten times likelier to suffer depression than people born in the first third.

One study, however—even one done as well as the ECA Study—does not entitle scientists to shout "Epidemic." Fortunately, the National Institute of Mental Health had done another study, called the Relatives Study, at the same time. It was similar to the ECA Study in design, and it too covered a considerable number of people. This time the people weren't randomly selected; they were chosen because they had close relatives who had been hospitalized for severe depression. The questioners started with 523 people who had already been severely depressed. Almost all the readily available first-degree relatives of these people—a total of 2,289 fathers, mothers, brothers, sisters, sons, and daughters—received an identical diagnostic interview. The aim was to find out if these relatives had ever been seriously depressed too, to see if relatives of seriously depressed people are at greater risk of depression than the population at large. Knowing this would help untangle the genetic from the environmental contribution to depression.

Again, as in the ECA Study, the findings turned expectations upside down. They showed a greater than tenfold increase in depression over the course of the century.

Consider just the women. Those studied who had been born during the

Korean War period (which means they were about thirty years old at the time of the ECA Study) were ten times likelier to have had an episode of depression than women born around World War I were, even though the older women (in their seventies at the time of the study) had had much more opportunity to become depressed.

Back when the women of the World War I generation were thirty (the age the Korean War women now were), only 3 percent of them had had a severe depression. Contrast this with the fate of the women of the Korean War period: By the time they were thirty, 60 percent of them had been severely depressed—a twentyfold difference.

The statistics on the males in the study showed the same surprising reversal. Though the men suffered only about half as much depression as the women (a crucial fact I'll discuss in the next chapter), the percentage of men who had been depressed displayed the same strong increase over the course of the century.

Not only is severe depression much more common now; it also attacks its victims much younger. If you were born in the 1930s and later had a depressed relative, your own first depression, if you had one, would likely strike between the ages of thirty and thirty-five. If you were born in 1956, your first depression would probably strike when you were between twenty and twenty-five—ten years sooner. Since severe depression recurs in about half of those who have had it once, the extra ten years of vulnerability to depression add up to an ocean of tears.

And there may be other oceans, for these studies are concerned only with severe depression. Milder depression, which so many of us have experienced, may show just the same trend: There may be a great deal more of it than there used to be. Americans, on average, may be more depressed, and at a younger age, than they have ever been: unprecedented psychological misery in a nation with unprecedented prosperity and material well-being.

In any case, there is more than enough to warrant shouting "Epidemic."

I HAVE spent the last twenty years trying to learn what causes depression. Here is what I think.

Bipolar depression (manic-depression) is an illness of the body, biological in origin and containable by drugs.

Some unipolar depressions, too, are partly biological, particularly the fiercest ones. Some unipolar depression is inherited. If one of two identical twins is depressed, the other is somewhat more likely to be depressed than if they'd been fraternal twins. This kind of unipolar depression can often be contained with drugs, although not nearly as successfully as bipolar depression can be, and its symptoms can often be relieved by electroconvulsive therapy.

But inherited unipolar depressions are in the minority. This raises the question of where the great number of depressions making up the epidemic in this country come from. I ask myself if human beings have undergone physical changes over the century that have made them more vulnerable to depression. Probably not. It is very doubtful that our brain chemistry or our genes have changed radically over the last two generations. So a tenfold increase in depression is not likely to be explained on biological grounds.

I suspect that the epidemic depression so familiar to all of us is best viewed as psychological. My guess is that most depression starts with problems in living and with specific ways of thinking about these problems. Those were my suppositions when I began my research on depression twenty years ago, but I wondered how we could prove that the cause of most depression is psychological.

By what psychological process do people become depressed? An analogy: How do birds fly? From the time of the ancient Greeks through the end of the nineteenth century, there had been controversies about that astounding and wonderful process. It was easy enough to watch birds fly and then concoct a theory, yet there was simply no way to know which theory was right. The question was settled once and for all in 1903, and the solution came from unexpected quarters.

Wilbur and Orville Wright built an airplane and it flew. So physicists resorted to modeling, a time-honored means of settling scientific disputes. Modeling involves creating a "logical model" having the properties of the phenomenon that is mysterious—flying, for the Wrights, and depression, for us. If the logical model has all the properties of the real thing, the process by which the model works will tell you how the real thing works.

The Wrights' airplane—the logical model of bird flight—took off and, *mirabile dictu*, flew. So physicists concluded birds must fly by the same process.

My challenge was to construct a logical model displaying all the properties of depression. This task had two parts: first, to build the model and, second, to show that it fit depression. I could see some similarities right off, but proving that they were the same thing, and that learned helplessness was a laboratory model of the real-world phenomenon called depression, was another matter.

Across the next twenty years, well over three hundred studies, done in many universities around the world, built the learned-helplessness model. The very first studies were done with dogs; rats soon replaced the dogs, and finally people replaced the rats. All the studies had the same form: They were experiments with three groups of subjects. One group was allowed to bring some event or item—noise, shock, money, food—under its voluntary control. For example, a rat controlled shock by pressing a bar; each time it pressed the bar, the shock stopped. A second group— the helpless group—was "yoked" to the first and got exactly the same shock, but nothing it did mattered. Shock stopped for a rat in this group whenever the first rat pressed the bar. A third group was left entirely alone.

The results were consistent. The helpless group gave up. They became so passive that even in new situations, they didn't try. Rats just sat there, not even trying to escape. People gazed at easy anagrams and made no attempt to solve them. (A sizable number of other symptoms also ensued, and I'll discuss them later.) The group able to control events remained active and chipper, as did the group that was left alone. The rats ran briskly out of shock, and the people unscrambled the anagrams in a few seconds.

These simple results directly identified the source of learned helplessness. It was caused by experience in which subjects learned that nothing they did mattered and that their responses didn't work to bring them what they wanted. This experience taught them to expect that, in the future and in new situations, their actions would once again be futile.

The symptoms of learned helplessness could be produced in several ways. Defeat and failure generated the same symptoms as uncontrollable events did. Being defeated in a fight by another rat produced symptoms identical to those caused by inescapable shock. Being told your job was to control noise, and then failing to do so, produced the same symptoms as unsolvable problems or inescapable noise did. So learned helplessness seemed to be at the core of defeat and failure.

Learned helplessness could be cured by showing the subject his own actions would now work. It could also be cured by teaching the subject to think differently about what caused him to fail. It could be prevented if, before the experience with helplessness occurred, the subject learned that his actions made a difference. The earlier in life such mastery was learned, the more effective the immunization against helplessness.

Thus was the learned-helplessness theory developed, tested, and perfected. But did it serve as a model for depression? Did the laboratory model fit the real-world phenomenon? The stakes in achieving a fit were large, for when a model exists, a disorder can be deliberately created in the laboratory, which means there is a good chance its hidden mechanisms can be identified and treatments devised. If it turned out we had discovered a laboratory model for one of mankind's oldest tormentors, depression, that would be scientific progress of a high order.

There was little to do to show that the principles of the Wright brothers' airplane flight matched those of bird flight. Their "symptoms" were patently the same: Both took off, flew, and landed. In the case of learned helplessness there was much more to do to show that the experiment reflected, point for point, all the symptoms of depression. A convincing fit is the crucial step for all laboratory models of mental illness. We needed to know whether the symptoms of learned helplessness produced in all those laboratories were the same as the symptoms depressed people had. The closer the parallel, the better the model.

Let's start with the toughest case: full-blown unipolar depression, like that of Sophie, the young patient I spoke of earlier in this chapter.

If you walk into a psychiatrist's or psychologist's office for help, he will soon attempt a diagnosis, and to help him do that he'll pull out a copy of something called *DSM-III-R* (which stands for *Diagnostic and Statistical Manual of the American Psychiatric Association*, third edition, revised). It is the official bible of the profession, a codification of what we know about how to diagnose mental illness. In your first interview the therapist will try to see if your symptoms let him place you in any of the categories of mental disorder.

Making a diagnosis by *DSM-III-R* is a little like ordering dinner from a Chinese menu. To be diagnosed as suffering a "major depressive episode" you must have five of the following nine symptoms:

1. Depressed mood
2. Loss of interest in usual activities
3. Loss of appetite
4. Insomnia
5. Psychomotor retardation (slow thought or movement)
6. Loss of energy
7. Feelings of worthlessness and guilt
8. Diminished ability to think and poor concentration
9. Suicidal thought or action

Sophie was a good example of someone suffering a major depressive episode. She had six of the nine symptoms, lacking only suicidal thoughts, psychomotor retardation, and insomnia.

When we took the list of symptoms from *DSM-III-R* and applied them to the people and animals that had taken part in the learned-helplessness experiments, we found that the groups allowed to control events had none of the nine critical symptoms, but the groups not permitted to control these very same events showed no less than eight of the nine—two more than the seriously depressed Sophie had had.

1. People given inescapable noise or unsolvable problems reported that a *depressed mood* descended on them.

2. Animals that suffered inescapable shock *lost interest in their usual activities*. They no longer competed with each other, fought back when attacked, or cared for their young.

3. Animals that suffered inescapable shock *lost their appetites*. They ate less, drank less water (and more alcohol when offered it), and lost weight. They lost interest in copulation.

4. Helpless animals had *insomnia*, particularly the early-morning awakening that depressed people have.

5. and 6. Helpless people and animals *showed psychomotor retardation and lost energy*. They didn't try to escape shock, get food, or solve problems. They didn't fight back when attacked or insulted. They readily gave up on new tasks. They wouldn't explore new environments.

7. Helpless people blamed their failure to solve problems on their *lack of ability and worthlessness*. The more depressed they got, the worse was this aspect of their pessimistic explanatory style.

8. Helpless people and animals *didn't think very well* and were *inattentive*. They had extraordinary difficulty learning anything new and had trouble paying attention to the crucial cues that signal rewards or safety.

The only symptom we didn't see was suicidal thought and action, and this was probably only because the laboratory failures were so minor: e.g., failure to turn off noise or solve anagrams.

So the fit between the model and the real-life phenomenon was exceedingly close. Inescapable noise, unsolvable problems, and inescapable shock produced eight of the nine symptoms which contribute to the diagnosis of major depression.

The closeness of this fit inspired researchers to test the theory still another way. A number of drugs can break up depression in people; the researchers gave all of them to the helpless animals. Again the results were dramatic: Each of the antidepressant drugs (and electroconvulsive therapy as well) cured learned helplessness in animals. They probably did so by raising the amount of crucial neurotransmitters available in the brain. The researchers also found that drugs that do not break up depression in people, like caffeine, Valium, and amphetamines, do not break up learned helplessness either.

The fit, then, seemed almost perfect. In its symptoms, learned helplessness produced in the laboratory seemed almost identical to depression.

When we now looked at the upsurge of depression, we could view it as an epidemic of learned helplessness. We knew the cause of learned helplessness, and now we could see it as the cause of depression: *the belief that your actions will be futile*. This belief was engendered by defeat and failure as well as by uncontrollable situations. Depression could be caused by defeat, failure, and loss and the consequent belief that any actions taken will be futile.

I think this belief is at the heart of our national epidemic of depression. The modern self must be more susceptible to learned helplessness, to an ever-growing conviction that nothing one does matters. I think I know why, and I'll discuss it in the final chapter.

This all sounds pretty bleak. Yet there is also a hopeful side, and this is where explanatory style becomes important.

5

How You Think, How You Feel

IF SOPHIE had suffered her depression twenty years ago, she would have been out of luck. She would have had to wait until the depression ran its course—months, even a year or more. But because she became depressed within the last decade, she stood a much better chance, for in the last ten years a treatment has been developed that works quickly and well. Its discoverers were a psychologist, Albert Ellis, and a psychiatrist, Aaron T. Beck. When the history of modern psychotherapy is written, I believe their names will appear on the short list with Freud and Jung. Together they took the mystery out of depression. They showed us it was much simpler and more curable than it was thought to be.

Before Ellis and Beck spun their theories, it was dogma that all depression was manic-depressive illness. There were two opposing theories of manic-depression illness: The biomedical school held that it was a disease of the body; the alternative was Freud's notion that depression was anger turned upon the self. Dutifully incorporating this insidious bit of nonsense into their treatment of patients, the Freudians urged depressives to let all their emotions hang out—with the common result of increased depression and even suicide.

Ellis was a very different apostle of letting it all hang out. After getting his Ph.D. from Columbia University in 1947, Ellis undertook a private practice in psychotherapy, specializing in marriage and family therapy. Perhaps stirred by his patients' disclosures, he soon launched what became a lifelong campaign against sexual repression. He began writing book after book with titles like *If This Be Sexual Heresy*, *The Case for Sexual Liberty*, and *The Civilized Couple's Guide to Extramarital Adventure*. Quite naturally Ellis became a charter member of, and guru to, the Kerouac generation, providing its rationale. I first came across his work in the early 1960s when, as a Princeton sophomore, I helped organize a student program on sexuality. Ellis, invited to speak, proposed some such title as "Masturbate Now" for his presentation. The president of Princeton, usually a man of unflappable fairness, had him disinvited.

Many colleagues viewed Ellis as an embarrassment, but others recognized that he was endowed with an extraordinary clinical sense. When his patients were talking, he was listening acutely and thinking hard and iconoclastically. By the 1970s he had taken his charisma and his directness into the field of depression, an area filled with nearly as much prejudice and misconception as sexuality was. Depression was never the same again.

Ellis was as outrageous in his new field as he'd been in the old. Gaunt and angular, always in motion, he sounded like a (very effective) vacuum-cleaner salesman. With patients, he pushed and pushed until he had persuaded them to give up the irrational beliefs that sustained their depression. "What do you mean you can't live without love?" he would cry. "Utter nonsense. Love comes rarely in life, and if you waste your life mooning over its all too ordinary absence, you are bringing on your own depression. You are living under a tyranny of *should*'s. Stop 'should-ing' on yourself!"

Ellis believed that what others thought of as deep neurotic conflict was simply bad thinking—"stupid behavior on the part of nonstupid people," he called it—and in a loud, propagandistic way (he called himself a counterpropagandist) he would demand that his patients stop thinking wrong and start thinking right. Surprisingly, most of his patients got better. Ellis successfully challenged the hallowed belief that mental illness is an enormously intricate, even mysterious phenomenon, curable only when deep unconscious conflicts are brought to light or a medical illness is rooted out. In the complexified world of psychology, this stripped-down approach came off as revolutionary.

Meanwhile, Beck, a Freudian psychiatrist with immense clinical gifts, was also having trouble with the orthodox approach. Beck and Ellis couldn't have contrasted more sharply. Ellis's manner was Trotskyite, Beck's was Socratic. A friendly, folksy man with a cherubic face and the look of a New England country doctor, given to wearing red bow ties, Beck conveyed gentleness and bedrock common sense. Haranguing patients was not his style. He would listen carefully, softly question, mildly persuade.

Like Ellis, Beck found himself intensely frustrated in the 1960s because of the stranglehold the Freudian and biomedical views had on the treatment of depression. After his medical studies at Yale, he spent years as a conventional analyst, waiting for the lonely figure on the couch to come up with some insight about his depression: how he had been turning his anger on himself instead of expressing it, and how depression had resulted. Beck's wait was rarely rewarded. He had then tried treating groups of depressives, encouraging them to give vent to their anger and their sadness rather than holding them in. This was worse than unrewarding. Depressives would unravel before his eyes, and he could not easily knit them up again.

In 1966, when I met Tim Beck (his middle name is Temkin and his friends call him Tim), he was writing his first book about depression. His common sense had asserted itself. He had decided he would merely describe what a depressed person consciously thinks and leave to others the deep theorizing about where these thoughts come from. Depressives think awful things about themselves and their future. Maybe that's all there is to depression, Tim reasoned. Maybe what looks like a symptom of depression—negative thinking—*is* the disease. Depression, he argued courageously, is neither bad brain chemistry nor anger turned inward. It is a disorder of conscious thought.

With this battle cry, Tim lit into the Freudians. "The troubled person," he wrote, "is led to believe that he can't help himself and must seek out a professional healer when confronted with distress related to everyday problems of living. His confidence in using the 'obvious' techniques he has customarily used in solving his problems is eroded because he accepts the view that emotional disturbances arise from forces beyond his grasp. He can't hope to understand himself through his own efforts, because his own notions are dismissed as shallow and insubstantial. By debasing the value of common sense, this subtle indoctrination inhibits him from using his own judgment in analyzing and solving his problems."

Tim liked to quote a remark by the great mathematician and philosopher Alfred North Whitehead: "Science is rooted in . . . common sense thought. That is the datum from which it starts, and to which it must recur. . . . You may polish up common sense, you may contradict it in detail, you may surprise it. But ultimately your whole task is to satisfy it."

A progenitor of this revolution in psychology, also today in his seventies, was Joseph Wolpe. A psychiatrist in South Africa and a born dissenter (his own brother, a leading South African Communist, had been persecuted and jailed), Wolpe had chosen to confront the psychoanalytic establishment. In South Africa, that was almost like opposing apartheid, such was psychoanalysis's grip on the profession. In the 1950s Wolpe astounded the therapeutic world, and infuriated his colleagues, by finding a simple cure for phobias. The psychoanalytic establishment held that a phobia—an irrational and intense fear of certain objects, such as cats—was just a surface manifestation of a deeper, underlying disorder. The phobia's source, it was said, was the buried fear that your father would castrate you in retaliation for your lust for your mother. (No alternative mechanism is suggested for women. Remarkably, Freudians never paid much attention to the fact that the vast majority of phobics are women, and therefore lack the genital configuration required by their theory.) The biomedical theorists, on the other hand, claimed that there must be some, as yet undiscovered, disordered brain chemistry that was the underlying problem. (Even now, forty years later, this malfunction of brain chemistry has not been found.) Both groups insisted that to treat only the patient's fear of cats would do no more good than it would to put rouge over measles.

Wolpe, however, reasoned that irrational fear of something isn't just a symptom of a phobia; it's the whole phobia. If the fear could be removed (and it could, through various Pavlovian extinction procedures involving punishment and reward), that would extinguish the phobia. If you could get rid of your fear of cats, the problem would be solved. The phobia wouldn't, as the psychoanalytic and biomedical theorists claimed, reappear in some other form. Wolpe and his followers, who called themselves behavior therapists, routinely cured fears in a month or two, and the phobias didn't reappear in any other form.

For this impertinence—for implying there was nothing particularly complex about psychiatric disorders—Wolpe was made exceedingly uncomfortable in South Africa. He exiled himself, going to Maudsley Hospital in London, then the University of Virginia, and finally Temple University in Philadelphia, where he continued to apply behavior therapy to mental illness. Feisty and opinionated, he regularly got into huge fights with everyone. When followers deviated from his ideas even in small ways, he wrote them off. If this trait was reminiscent of the psychoanalytic orthodoxy by which he himself had been persecuted, the other side of the trait was courage.

By the late 1960s Philadelphia was becoming the Athens of the new psychology. Joseph Wolpe was fulminating up at Temple, and Tim Beck was now at the University of Pennsylvania, gathering an increasing number of adherents. He quietly drew the same conclusion about depression that Wolpe had drawn about phobia. Depression is nothing more than its symptoms. It is caused by conscious negative thoughts. There is no deep underlying disorder to be rooted out: not unresolved childhood conflicts, not our unconscious anger, and not even our brain chemistry. Emotion comes directly from what we think: Think "I am in danger" and you feel anxiety. Think "I am being trespassed against" and you feel anger. Think "Loss" and you feel sadness.

I was an early adherent, believing that the same process—conscious thought gone awry—might be at work in both learned helplessness and depression. I had gone to Cornell University to teach in 1967, right after taking my Ph.D. at the University of Pennsylvania. In 1969 Tim asked me to come back to the University of Pennsylvania and spend a year or two with him to learn his new approach to depression. I returned gladly and found myself in the middle of a group excitedly designing a new kind of therapy for depression.

Our reasoning was straightforward. Depression results from lifelong habits of conscious thought. If we change these habits of thought, we will cure depression. Let's make a direct assault on conscious thought, we said, using everything we know to change the way our patients think about bad events. Out of this came the new approach, which Beck called cognitive therapy. It tries to change the way the depressed patient thinks about failure, defeat, loss, and helplessness. The National Institute of Mental Health has spent millions of dollars testing whether the therapy works on depression. It does.

HOW YOU THINK about your problems, including depression itself, will either relieve depression or aggravate it. A failure or a defeat can teach you that you are now helpless, but learned helplessness will produce only momentary symptoms of depression—unless you have a pessimistic explanatory style. If you do, then failure and defeat can throw you into a full-blown depression. On the other hand, if your explanatory style is optimistic, your depression will be halted.

Women are twice as likely to suffer depression as men are, because on the average they think about problems in ways that amplify depression. Men tend to act rather than reflect, but women tend to contemplate their depression, mulling it over and over, trying to analyze it and determine its source. Psychologists call this process of obsessive analysis *rumination*, a word whose first meaning is "chewing the cud." Ruminant animals, such as cattle, sheep, and goats, chew a cud composed of regurgitated, partially digested food—not a very appealing image of what people who ruminate do with their thoughts, but an exceedingly apt one. Rumination combined with pessimistic explanatory style is the recipe for severe depression.

This ends the bad news. The good news is that both pessimistic explanatory style and rumination can be changed, and changed permanently. Cognitive therapy can create optimistic explanatory style and curtail rumination. It prevents new depressions by teaching the skills needed to bounce back from defeat. You will see how it works on others, and then you will learn how to use its techniques on yourself.

Learned Helplessness and Explanatory Style

WE ALL BECOME momentarily helpless when we fail. The psychological wind is knocked out of us. We feel sad, the future looks dismal, and putting out any effort seems overwhelmingly difficult. Some people recover almost at once; all the symptoms of learned helplessness dissipate within hours. Others stay helpless for weeks or, if the failure is important enough, for months or longer.

This is the critical difference between brief demoralization and an episode of depression. You will recall that eight of the nine symptoms of depression in the DSM-III-R "Chinese menu" (described in chapter four) are produced by learned helplessness. You must have five of the nine to be diagnosed as suffering a major depressive episode. However, one more factor is needed: The symptoms cannot be momentary; they have to last at least two weeks.

The difference between people whose learned helplessness disappears swiftly and people who suffer their symptoms for two weeks or more is usually simple: Members of the latter group have a pessimistic explanatory style, and a pessimistic explanatory style changes learned helplessness from brief and local to long-lasting and general. Learned helplessness becomes full-blown depression when the person who fails is a pessimist. In optimists, a failure produces only brief demoralization.

The key to this process is hope or hopelessness. Pessimistic explanatory style, you will recall, consists of certain kinds of explanations for bad events: personal ("It's my fault"), permanent ("It's always going to be like this"), and pervasive ("It's going to undermine every aspect of my life"). If you explain a failure permanently and pervasively, you project your present failure into the future and into all new situations. For example, if rejected by someone you love, you may tell yourself, "Women [men] hate me" (a pervasive explanation) and "I'm never going to find anybody" (a permanent explanation). Both of these factors, permanence and pervasiveness, create your expectation that you will be rejected again and again—that it is not just this lover who will reject you but all lovers. Explaining romantic setbacks to yourself this way will undercut all your future quests for love.

If, in addition, you believe the cause is personal ("I'm unlovable"), your self-esteem will suffer as well.

Put all this together and you can see there is one particularly self-defeating way to think: *making personal, permanent, and pervasive explanations for bad events*. People who have this most pessimistic of all styles are likely, once they fail, to have the symptoms of learned helplessness for a long time and across many endeavors, and to lose self-esteem. Such protracted learned helplessness amounts to depression. This is the central prediction from my theory: People who have a pessimistic explanatory style and suffer bad events will probably become depressed, whereas people who have an optimistic explanatory style and suffer bad events will tend to resist depression.

If this is so, then pessimism is a risk factor for depression in just the same sense as smoking is a risk factor for lung cancer or being a hostile, hard-driving man is a risk factor for heart attack.

Does Pessimism Cause Depression?

I HAVE SPENT much of the last ten years testing this prediction. The first thing the University of Pennsylvania group did was the simplest. We gave the explanatory-style questionnaire to depressed people, thousands of them, people with all kinds and degrees of depression. We consistently found that when people are depressed they are also pessimistic. The finding was so consistent and was repeated so often that, according to one estimate, it would take over ten thousand negative studies to cast doubt on it.

This does not show that pessimism causes depression, only that depressed people happen to be pessimistic at the same time they are depressed. You'd get this same coincidence of pessimism and depression if (to reverse things) it were depression that caused pessimism, or if something else (like brain chemistry) caused both conditions. Finally, part of the way we diagnose depression is to listen to what pessimistic people say. If a patient tells us he is worthless, this pessimistic explanation is part of the reason we diagnose him as depressed. So, the association between pessimistic explanatory style and depression could simply be circular.

To show that pessimism causes depression, we needed to take a group of people who were not depressed and show that, after some catastrophe, the pessimistic ones became depressed more easily than the optimistic ones. The ideal experiment would have been something like this: to test everyone in a small town on the Gulf Coast of Mississippi for depression and explanatory style and then wait for a hurricane to hit. After the hurricane passed, we'd go see who lay there passively in the mud and who got up and rebuilt the town. There were both ethical and funding problems involved in conducting this "experiment of nature." So we had to find other ways of testing the causal chain.

One of my most brilliant undergraduates, Amy Semmel, then a sophomore, solved the dilemma by pointing out natural disasters that hit much closer to home—hit my own classes, in fact, twice a semester. Exams. When my classes began in September, we tested all the students both for depression and for their explanatory style. In October, as the midterm approached, we asked them all what would count as a "failure" for them. On average, they said getting a B+ would constitute failure. (You can see what a bunch of high achievers they were.) This was fine for the experiment since the average grade on my exams is C, which meant most of my students would be subjects. One week later, they took the midterm, and the next week they got their midterm grades back, along with a copy of the Beck Depression Inventory.

Thirty percent of the people who (by their own definition of failure) failed the midterm got very depressed. And 30 percent of the people who were pessimists in September did, too. But 70 percent of the people who both were pessimists in September *and* failed the exam got depressed. So a recipe for severe depression is preexisting pessimism encountering failure. In fact, those of this group who made the most permanent and pervasive explanations for why they failed were the people who were still depressed when we tested them again in December.

A much grimmer setting for an "experiment of nature" took place in prison. We measured the depression level and explanatory style of male prisoners before and after incarceration. Because suicide in prison is such a prevalent problem, we wanted to try to predict who was at most risk for becoming depressed. To our surprise, no one was seriously depressed upon entering prison. To our dismay, almost everyone was depressed on leaving. Some might say this means the prisons are doing their job, but it seems to me something deeply demoralizing is happening during imprisonment. At any rate, we once again correctly predicted who became most depressed of all: those who entered as pessimists. This means pessimism is fertile soil in which depression grows, particularly when the environment is hostile.

These various findings all pointed to pessimism as a cause of depression. We knew we could take a group of normal people and predict, far in advance, who among them were most likely to succumb to depression when bad events struck.

Another way of finding out if pessimism causes depression was to look at a group of people across time, in the course of their natural lives. This is called conducting a longitudinal study. We followed a group of 400 third-graders right on through the sixth grade (we're still following them), measuring their explanatory style, their depression, their school achievement, and their popularity twice a year. We found that the children who started out as pessimists were the ones most likely, over the four years, to get depressed and stay depressed. Those children who started out as optimists stayed nondepressed or, if they did get depressed, they recovered rapidly. When major bad events occurred, like parents separating or getting divorced, the pessimists went under most readily. We also studied young adults and found the same pattern.

Do these studies really prove that pessimism causes depression, or only that pessimism precedes depression and predicts it? Here's a particularly devilish argument. Let's assume people have a great deal of insight into how they react to bad events. Some people have repeatedly seen how devastated they become when bad things happen. This knowledge makes them pessimists. Others, those who will become optimists, have seen how promptly they bounce back. These two groups become pessimists or optimists because they have observed their own reaction to bad events. On this account, pessimism is no more a cause of depression than a speedometer's reading 60 miles an hour causes the car to speed along: The speedometer and the pessimism merely reflect more basic underlying states.

I know of only one way to dispatch this argument: Study the way therapy works.

Explanatory Style and Cognitive Therapy

TANYA CAME into therapy with a marriage going downhill day by day, three children she saw as wild and uncontrollable, and a very severe depression. She agreed to participate in a study of different therapies for depression and was assigned to receive both cognitive therapy and antidepressant drugs. She allowed the investigators to tape-record her therapy sessions. In these quotes, the italics emphasize the sorts of explanations she gave for her problems. I will attach numbers to each quote. These numbers are her pessimism scores (related to the test in chapter three). They range from 3 (completely temporary, specific, and external) to 21 (completely permanent, pervasive, and personalized). Each individual dimension is coded on a 1 to 7 scale, so the three dimensions added together range from 3 to 31. Numbers in the 3 to 8 range are very optimistic. Numbers above 13 are very pessimistic.*

> Tanya felt disgusted with herself *"because I always yell at my kids and never apologize"* (permanent, rather pervasive, and personal: 17).
> She had no hobbies *"because I'm no good at anything"* (permanent, pervasive, and personal: 21).
> She failed to take her antidepressant medicine "because I can't handle it, *I'm not strong enough"* (permanent, pervasive, and personal: 15).

Tanya's explanations were uniformly pessimistic. Whatever it was, if it was bad, it was going to last forever, it was going to destroy everything, and it was her fault.

Like everyone else in her group, she received twelve weeks of treatment. She did beautifully. Her depression began to lift markedly within a month, and by the end of treatment she was free of depression. Her life wasn't outwardly much better. Her marriage continued to fall apart by inches. Her children still didn't behave themselves at school or at home. But she looked at the causes of her problems in a much more optimistic way. Here's the way she now talked:

> "I had to go to church alone *because my husband was being mean and wouldn't go"* (temporary, specific, and external: 8).
> "I run around looking like rags *because the kids have to get their school clothes"* (quite temporary, specific, and external: 8).
> *"He took all my money out of the savings account and spent it on himself.* If I'd had a gun, I would have shot him" (temporary, specific, and external: 9).
> She had been having trouble driving *"because my glasses aren't dark enough"* (temporary, specific, and external: 6).

When bad events occurred, as they did almost daily, Tanya no longer saw them as unchangeable, pervasive, and her fault. She now began to take action to change things.

What caused Tanya's remarkable change from pessimistic to optimistic

---

*The method of coding the pessimism of people who cannot or did not take explanatory-style questionnaires is called content analysis of verbatim explanations, or CAVE. It is described on page 132.

explanatory style? Was it the drugs or was it the cognitive therapy? Was the change just a sign she had gotten less depressed, or was it the cause of her getting less depressed? Because Tanya was one of many patients assigned to different treatments, these questions could be answered.

First, both treatments worked very well. Antidepressant drugs alone and cognitive therapy alone broke up depression reliably. The combination worked even better than either alone, but only slightly better.

Second, the active ingredient in cognitive therapy was a change in explanatory style from pessimistic to optimistic. The more cognitive therapy done and the more expertly it was delivered, the more thorough the change to optimism. In turn, the greater the change toward optimism, the greater the relief from depression. Drugs, on the other hand, even though they relieved the depression fairly effectively, did not make patients more optimistic. It was reasonable to conclude that although drugs and cognitive therapy both relieve depression, they probably work in quite different ways. Drugs seem to be activators; they push the patient up and out, but they do not make the world look any brighter. Cognitive therapy changes the way you look at things, and this new, optimistic style gets you up and around.

The third and most important set of findings was about relapse. How permanent was the relief of depression? Tanya's depression did not recur, although those of many of the other patients in this study did. The results showed that the key to permanent relief of depression was a change in explanatory style. Many of the patients in the drug groups relapsed, but patients who got cognitive therapy did not relapse at nearly that rate. Patients whose explanatory style became optimistic were less likely to relapse than patients whose style remained pessimistic.

This means cognitive therapy specifically works by making patients more optimistic. It prevents relapse because patients acquire a skill they can use again and again without relying on drugs or doctors. Drugs relieve depression, but only temporarily; unlike cognitive therapy, drugs fail to change the underlying pessimism which is at the root of the problem.

I concluded from these studies that among people who are not now depressed, pessimistic explanatory style predicts who is going to get depressed. It also predicts who will stay depressed, and it predicts who will relapse after therapy. Changing explanatory style from pessimism to optimism relieves depression markedly.

Remember our concern that pessimism might merely display the fact that you are easily depressed by bad events, but not itself be a cause of depression. The way to test whether pessimism is a cause is to change pessimism to optimism. If pessimism was only an indicator, like a speedometer, changing to optimism shouldn't affect how you react to bad events any more than changing the speedometer would change the speed of the car. However, if pessimism is a cause of why you get depressed so easily, changing pessimism into optimism should relieve depression. That is, in fact, what happened. This outcome sews up a causal role for pessimism in depression. It is surely not the *only* cause of depression—genes, bad events, hormones also put people at risk—but that it is one of the major causes now seems undeniable.

Rumination and Depression

IF YOU WALK around disposed to believe of any problem that "it's me, it's going to last forever, it's going to undermine everything I try," you are set up for depression. But just because you may be disposed to think this way doesn't necessarily mean you frequently utter such thoughts to yourself. Some people do, some don't. People who mull over bad events are called ruminators.

A ruminator can either be an optimist or a pessimist. Ruminators who are pessimists are in trouble. Their belief structure is pessimistic, and they repeatedly tell themselves how bad things are. Other pessimists are action-oriented and do not ruminate: They have pessimistic explanatory style, but they do not talk to themselves much at all. When they do, it is usually about what they plan to do, not about how bad things are.

When Tanya came into therapy, she was not only a pessimist, she was a ruminator as well. She brooded about her marriage, her children, and most destructively, her depression itself.

> "But now, I don't want to do nothing. . . ."
> "It's just really bad for me, I've got the blues constantly. I'm not a crying person—I don't cry unless there's a real good reason—but, jeez, this time when somebody says something I don't like, I start crying. . . ."
> "I can't take this. . . ."
> "I'm not a very affectionate person. . . ."
> "My husband won't leave me alone. He just bugs me. I wish he wouldn't be like that."

Tanya had succumbed to nonstop rumination, an unbroken string of sour musings with no action statements at all. It wasn't her pessimism alone that was fueling her depression; it was rumination too.

Here's how the pessimism-rumination chain leads to depression: First, there is some threat against which you believe you are helpless. Second, you look for the threat's cause, and, if you are a pessimist, the cause you arrive at is permanent, pervasive, and personal. Consequently, you expect to be helpless in the future and in many situations, a conscious expectation that is the last link in the chain, the one triggering depression.

The expectation of helplessness may arise only rarely, or it may arise all the time. The more you are inclined to ruminate, the more it arises. The more it arises, the more depressed you will be. Brooding, thinking about how bad things are, starts the sequence. Ruminators get this chain going all the time. Any reminder of the original threat causes them to run off the whole pessimism-rumination chain, right through to the expectation of failure and into depression.

People who do not ruminate tend to avoid depression even if they are pessimists. For them the sequence runs itself off infrequently. Optimists who ruminate also avoid depression. Changing either rumination or pessimism helps relieve depression. Changing both helps the most.

We find, then, that pessimistic ruminators are most at risk for depression. Cognitive therapy limits rumination as well as creating an optimistic explanatory style. Here's what Tanya sounded like at the end of therapy:

"I don't want a full-time job again, I just want something part-time, four hours a day so I don't have to sit in the house all day . . ." (action).

"I will feel like I am contributing to the income so if we want to go somewhere, we can go" (action).

"I kind of like to do spur-of-the-moment things every once in a while" (action).

She no longer ruminated about bad events continually, and her speech was now peppered with action statements.

The Other Side of the Epidemic: Women vs. Men

THE CRUCIAL ROLE rumination plays in depression may be responsible for the arresting fact that depression is primarily female. Study after study has found that during the twentieth century, depression has struck women more frequently than men. The ratio is now two to one.

Why should women suffer so much more?

Is it because women are more willing to go to therapy than men and thus show up more frequently in the statistics? No. The same preponderance of women shows up in door-to-door surveys.

Is it because women are more willing to talk openly about their troubles? Probably not. The two-to-one ratio shows up in both public and anonymous conditions.

Is it because women tend to have worse jobs and less money than men do? No. The ratio stays two-to-one even when groups of women and men are matched for the same jobs and the same income: Rich women have twice as much depression as rich men, and unemployed women twice as much as unemployed men.

Is it some sort of biological difference that produces more depression? Probably not. Studies of premenstrual and postpartum emotionality show that while hormone fluctuations do tend to affect depression, the effect isn't nearly big enough to make a two-to-one difference.

Is it a genetic difference? Careful studies of how much depression occurs among the sons and daughters of male and female depressives show there is substantial depression among the sons of male depressives—too much, considering the way chromosomes are passed from father to son and from mother to daughter, for it to be true that genetics underpins the lopsided sex ratio. There is evidence of a genetic contribution to depression, but there is no evidence that genes contribute more to depression in women than in men.

Three interesting theories remain.

The first concerns sex roles—that there is something about a woman's role in our society that makes her fertile ground for depression.

One fashionable argument in this category is that women are brought up to invest in love and in social relations, while men are brought up to invest in achievement. A woman's self-esteem, runs the argument, depends on how love and friendship go; social failure, therefore—from divorce and separation, to children leaving the nest, to a wasted evening with an awful blind date—hits women harder than men. This may be true, but it does not explain why women are twice as likely to be depressed. For the argument can be turned around: By this hypothesis, men take failure at work more seriously. Bad grades, no promotion, the softball team losing—these too deplete a man's self-esteem. And failure seems just as common in work as in love, so the net effect would be just as much depression in men as in women.

Another fashionable sex-role argument dwells on role conflict: There are more conflicting demands on women than on men in modern life. A woman not only has the traditional role of mother and wife but now must hold down a job as well. This extra demand produces more pressure than ever before and therefore more depression. The argument sounds plausible; but, like many plausible and ideologically congenial theories, it dashes against the rocks of fact. Working wives are less depressed, on average, than wives who do not work outside the home. So sex-role explanations do not seem to account for the two-to-one female preponderance of depression.

The second of the remaining theories involves learned helplessness and explanatory style. In our society, it is argued, women receive abundant experience with helplessness over the course of their lives. Boys' behavior is lauded or criticized by their parents and their teachers, while girls' is often ignored. Boys are trained for self-reliance and activity, girls for passivity and dependence. When they grow up, women find themselves in a culture that depreciates the role of wife and mother. If a woman turns to the world of work, she finds her achievements are given less credit than men's. When she speaks in a meeting, she gets more bored nods than a man would. If despite all this she manages to excel and is promoted to a position of power, she is seen as being out of place. Learned helplessness at every turn. If women tend to have a more pessimistic explanatory style than men do, any given helplessness experience will tend to produce more depression in a woman than in a man. And indeed there are data showing that any given stressful factor causes more depression in women than in men.

This theory is also plausible, but not without its holes. One hole is that no one has ever proven that women are more pessimistic than men. Indeed the only relevant study of randomly sampled males and females is among grade-school children, and it comes out the opposite way. Among third-, fourth-, and fifth-graders, boys are more pessimistic than girls and more depressed. When parents divorce, the boys get more depressed than the girls do. (All this may change at puberty, and indeed it does seem the two-to-one depression ratio begins in the teenage years. Something may happen at puberty that flips young women into depression and young men out of it. More of this later, when we talk about parenting and about school in chapters seven and eight.) Another problem is that no one has ever shown that women see their lives as more uncontrollable than men do.

The last of the three theories involves rumination. In this view, when trouble strikes, women think and men act. When a woman gets fired from her job, she tries to figure out why; she broods, and she relives the events over and over. A man, upon getting fired, acts: He gets drunk, beats someone up, or otherwise distracts himself from thinking about it. He may even go right out and look for another job, without bothering to think through what went wrong. If depression is a disorder of thinking, pessimism and rumination stoke it. The tendency to analyze feeds right into it; the tendency to act breaks it up.

In fact, depression itself may set off rumination more in women than men. When we find ourselves depressed, what do we do? Women try to figure out where the depression came from. Men go out to play basketball, or leave for the office to work to distract themselves. Men are more often alcoholic than women are; perhaps the difference is great enough to enable us to say: Men drink, women get depressed. It might be that men drink to forget their troubles while women ruminate. The woman, ruminating away about the source of the depression, will only get more depressed, whereas the man, responding by taking action, may cut depression off.

The rumination theory just might be able to explain the depression epidemic in general as well as the lopsided sex ratio. If we now live in an age of self-consciousness, in which we are encouraged to take our problems more earnestly and analyze them endlessly rather than act, more depression might well be the result. I'll talk more about this speculation in chapter fifteen.

Evidence has poured in recently that supports the role of rumination in producing the sex differences in depression. Susan Nolen-Hoeksema of Stanford University, who originated the rumination theory, has led the way in testing it. When women rate what they actually do (not what they *should* do) when they are depressed, the majority say, "I tried to analyze my mood" or "I tried to find out why I felt the way I did." The majority of men, on the other hand, say they did something they enjoyed, like sports or playing a musical instrument, or they say, "I decided not to concern myself with my mood."

The same pattern held in a diary study in which men and women wrote down everything they did as bad moods struck: Women thought and analyzed their mood; men distracted themselves. In a study of couples in conflict, each person dictated into a tape recorder what he or she did every time there was marital trouble. In overwhelming proportions the women focused on and expressed their emotion, and the men distracted themselves or decided not to be concerned with their mood. Finally, in a laboratory study, men and women were offered a choice of two tasks when they were sad. They could choose to list the words that best described their mood (a task focusing on the depression) or rank a list of nations in order of their wealth (a distracting task). Seventy percent of the women chose the emotion-focused task, listing the words that described their mood. With men, however, the percentages were reversed.

So analyzing and wallowing in emotion when distressed seems a likely explanation for why women are more depressed than men. This implies that men and women experience mild depression at the same rate, but in women, who dwell on the state, the mild depression escalates; men, on the other hand, dissolve the state by distracting themselves, by action or perhaps by drinking it away.

We are left with two plausible views that have some support. One is that women learn more helplessness and pessimism, and the second is that women's likelier first reaction to trouble—rumination—leads right into depression.

Depression as Curable

ONE HUNDRED years ago, the most fashionable explanation for human action, particularly bad human action, was character. Words like *mean*, *stupid*, *criminal*, *evil*—these were considered satisfactory explanations for bad behavior. *Crazy* was accepted as an explanation for mental illness. These terms denote traits that can't be changed easily, if at all. As prophecy, they are also self-fulfilling. People who believe themselves stupid, rather than uneducated, don't take action to improve their minds. A society that views its criminals as evil and the mentally ill as crazy does not support institutions truly designed for rehabilitation but supports, instead, institutions meant for vengeance or for warehousing human beings to keep them out of sight.

Toward the end of the nineteenth century, the labels and the concepts behind them began to change. The growing political clout of the massive labor force probably began the transformation. Then came wave after wave of European and Asian immigrants who visibly bettered themselves in less than a generation. Explanations of human failure in terms of abiding bad character gave way to suggestions of bad upbringing or bad environment. Ignorance began to be seen as lack of education, not stupidity, and crime as issuing from poverty, not evil. Poverty itself was now thought of as lack of opportunity, not sloth. Madness began to be seen as consisting of maladaptive habits that could be unlearned. This new ideology, which stressed one's environment, was the backbone of the behaviorism that dominated American (and Russian) psychology from 1920 to 1965, from Lenin to LBJ.

Behaviorism's successor, cognitive psychology, retained the optimistic belief in change and wed it to an expanded view of the self, developing the thesis that the self could improve itself. People who wanted to reduce the amount of human failure in this world could look beyond the difficulties of changing the conditions of upbringing and environment; they could embrace the prospect that the individual could choose to act on himself. For example, curing mental illness no longer rested solely in the hands of therapists, social workers, and asylums. It now passed in part into the hands of the sufferers.

This belief is the intellectual underpinning of the self-improvement movement, the wellspring of all those diet books, exercise books, and books on changing your personality: your Type A risk for heart attack, your airplane phobia, your depression. What is remarkable is that much of this self-improving ideology is not claptrap. A society that exalts the self to the extent ours does produces an entity that is not a chimera. The self-improving self actually improves itself. You can indeed lose weight, lower your cholesterol level, be physically stronger and more attractive, less compulsively time-urgent and reflexively hostile, less pessimistic.

The belief in self-improvement is a prophecy just as self-fulfilling as the old belief that character could not be changed. People who believe they don't have to be sedentary or hostile will try to take the steps that get them jogging or make them think twice when trespassed against; people who don't believe change is possible will indeed remain incapable of change. A culture believing in self-improvement will support health clubs, Alcoholics Anonymous, and psychotherapy. A culture believing that bad action stems from bad character and is permanent won't even try.

Scientists who speak of a self that can act to change the self are not spouting metaphysical boosterism. The computer provides the physical model for such claims. A computer, even a PC, can compare its output to that of a template (an ideal situation), find the places where the fit is imperfect, and move to correct the imperfections. Having done this, it can once again compare what it has done to what it should do and, if still wrong, act to correct itself again. When the match is perfect, it will stop. If a home computer can bring this off, self-improvement should be a breeze for the vastly more complex human brain.

Human beings have been getting severely depressed ever since failure began—perhaps not in the droves they do today, but depressed nevertheless. And when the medieval swain failed to conquer a fair maiden's heart, his mother told him not to obsess about it, probably without any more effect than mothers today have on the depressions their children bring home. Then, in the 1980s, along came cognitive therapy, which tries to change the way people think about their failures. Its maxims aren't terribly different from the wisdom the grandmothers and preachers of yore had tried, without notable success, to impart. But cognitive therapy works.

What does cognitive therapy do, and why does it work?

Cognitive Therapy and Depression

To AN AUDIENCE that swelled over the 1970s, Aaron Beck and Albert Ellis both argued that what we consciously think is what mainly determines how we feel. From this thesis a therapy developed that sought to change the way the depressed patient consciously thinks about failure, defeat, loss, and helplessness.

Cognitive therapy uses five tactics.

First, you learn to recognize the automatic thoughts flitting through your consciousness at the times you feel worst. Automatic thoughts are very quick phrases or sentences, so well practiced as to be almost unnoticed and unchallenged. For example, a mother of three children sometimes screams at them as she sends them off to school. She feels very depressed as a consequence. In cognitive therapy she learns to recognize that right after these screaming incidents she always says to herself, "I'm a terrible mother—even worse than my own mother." She learns to become aware of these automatic thoughts, and learns that they are her explanations, and that those explanations are permanent, pervasive, and personal.

Second, you learn to dispute the automatic thoughts by marshaling contrary evidence. The mother is helped to remember and acknowledge that when the kids come home from school, she plays football with them, tutors them in geometry, and talks to them sympathetically about their problems. She focuses on this evidence and sees that it contradicts her automatic thought that she is a bad mother.

Third, you learn to make different explanations, called reattributions, and use them to dispute your automatic thoughts. The mother might learn to say something like: "I'm fine with the kids in the P.M. and terrible in the A.M. Maybe I'm not a morning person." That's a much less permanent and pervasive explanation for screaming at the kids in the morning. As for the chain of negative explanations that goes, "I'm a terrible mother, I'm not fit to have kids, therefore I don't deserve to live," she learns to interrupt it by inserting the contrary, new explanation.

Fourth, you learn how to distract yourself from depressing thoughts. The mother learns that thinking these negative things now is not inevitable. Rumination, particularly when one is under pressure to perform well, makes the situation even worse. Often it is better to put off thinking, in order to do your best. You can learn to control not only what you think but when you think it.

Fifth, you learn to recognize and question the depression-sowing assumptions governing so much of what you do:

"I can't live without love."
"Unless everything I do is perfect, I'm a failure."
"Unless everybody likes me, I'm a failure."
"There is a perfect right solution for every problem. I must find it."

Premises like these set you up for depression. If you choose to live by them—as so many of us do—your life will be filled with black days and blue weeks. But just as a person can change his explanatory style from pessimistic to optimistic, he can also choose a new set of more human premises to live by:

"Love is precious but rare."
"Success is doing my best."
"For every person who likes you, one person doesn't like you."
"Life consists of putting my fingers in the biggest leaks in the dam."

The depression suffered by Sophie—the former "golden girl" who had come to consider herself unlovable, untalented, "a washout"—is typical of the depressions young people are experiencing in unprecedented numbers. Her depression had at its core a pessimistic explanatory style. After she began cognitive therapy, life quickly turned around for her. Her treatment took a total of three months, one hour per week. Her outside world did not change, at least not at first, but the way she thought about it changed mightily.

First, she was helped to see that she had been conducting an unrelievedly negative dialogue with herself. She remembered that when she'd made a comment in class and had been complimented by the professor, she had immediately thought: "She's just trying to be nice to all the students." When she'd read about Indira Gandhi's assassination, she'd thought: "All women leaders are doomed, one way or another." When her friend had been impotent late one night, she'd thought: "I'm repulsive to him."

I asked her, "If a drunk reeling on the street told you you were repulsive, would you discount it?"

"Sure."

"But when you say equally groundless things to yourself, you believe them. This is because you think the source, yourself, is more credible. It isn't. Often we distort reality more than drunks do."

Sophie soon learned to marshal evidence against her automatic thoughts and thus challenge them: She remembered that the professor who had complimented her did not in fact flatter everyone but had been quite cutting when another student commented in class. She focused on the fact that the lover who'd been impotent had drunk an entire six-pack in the hour before they made love. She learned a crucial skill: how to conduct an optimistic personal dialogue. She learned how to talk to herself when she failed and how not to talk to herself when things went well. She learned that when she expected to fail, failure became more likely. Her explanatory style changed permanently from pessimistic to optimistic.

Sophie caught fire again academically, and she graduated with high honors. She began a love affair which is now a fulfilling marriage.

Unlike most people who are prone to depression, Sophie learned how to prevent its return. The difference between Sophie and someone who takes antidepressant drugs is that she learned a set of skills to use whenever she is faced with failure or defeat—skills she always carries with her. Her victory over depression is hers alone, not something she must credit to doctors and the latest medication.

Why Does Cognitive Therapy Work?

THERE ARE two kinds of answers to this question. On a mechanical level, cognitive therapy works because it changes explanatory style from pessimistic to optimistic, and the change is permanent. It gives you a set of cognitive skills for talking to yourself when you fail. You can use these skills to stop depression from taking hold when failure strikes.

At a philosophical level, cognitive therapy works because it takes advantage of newly legitimized powers of the self. In an era when we believe the self can change itself, we are willing to try to change habits of thought which used to seem as inevitable as sunrise. Cognitive therapy works in our era because it gives the self a set of techniques for changing itself. The self chooses to do this work out of self-interest, to make itself feel better.

Part Two

The Realms of Life

Meanwhile, the Ice Kings trembled in their chairs
But not from the cold—they'd seen a man hoist high
The Great Horn-Cup that ends deep in the ocean
And lower all Seven Seas by his own stature;

They'd seen him budge the Cat of the World and heft
The pillar of one paw, the whole north corner;
They'd seen a mere man wrestle with Death herself
And match her knee for knee, grunting like thunder.

David Wagoner
"The Labors of Thor"

6

Success at Work

ON LONG FLIGHTS, I usually take the window seat and curl up facing the window, mostly to avoid having to make conversation with my seatmate. I was annoyed one day in March 1982, at the beginning of flight 79 from San Francisco to Philadelphia, to find that my tactics were of no avail. "Hi," my seatmate, a balding sixty-year-old, said heartily. "My name is John Leslie. What's yours?" He pushed his hand at mine. "Oh no," I said to myself, "a gabby one." I mumbled my name and gave him a perfunctory handshake, hoping he'd get the message.

Leslie would not be denied. "I raise horses," he said as the plane taxied down the runway. "When I come to a crossroad, all I have to do is think which way I want the horse to go, and he goes that way. In my job, I raise men—and all I have to do is think what I want them to do, and they do it."

Thus began the chance, uninvited conversation which started a dramatic shift in the focus of my work.

Leslie was persistent, a full-blown optimist who seemed to have no doubt that I would be enthralled by his words of wisdom. And in fact, as the plane neared Nevada, with the snowcapped Sierras beneath us, I found myself being drawn in. "My people," he announced, "developed the video recorder for Ampex. That was the most creative group I ever led."

"What separates your creative groups from your turkeys?" I asked.

"Each person," he said, "every one of them, believes he can walk on water."

By Utah, I was hooked. What he was telling me matched what I had been seeing in people who resisted depression.

"How can you make someone creative?" I asked him.

"I'll show you," he replied. "But first, what do you do for a living?"

I gave him a brief rundown on what I had been up to for the last fifteen years. I told him about helpless people and animals and how helplessness had proved to be a model for depression. I told him about pessimistic explanatory style and the pessimists who gave up so easily moments after experiencing loss of control. "These were the people," I said, "who, outside the lab, came down with serious depression."

"Have you done much work about the other side of the coin?" Leslie asked. "Can you predict who'll never give up and who won't become depressed no matter what you do to them?"

"I haven't thought about them enough," I confessed.

Actually, I had been uneasy for some time about psychology's fixation upon disease. My profession spends most of its time (and almost all of its money) trying to make the troubled less troubled. Helping troubled people is a worthy goal, but somehow psychology almost never gets around to the complementary goal of making the lives of well people even better. With Leslie's prompting I was beginning to see that my work was germane to the other goal. If I could identify in advance the people who would get depressed, I should also be able to identify those who never would.

John asked whether I could think of some business pursuits in which it was essential to keep going in the face of constant rejection and failure.

"Maybe sales," I replied, thinking of a speech I'd given a few months before to a group of insurance-company presidents. "Selling life insurance, say." In life insurance, they'd told me, nine out of ten prospects brush you off. You have to pick yourself up and keep going just to get to the tenth. It's like hitting against a great pitcher: Most of the time you swing and miss, but to get on base you've got to keep swinging. If you keep the bat on your shoulder, you always strike out.

I thought back to a conversation I'd had that weekend with John Creedon, the head of Metropolitan Life. After my speech Creedon asked me if psychology had anything to tell the corporation manager. Could we, for example, help him pick out the people who could successfully sell insurance? And could we develop ways to change foot-dragging pessimists into "Yes, I can" optimists? I had told Creedon I did not know. I now narrated that conversation to Leslie, and by the time we began our descent to Philadelphia, he had me promising to write Creedon a letter. And I did write him, to say that I thought we could perhaps pick out future successes.

I never saw Leslie again. Soon after he buoyantly suggested that I shift my attention from pessimism to optimism, from failure to success, I did just that. My subsequent research showed repeatedly that optimists do better in school, win more elections, and succeed more at work than pessimists do. They even seem to lead longer and healthier lives. As a therapist and a teacher of therapists I found that pessimism can be changed into optimism, not just in depressed people but in normal people as well.

It often occurred to me that I owed Leslie a letter. If I'd written it, I'd have told him about my research on optimism.

Consider the rest of this book that letter.

THREE WEEKS after that flight, I found myself high in one of Metropolitan Life's twin towers in Manhattan, treading the deepest-pile woolen carpets I had ever trod into the gleaming, oak-paneled inner sanctum of John Creedon. A cheerful and perceptive man in his mid-fifties, he had grasped the potential of optimism for his industry long before I had. He explained the perennial problem that Metropolitan and all insurance companies have with their sales forces.

"Selling is not easy," he began. "It requires persistence. It's an unusual person who can do it well and stick with it. Every year we hire five thousand new agents. We select them very carefully out of the sixty thousand people who apply. We test them, we screen them, we interview them, we give them extensive training. But half of them quit anyway in the first year. Most of those who stay on produce less and less. By the end of the fourth year eighty percent are gone. It costs us more than thirty thousand dollars to hire a single agent. So we lose over seventy-five million dollars every year in hiring costs alone. And our figures are typical of the whole industry.

"I'm not just talking about money Met Life loses, Dr. Seligman," he continued. "Whenever an employee quits a job, I'm talking about human misery, about your field—depression. When fifty percent of a whole industry quits every year, there's an important humanitarian mission here—to try to better the 'person-environment fit.'

"What I want to know is, can your test pick out in advance the people who will make the best agents, so we can stem this flow of wasted human capital?"

"Why does quitting typically happen?" I asked.

Creedon outlined the process of giving up. "Every single day even the best agent has quite a few people say no, usually a number of them right in a row. So it s easy for the average agent to get discouraged. Once they get discouraged, they take the no's harder and harder; it takes more and more effort for them to get up and make the next call. They put off making that next call. They spend more and more time fiddling around and doing things that keep them away from the telephone and off the road. This makes it even harder to make the next call. Their production falls off, and they start to think about quitting. When they hit that wall, few of them know how to get over, under, or around it.

"Remember," he said, "these are people with a lot of independence—that's one of the attractions of the business—so we aren't looking over their shoulders constantly and prodding them when they slow down. Remember this, too: Only those agents who keep making their ten calls each day, and don't get fazed by rejection, succeed."

The Explanatory Style of Success

I EXPLAINED the theory of learned helplessness and explanatory style to Creedon. Then I told him about the optimism/pessimism questionnaire (see chapter three). Time and time again, I said, it has been shown that people who score pessimistically on the questionnaire give up easily and become depressed.

But the questionnaire, I went on, doesn't identify just pessimists. Its scores are continuous and range from deeply pessimistic to irrepressibly optimistic. The people who score at the very optimistic end, I said, should be the most persistent. They're the most immune to helplessness. They should never give up, no matter how much rejection and failure they encounter.

"These invulnerable optimists have never really been looked at before," I said, "and they may be exactly the people who'll succeed in a job as challenging as selling insurance."

"Tell me exactly how optimism could help," Creedon replied. "Let's take cold calling, a crucial part of selling life insurance. In cold calling, you have a list of possible prospects, like the names of all the parents of new babies in a town. You start calling, from the top of the list, and you try to make a face-to-face appointment. Most people say, 'No, I'm not interested'—or even just hang up on you."

I explained that optimistic explanatory style should affect not what the insurance agent says to prospects but what he says to himself when the prospect says no. Pessimistic salesmen, I told Creedon, will say permanent, pervasive, and personal things to themselves, like "I'm no good" or "No one wants to buy insurance from me" or "I can't even get to first base." This undoubtedly will produce the giving-up response and make it harder to dial the next prospect. After several such episodes, I predicted, the pessimistic agent will quit for the evening—and eventually quit altogether.

The optimistic agent, on the other hand, will talk to himself in more constructive ways: "He was too busy right now," or "They already have insurance, but eight of ten people are underinsured," or "I called during supper." Or he'll say nothing at all to himself. The next call won't be any harder to make, and within a few minutes the agent will have gotten through to the one person in ten, on average, who makes an appointment. This will energize the agent, so he'll breeze through the next ten calls and get another appointment. In this way he'll live up to his selling potential.

Even before I walked in his door, Creedon, like many other insurance executives, knew that optimism was the key to sales success. He had been waiting for someone who could measure it. We decided to start with a simple correlational study, to see if already successful salesmen were also extremely optimistic. If they were, we would proceed step by step. Our eventual aim was to create a whole new way of selecting the sales force. We used a questionnaire different from the questionnaire you took in chapter three. In this open-ended ASQ (Attributional Style Questionnaire) are twelve vignettes, little scenarios. Half are about bad events (e.g., "You go out on a date, and it goes badly...."), and half are about good events (e.g., "You suddenly become rich...."). You are asked to imagine the event happening to you and to fill in the most likely cause. For example, to explain the first vignette you might say, "I have bad breath," and for the second, "I'm a brilliant investor."

You are then asked to rate the cause you supplied, on a one-to-seven scale, for personalization. ("Is this cause something about other people or circumstances [external], or is it something about you [internal]?") You're then asked to rate it for permanence. ("Will this cause never again be present when looking for a job [temporary] or always be present [permanent]?") And finally you rate it for pervasiveness. ("Does this cause affect only looking for a job [specific] or all other areas of your life [pervasive]?")

For our first try, we gave the questionnaire to two hundred experienced sales agents, half of whom were eagles (very productive) and half turkeys (unproductive). The eagles scored much more optimistically on the questionnaire than the turkeys did. When we matched test scores to actual sales records, we found that agents who scored in the most optimistic half of the ASQ had sold 37 percent more insurance on average in their first two years of work than agents who scored in the pessimistic half.

Agents who scored in the top 10 percent sold 88 percent more than the most pessimistic tenth. In our quest to find out how useful our test might be in the world of business, this was an encouraging beginning.

Testing for Talent

OVER MANY YEARS the insurance industry developed a test meant to discover a person's suitability for a sales career. The Career Profile is published by the Life Insurance Management Research Association. All applicants to Met Life must take a Career Profile, and to be hired they need to score 12 or better. Only the top 30 percent of applicants attain this score. Those who get a 12 or better are interviewed, and if the manager likes what he sees, they are offered a job.

In general, for any line of work two kinds of questionnaires can predict potential for success: empirical and theory-based. An empirical test starts with people who have, in fact, succeeded on the job and people who have, in fact, failed. It throws a large number of random questions at them, covering all of life: "Do you like classical music?" "Do you want to earn a lot of money?" "Do you have a lot of relatives?" "How old are you?" "Do you like to go to parties?" Most of the questions don't separate the eagles from the turkeys, but a few hundred will turn out to. (You just determine which questions happen to work and use those; no theory at all is involved.) These few hundred questions become the test items used to predict future successes at that job. The suitable applicant will have to have the same "profile"—the same sets of ages, backgrounds and attitudes, in short, the same answers—as the typical successful worker already in that field. Empirical tests, then, in effect admit at the outset that why someone succeeds is a complete mystery; they merely use the questions that happen to separate eagles from turkeys.

Theory-based tests, on the other hand, like IQ tests or the SAT, ask only questions deduced from a theory—in this case, a theory of ability. The theory behind the SAT, for example, is that "intelligence" consists of verbal skills (reading comprehension, ability to understand analogies, etc.) and of mathematical-analytic skills (algebra, geometry, etc.). Since these skills are fundamental to how you do schoolwork, performing well on them should predict future success in school. And it does, quite respectably.

But both empirical and theory-based tests make a notoriously large number of mistakes, even though on the whole they predict with statistical accuracy. Many people who score poorly on the SATs will do well in college, and many people who score well will flunk out. Even more obvious was Met Life's problem: A great many people who score well on the Career Profile sell poorly. But could many of those who scored poorly on the Career Profile go on to sell insurance well? Met Life didn't know, since it hired almost none of them. The company was therefore left with jobs open, since not enough applicants could pass the Career Profile. If a substantial number of applicants failed the industry test but would sell as much insurance as those who passed it, Met Life could solve its severe manpower problem.

The ASQ is a theory-based test, but it is based on a theory very different from traditional wisdom about success. Traditional wisdom holds that there are two ingredients of success, and you need both to succeed. The first is ability or aptitude, and IQ tests and the SAT are supposed to measure it. The second is desire or motivation. No matter how much aptitude you have, says traditional wisdom, if you lack desire you will fail. Enough desire can make up for meager talent.

I believe the traditional wisdom is incomplete. A composer can have all the talent of a Mozart and a passionate desire to succeed, but if he believes he cannot compose music, he will come to nothing. He will not try hard enough. He will give up too soon when the elusive right melody takes too long to materialize. Success requires persistence, the ability to not give up in the face of failure. I believe that optimistic explanatory style is the key to persistence.

The explanatory-style theory of success says that in order to choose people for success in a challenging job, you need to select for three characteristics:

1. aptitude
2. motivation
3. optimism

All three determine success.

Testing Explanatory Style at Met Life

THERE ARE two possible explanations of why in our first study the good sales agents had more optimistic ASQ scores than the bad agents. One explanation confirms the theory that optimism produces success; it says that optimism causes you to sell well and pessimism makes you sell badly. The other explanation is that selling well makes you optimistic and selling badly makes you pessimistic.

Our next step was to find out which causes which, by measuring optimism at the time of hiring and seeing who went on to do best over the next year.

To test our theory, we took the first 104 agents hired in western Pennsylvania in January 1983. All had already passed the Career Profile and received their preappointment training. Each then took the ASQ. We thought we'd have to wait a year until the production data came in to find out anything important. As it happened, we had no wait.

We were stunned by how optimistic new insurance agents are. Their group average G – B score (the difference between explanatory style for good events and explanatory style for bad events) was over 7.00. This is far above the national average and suggests that all but the most optimistic need not apply. Life insurance agents, as a group, are more optimistic than people from any other walk of life we have ever tested: car salesmen, commodity traders who scream all day long in the pits, West Point plebes, managers of Arby's restaurants, the candidates for the office of President of the United States during this century, major-league baseball stars, or world-class swimmers.* We had picked exactly the right profession to start with, one that requires very strong optimism just to enter and extreme optimism to succeed in.

One year later we looked at how the agents fared. As John Creedon had warned us, more than half the agents had quit; 59 of the 104 quit during the first year.

Who quit?

Agents who scored in the less optimistic half of the ASQ were twice as likely to quit as agents who scored in the more optimistic half. Agents who scored in the least optimistic quarter were three times likelier to quit than agents who scored in the most optimistic quarter. In contrast, the people with the lowest scores on the Career Profile weren't any likelier to quit than those with high scores.

How about the bottom line, dollars produced?

The agents from the top half of the ASQ sold 20 percent more insurance than the less optimistic agents from the bottom half. The agents from the top quarter sold 50 percent more than the agents from the bottom quarter. Here the Career Profile was predictive as well. Agents who scored in the top half of the Career Profile sold 37 percent more than agents who scored in the bottom half. Taking the two tests together (they don't duplicate each other; each contributes its own distinct perspective), we saw that agents who scored in the upper half of both sold 56 percent more than agents who scored in the bottom half of both. So optimism predicted who survived, and it predicted who sold the most—and it did so about as well as the industry test.

---

* Our method of testing the optimism of people who cannot or did not take the ASQ is called content analysis of verbatim explanations, or CAVE. It is described on page 132.

Did this study adequately test the theory and the power of optimism to predict sales success? No. Several questions still needed answering before Met Life would be completely convinced that the ASQ predicts success as a salesman. First, only 104 people were studied, and the sample, coming entirely from western Pennsylvania, might have been unrepresentative. Second, the agents took the test under no pressure at all, because they had already been hired. What if Met Life now began to hire agents using the ASQ and some applicants, knowing that getting hired depended on how well they did, tried to fake their answers? If they succeeded, that would invalidate the test.

It was fairly easy to erase our worry about cheating. We ran a special study in which certain test-takers were told how to cheat ("Just appear as optimistic as you can") and given an incentive to cheat as well—a $100 reward for the best score. But even with knowledge and incentive, they scored no higher than their fellow test-takers. In other words, this is a hard test to cheat on, and being coached to appear as optimistic as possible doesn't work. Even if you study this book, you will find it difficult to cheat effectively on our optimism tests, since the right answers vary from test to test and we include "lie scales" to pick out cheaters.

The Special Force Study

WE WERE NOW ready for a full-blown study in which the applicants took the test under real hiring conditions. In early 1985, fifteen thousand applicants to Met Life nationwide took both the ASQ and the Career Profile.

We had two goals. The first was to hire one thousand agents by the usual criterion, passing the Career Profile. For these thousand agents, the ASQ score did not enter into the hiring decision. We wanted only to see if the optimists on this regular force would go on to outsell the pessimists.

The second goal was much riskier for Met Life. We decided to create a "special force" of optimistic agents—applicants who had barely failed the Career Profile (scoring from 9 to 11) but had scored in the top half of the ASQ. Over a hundred agents who no one else would hire, because they failed the industry test, would be taken on. They would not know they were special agents. If this group failed utterly, Met Life stood to lose about three million dollars in training costs.

So one thousand of the fifteen thousand applicants were hired into the regular force; half were optimists and half were pessimists. (I said above that as a rule applicants are very optimistic. But of course, half the applicants fall below the average, some of them well below, which is where we found the pessimistic applicants.) And 129 more—all of whom had scored in the top half of the ASQ, and thus were genuine optimists, but had failed the Career Profile—were hired as well. They made up the optimistic special force.

Over the next two years the new agents were monitored, and this is how they did:

In the first year, the optimists in the regular force outsold the pessimists, but only by 8 percent. In the second year, the optimists sold 31 percent more.

As for the special force, it did beautifully. They outsold the pessimists in the regular force by 21 percent during the first year, and by 57 percent in the second year. They even outsold the average of the regular force over the first *two* years, by 27 percent. In fact, they sold at least as much as the optimists in the regular force.

We also saw that the optimists kept improving over the pessimists. Why? Our theory had been that optimism matters because it produces persistence. At first, we expected, talent and motivation for selling should be at least as important as persistence. But as time goes on and the mountain of no's accumulates, persistence should become decisive. This proved to be exactly the pattern.

The optimism test predicted selling results as least as accurately as the Career Profile did.

The Special Force

WHO WAS HIRED into the special force? Let me tell you about Robert Dell¹, and the day my theory took on flesh and blood.

Success Magazine heard about the special-force study and interviewed me. In 1987 they published an article about optimism and the supersalesman, which began with a profile of a man named Robert Dell, who was supposed to be a typical member of Met Life's special force. Dell, said the article, had worked in a slaughterhouse and had gotten a pink slip after years on the job. He applied to Met Life and, in spite of failing the Career Profile, had been hired because of his high score on the ASQ. According to the article, he had become a star salesman, because he was not only persistent but imaginative. He found customers in places where no one else even looked.

I had assumed "Robert Dell" was a fictional character—a composite, typical special-force agent. But one day a few weeks after the article came out, my secretary told me I had a call from a Mr. Robert Dell. I snatched up the receiver. "Robert Dell?" I asked. "Robert Dell? You mean you really exist?"

"I'm real," said a deep voice on the other end of the line. "They didn't make me up."

Dell told me that what the magazine had reported was true, and added to the story. He had worked in an eastern Pennsylvania slaughterhouse for twenty-six years, all of his adult life. The work was grueling, but at least he was working in the scrapple kitchen, not quite as bad as some of the other jobs. Then demand went down. The union contract guaranteed him a minimum amount of work time, but he was told he'd have to put in that time on the killing floor. It was disturbing work for him. The company's business got worse, and one Monday morning he reported to work to find a small sign on the front door. It read CLOSED.

"I wasn't about to collect welfare for the rest of my life," Dell told me, "so I answered a blind ad three or four days later, for people who wanted to sell insurance. I'd never sold anything and didn't know if I could, but I took your test, and, what do you know, Met Life wanted to hire me."

Losing his slaughterhouse job, he said, proved to be a blessing in disguise. In his first year on the special force he earned 50 percent more than he had in the slaughterhouse. In his second year he had doubled his slaughterhouse salary. Furthermore, he loved the work, particularly the freedom to set his own limits and discipline himself.

"But I had a terrible morning today," he went on. "I'd written a huge policy. It had taken me months to nurse it along—the biggest policy I'd ever written. And then, a couple of hours ago, Met Life's underwriting department turned it down. So I decided to call you."

"That's great, Mr. Dell," I replied, not catching on. "I'm glad you did."

"Dr. Seligman, this article told me that you've picked out a whole force of winners for Met Life, people who keep going even when bad things happen, like what happened to me this morning. I assume you didn't do this for free."

"That's true."

"Well, I think you should return the favor and buy from me."

I did.

Met Life's New Hiring Policy

IN THE 1950s Met Life was the giant of the insurance industry, employing over 20,000 agents. Over the next thirty years, Met decided to cut back its sales force and rely on other means to sell insurance and other products.

By 1987, when we were just completing the special force study, Met Life had long ago been displaced by Prudential as the industry leader and its sales force had withered to just over eight thousand agents. A new, forceful leadership of the sales force was needed to reverse the slide. John Creedon brought in Bob Crimmins, a silver-haired dynamo with astonishing oratorical charisma. Crimmins in turn recruited Dr. Howard Mase, an enormously successful trainer and developer of managers for CitiCorp, to breathe new life into selection and training. Their ambitious goal was to increase the sales force dramatically—to ten thousand the next year and, if that worked, to twelve thousand the year after—and by so doing to increase Met Life's market share. But they wanted to keep the quality of the force high at the same time. It looked to them as if our special force study could help, since we had demonstrated on a massive scale that optimism predicts success, above and beyond traditional criteria for hiring.

So Met Life decided to give the ASQ to all its applicants from then on, and as a major part of their bold strategy started hiring people according to their optimism. They used us well.

Under Crimmins's and Mase's leadership, Met Life adopted a two-pronged strategy for selecting new agents. The company hires applicants who score in the top half of the ASQ and fail the Career Profile by just a little. This makes for a large number of agents who would not even have been considered using the old strategy. In addition, the most pessimistic 25 percent aren't hired even if they pass the Career Profile. So the predicted problem employees, who used to be such expensive failures for the company, now are not hired. With this strategy, Met Life has exceeded its goal and expanded the sales force to more than twelve thousand. I'm told that by doing so Met has increased its share of the personal-insurance market by almost 50 percent. The company has not only a larger sales force, but a better one. By one measure of production, they have now regained the lead in the industry.

By using the ASQ, Bob Crimmins and Howard Mase had gone a long way to satisfying Met Life's manpower needs in less than two years.

Changing Pessimists into Optimists

I WAS IN John Creedon's office again. The pile of the carpets was still deep, the oak paneling still glowed, but all of us were somewhat older. When we'd first met seven years before, at my talk to the chief executive officers of life-insurance companies, John had just become CEO of Met

Life and I'd had a gleam in my eye about optimism and success. John had risen to national prominence as a leader of the American business community. Now he told me he was retiring in a year.

We reviewed what we had accomplished. We had found that optimism could be measured and, as we hoped, could predict a person's success as a life-insurance agent. Not only had we changed the selection strategy of this immense company, but the selection policy of the whole industry was now showing signs of change.

"One thing bothers me still," John said. "Every business is stuck with some pessimists. Some are entrenched by seniority, others are around because they're good at what they do. As I've gotten older," he continued, "I find the pessimists weigh on me more and more. They always tell me what I can't do. They only tell me what's wrong. I know it's not their intention, but they curdle action, imagination, and initiative. I believe that most of them—and certainly the company—would be better off if they were more optimistic.

"So, here's my question. Can you take a person who's had thirty or even fifty years of practice at thinking pessimistically and change him into an optimist?"

The answer to that question is yes. But Creedon was now talking not about sales agents but about his executive corps, particularly the conservative bureaucracy that, whoever the CEO, has so much practical control over any institution. I didn't know exactly how to go about reforming a bureaucracy. Executives can't be ordered to take tests and seminars the way agents can. Not even Creedon, perhaps, could require them to undergo cognitive therapy, singly or en masse. But, even if he could, would it be wise to teach them optimism?

That night, and for many nights after, I thought about John's request. Is there a proper role for pessimism in a well-run corporation? Is there a proper role for pessimism in a well-run life?

Why Pessimism?

PESSIMISM is all around us. Some people are continually afflicted with it. All but the most optimistic among us have bouts of it. Is pessimism one of nature's colossal mistakes, or does it have a valuable place in the scheme of things?

Pessimism may support the realism we so often need. In many arenas of life, optimism is unwarranted. At times we do fail irretrievably, and seeing those times through rose-colored glasses may console us but will not change them. In some situations—the cockpit of an airliner, for example—what's needed is not an upbeat view but a mercilessly realistic one. Sometimes we need to cut our losses and invest elsewhere rather than find reasons to hold on.

When Creedon asked me if I could change the pessimism of Metropolitan Life executives, I was less worried about my ability to change pessimism into optimism than I was about the harm I might do. Maybe some of the pessimism his executives brought to their jobs accomplished something important. Someone has to dampen overly enthusiastic plans. These pessimists had risen to the top of America's corporate ladder—they had to be doing something right.

That evening, thinking back over John's complaint, I once again pondered a question that had long nagged at me: Why has evolution allowed depression and pessimism to exist at all? Certainly optimism seems to have an evolutionary role. In his acute, speculative book *Optimism: The Biology of Hope* Lionel Tiger argues that the human species has been selected by evolution because of its optimistic illusions about reality. How else could a species have evolved that plants seeds in April and holds on through drought and famine until October, that stands up alone before charging mastodons and waves small sticks, that commences to build cathedrals that will take several lifetimes to complete? The capacity to act on the hope that reality will turn out better than it usually does is behind such courageous, or foolhardy, behavior.

Or consider this: Many people believe there is no God, that the only purposes in life are those people manage to create for themselves, and that when they die, they rot. If this is so, why are so many of these same people cheerful? The capacity to blind ourselves to our own deeply held negative beliefs may be our remarkable defense against succumbing continually to depression.

But what, then, is the role of pessimism? Perhaps it corrects for something we do only poorly when we are optimistic and not depressed—namely, appreciating reality accurately.

It's a disturbing idea, that depressed people see reality correctly while nondepressed people distort reality in a self-serving way. As a therapist I was trained to believe that it was my job to help depressed patients both to feel happier and to see the world more clearly. I was supposed to be the agent of happiness *and* of truth. But maybe truth and happiness antagonize each other. Perhaps what we have considered good therapy for a depressed patient merely nurtures benign illusions, making the patient think his world is better than it actually is.

There is considerable evidence that depressed people, though sadder, are wiser.

Ten years ago Lauren Alloy and Lyn Abramson, then graduate students at the University of Pennsylvania, did an experiment in which people were given differing degrees of control over the lighting of a light. Some were able to control the light perfectly: It went on every time they pressed a button, and it never went on if they didn't press. The other people, however, had no control at all: The light went on regardless of whether they pressed the button.

The people in both groups were asked to judge, as accurately as they could, how much control they had. Depressed people were very accurate, both when they had control and when they didn't. The nondepressed people shocked us. They were accurate when they had control, but when helpless they were undeterred: they still judged that they had a great deal of control.

Wondering if lights and button pushing just didn't matter enough to the people, Alloy and Abramson added monetary incentives to the test: When the light went on the subjects won money, but when the light didn't go on they lost money. But the benign distortions of nondepressed people did not go away; rather, they got even bigger. Under one condition all the people had some control, but the task was rigged so that everyone lost money. In this situation, nondepressed people said they had less control than they actually had. When the task was rigged so that they won money, nondepressed people said they had more control than they actually had. Depressed people, on the other hand, were rock solid, exactly accurate whether they won or lost.

These have been the consistent findings over the last decade. Depressed people—most of whom turn out to be pessimists—accurately judge how much control they have. Nondepressed people—optimists, for the most part—believe they have much more control over things than they actually do, particularly when they are helpless and have no control at all.

Another kind of evidence for the thesis that depressed people, though sadder, are wiser involves judgments of skill. Several years ago, *Newsweek* reported that 80 percent of American men think they are in the top half of social skills. They must have been nondepressed American men, if the results of Peter Lewinsohn, a psychologist at the University of Oregon, and his colleagues are valid. These investigators put depressed and non-depressed patients in a panel discussion and later had the patients judge how well they did. To what extent were they persuasive? Likable? As judged by a panel of observers, depressed patients weren't very persuasive or likable; poor social skills are a symptom of depression. Depressed patients judged their lack of skill accurately. The surprising finding was from the nondepressed group. They markedly overestimated their skills, judging themselves as much more persuasive and appealing than the judges thought they were.

Still another variety of evidence concerns memory. In general, depressed subjects recall more bad events and fewer good events than nondepressed subjects, who show the reverse pattern. But who is right? That is, if the real number of good and bad events in the world could be known, who would see the past accurately and who would distort the past?

When I first became a therapist, I was taught that it was useless to ask depressed patients about their past, if you wanted to get an accurate picture of their lives. All you would ever hear was how their parents didn't love them, how their business ventures always failed, and how dreadful their hometown was. But could it be they were right? This could easily be tested in the laboratory by having people take a test, managed so that they are wrong twenty times and right twenty times. Later you ask them how they did. The evidence seems to be that depressives are accurate: they tell you, for example, that they got twenty-one right and nineteen wrong. It is the nondepressed people who distort the past: They may tell you they got twelve wrong and twenty-eight right.

A final category of evidence in the matter of whether depressed people are sadder but wiser involves explanatory style. Judging by the explanations of nondepressed people, failure is indeed an orphan, as the saying goes, and success has a thousand fathers. Depressives, however, own up to both failure and success.

This pattern has consistently emerged in all of our studies of explanatory style: lopsidedness among nondepressives and evenhandedness among depressives. The questionnaire you took in chapter three had half bad events and half good events, to which you assigned causes. You computed an overall $G - B$ score, which was your average for good events minus your average for bad events. How did your total compare to that of depressives? A depressive's explanatory style is roughly the same for good and bad events; that is, to the extent a depressive is a bit above average on personal, permanent, and pervasive explanations for good events, he is also a bit above average on personal, permanent, and pervasive explanations for bad events. A depressive's total $G - B$ score is around 0; he is evenhanded.

A nondepressive's score is well above 0, very lopsided. If it's bad, you did it to me, it'll be over soon, and it's only this situation. But if it's good, I did it, it's going to last forever, and it's going to help me in many situations. For nondepressives, bad events tend to be external, temporary, and specific, but good events are personal, permanent and pervasive. The more optimistic their judgments are, the more lopsided. A depressed person, in contrast, sees his successes as caused by the same sorts of factors as his failures.

Overall, then, there is clear evidence that nondepressed people distort reality in a self-serving direction and depressed people tend to see reality accurately. How does this evidence, which is about depression, tie into optimism and pessimism? Statistically, most depressed people score in the pessimistic range of explanatory style, and most nondepressed people score optimistically. This means that, on average, optimistic people will distort reality and pessimists, as Ambrose Bierce defined them, will "see the world aright." The pessimist seems to be at the mercy of reality, whereas the optimist has a massive defense against reality that maintains good cheer in the face of a relentlessly indifferent universe. It is important to remember, however, that this relationship is statistical, and that pessimists do not have a lock on reality. Some realists, the minority, are optimists, and some distorters, also the minority, are pessimists.

Is depressive accuracy just a laboratory curiosity? I don't think so. Rather it leads us to the very heart of what pessimism is really about. It is our first solid clue about why we have depression at all, the closest we've come to an answer to the question asked earlier: why evolution has allowed pessimism and depression to survive and prosper. If pessimism is at the base of depression and suicide, if it results in lower achievement, and as we will see, in poor immune function and in ill health, why didn't it die out epochs ago? What counterweighting function does pessimism serve for the human species?

The benefits of pessimism may have arisen during our recent evolutionary history. We are animals of the Pleistocene, the epoch of the ice ages. Our emotional makeup has most recently been shaped by one hundred thousand years of climactic catastrophe: waves of cold and heat; drought and flood; plenty and sudden famine. Those of our ancestors who survived the Pleistocene may have done so because they had the capacity to worry incessantly about the future, to see sunny days as mere prelude to a harsh winter, to brood. We have inherited these ancestors' brains and therefore their capacity to see the cloud rather than the silver lining.

Sometimes and in some niches in modern life, this deep-seated pessimism works. Think about a successful large business. It has a diverse set of personalities serving different roles. First, there are the optimists. The researchers and developers, the planners, the marketers—all these need to be visionaries. They have to dream things that don't yet exist, to explore boundaries beyond the company's present reach. If they don't, the competition will. But imagine a company that consisted only of optimists, all of them fixed upon the exciting possibilities ahead. It would be a disaster.

The company also needs its pessimists, the people who have an accurate knowledge of present realities. They must make sure grim reality continually intrudes upon the optimists. The treasurer, the CPAs, the financial vice-president, the business administrators, the safety engineers—all these need an accurate sense of how much the company can afford, and of danger. Their role is to caution, their banner is the yellow flag.

One should hasten to say that these people may not be the full-blown, high-octane pessimists whose explanatory style continually undermines their achievement and health. Some among them may be depressives, but others, perhaps even the majority, may for all their somber caution at their desks otherwise be cheery and sanguine. Some are merely prudent and measured people, who have nurtured their pessimistic side in the service of their careers. John Creedon was never suggesting that his executive corps was full of severe pessimists incapacitated by helplessness. But the difference is only in degree. These executives would, as a group, test out as pessimists, and their outlook would be basically, though not drastically, pessimistic.

These mild pessimists—call them professional pessimists—seem to make good use of pessimistic accuracy (it's their stock-in-trade) without suffering unbearably from the costs of pessimism: the bouts of depression and the lack of initiative we have seen so far in this book, and the ill health and failure to attain high office that we will see in the later chapters.

So the successful corporation has its optimists, dreamers, salesmen, and creators. But the corporation is a form of modern life that also needs its pessimists, the realists whose job is to counsel caution. I want to underline, however, the fact that at the head of the corporation must be a CEO, sage enough and flexible enough to balance the optimistic vision of the planners against the jeremiads of the CPAs. Creedon was just such a CEO, and his complaint to me about his corporate pessimists came from his daily task of reconciling the polarities.

The Balance Sheet:
Optimism vs. Pessimism

PERHAPS a successful life, like a successful company, needs both optimism and at least occasional pessimism, and for the same reason a corporation does. Perhaps a successful life also needs a CEO who has *flexible optimism* at his command.

I have just made the case for pessimism. It heightens our sense of reality and endows us with accuracy, particularly if we live in a world filled with unexpected and frequent disasters. Let me now review the case against pessimism (the other side of the case for optimism) so that we can compare its costs to its benefits.

- Pessimism promotes depression.
- Pessimism produces inertia rather than activity in the face of setbacks.
- Pessimism feels bad subjectively—blue, down, worried, anxious.
- Pessimism is self-fulfilling. Pessimists don't persist in the face of challenges, and therefore fail more frequently—even when success is attainable.
- Pessimism is associated with poor physical health (see chapter ten).
- Pessimists are defeated when they try for high office (see chapter eleven).
- Even when pessimists are right and things turn out badly, they still feel worse. Their explanatory style now converts the predicted setback into a disaster, a disaster into a catastrophe.

The best thing one can say about a pessimist is that his fears were founded.

The balance sheet seems to come out heavily on the side of optimism, but there are times and places where we need our pessimism. Chapter twelve presents guidelines on who should not use optimism and in what circumstances pessimism is best deployed.

All of us—extreme pessimists and extreme optimists alike—experience both states. Explanatory style probably has built-in flux. Circadian cycles ensure occasional mild depression. Depression has a rhythm through the day and, at least among some women, through the month. Typically we are more depressed when we wake up, and as the day goes on we become more optimistic. But superimposed on this is our BRAC, our Basic Rest and Activity Cycle. As noted previously, it hits its lows at roughly four in the afternoon and again at four in the morning. Its highs occur in late morning and early evening, although the exact timing varies from person to person.

During the highs, we are more optimistic than usual. We formulate adventurous plans: our next romantic conquest, the new sports car. During the lows, we are more inclined to depression and pessimism than usual. We see the stark realities that our plans entail: She'd never be interested in someone who is divorced and has three kids. A new Jaguar costs more than I make in a year. If you are an optimist and want to see this graphically, just remember the last time you woke up at four in the morning and couldn't get back to sleep. Worries that you easily dismiss during the day now overwhelm you: The argument with your spouse means divorce, the frown from the boss means you'll be fired.

During these daily bouts of pessimism we can see its constructive role in our lives. In these mild forms, pessimism serves the purpose of pulling us back a bit from the risky exaggerations of our optimism, making us think twice, keeping us from making rash, foolhardy gestures. The optimistic moments of our lives contain the great plans, the dreams, and the hopes. Reality is benignly distorted to give the dreams room to flourish. Without these times we would never accomplish anything difficult and intimidating, we would never even attempt the just barely possible. Mount Everest would remain unscaled, the four-minute mile unrun; the jet plane and the computer would be blueprints sitting in some financial vice-president's wastebasket.

The genius of evolution lies in the dynamic tension between optimism and pessimism continually correcting each other. As we rise and fall daily with the circadian cycle, that tension permits us both to venture and to retrench—without danger, for as we move toward an extreme, the tension pulls us back. In a sense it is this perpetual fluctuation that permits human beings to accomplish so much.

Evolution, however, has also given us our ancestors' Pleistocene brain. Through it come the naggings of pessimism: Success is fleeting; danger lurks around the next corner; tragedy awaits us; optimism is hubris. But the brain that accurately mirrored the grim realities of the ice ages now lags behind the less grim realities of modern life. Agriculture, and then the leap of industrial technology, put human beings in developed countries much less at the mercy of the next harsh winter. No longer do two out of three of our children die before they reach their fifth birthday. No longer is it reasonable for a woman to expect her own death during childbirth. No longer does massive starvation follow prolonged cold or drought. Certainly modern life has its own abundant menaces and tragedies: crime, AIDS, divorce, the threat of nuclear war, the undermining of the ecosystem. But it is only the most willfully negative manipulation of the statistics that has modern life in the West even approach the level of disaster that shaped the ice-age brain. And so we do well to recognize the insistent voice of pessimism for the vestige it is.

It does not follow that we should become lotus-eaters. It does follow that we are entitled to more optimism than we may naturally feel. Do we have a choice about using optimism? Can we learn the skills of optimism, superimpose them on the Pleistocene brain to enjoy their benefits, but still retain pessimism when we need it?

I believe we can, for evolution has allowed one thing more. Like the successful company, we each have in us an executive who balances the counsels of daring against the counsels of doom. When optimism prompts us to chance it and pessimism bids us to cower, a part of us heeds both. This executive is sapience. It is this entity to whom is addressed the most basic point of this book: By understanding the single virtue of pessimism along with its pervasive, crippling consequences, we can learn to resist pessimism's constant callings, as deep-seated in brain or in habit as they may be. We can learn to choose optimism for the most part, but also to heed pessimism when it is warranted.

How to learn the skills of optimism and the guidelines for deploying such flexible optimism are the topics of "Changing: From Pessimism to Optimism," the concluding section of this book.

7

Children and Parents:
The Origins of Optimism

EXPLANATORY STYLE has a sweeping effect on the lives of adults. It can produce depression in response to everyday setbacks, or produce resilience even in the face of tragedy. It can numb a person to the pleasures of life, or allow him to live fully. It can prevent him from achieving his goals, or help him exceed them. As we will see, a person's explanatory style influences the way other people perceive him, disposing them to work against him or with him. And it affects physical health.

Explanatory style develops in childhood. The optimism or pessimism developed then is fundamental. New setbacks and victories are filtered through it, and it becomes an entrenched habit of thinking. In this chapter we will ask what explanatory style's source is, what its consequences are for children, and how it can be changed.

Test Your Child's Optimism

If your child is over seven, he has probably developed an explanatory style, which is in the process of crystallizing. You can measure your child's explanatory style with a test called the Children's Attributional Style Questionnaire, or CASQ, which has been taken by thousands of children. The CASQ is very much like the test you took in chapter three. It takes a child between the ages of eight and thirteen about twenty minutes to finish. If your child is older, give him the test from chapter three. For children under eight, there is no wholly reliable paper-and-pencil test, but there is another way of measuring their explanatory style, which I'll tell you about later in this chapter.

To give your child the test, set aside twenty minutes, sit down at a table with him, and say something like:

"Different kids think in different ways. I've been reading a book about this, and I've been wondering how you think about some things that might happen to you.

"Look at this. It's really interesting. It asks you a bunch of questions about what you think. Each question is like a little story, and for each story, there are two ways you might react. You're supposed to choose one way or the other, the one that's closest to the way you'd really feel if that particular thing happened to you.

"So here's a pencil. I want you to give it a try. Imagine that each of these little stories happened to you, even if they never have. And then check either the 'A' answer or the 'B' answer—the one that best describes the way you would feel. But the great thing about this test is that there are no wrong answers! Isn't that terrific? Now, here, let's take a look at number one."

Once you get him going, your child can probably take it without any assistance. But for younger children who are not skilled readers, you should read each item aloud at the same time the child is reading it to himself.

CHILDREN'S ATTRIBUTIONAL STYLE QUESTIONNAIRE (CASQ)

1. You get an *A* on a test.

		PvG
A.	*I am smart.*	I
B.	*I am good in the subject that the test was in.*	0

2. You play a game with some friends and you win.

		PsG
A.	*The people that I played with did not play the game well.*	0
B.	*I play that game well.*	I

3. You spend a night at a friend's house and you have a good
time.

PvG

A. *My friend was in a friendly mood that night.*   0
B. *Everyone in my friend's family was in a friendly
    mood that night.*   I

4. You go on a vacation with a group of people and you have
fun.

PsG

A. *I was in a good mood.*   I
B. *The people I was with were in good moods.*   0

5. All of your friends catch a cold except you.

PmG

A. *I have been healthy lately.*   0
B. *I am a healthy person.*   I

6. Your pet gets run over by a car.

PsB

A. *I don't take good care of my pets.*   I
B. *Drivers are not cautious enough.*   0

7. Some kids you know say that they don't like you.

PsB

A. *Once in a while people are mean to me.*   0
B. *Once in a while I am mean to other people.*   I

8. You get very good grades.

PsG

A. *Schoolwork is simple.*   0
B. *I am a hard worker.*   I

9. You meet a friend and your friend tells you that you look
nice.

PmG

A. *My friend felt like praising the way people looked
    that day.*   0
B. *Usually my friend praises the way people look.*   I

10. A good friend tells you that he hates you.

	PsB
A. *My friend was in a bad mood that day.*	0
B. *I wasn't nice to my friend that day.*	1

11. You tell a joke and no one laughs.

	PsB
A. *I don't tell jokes well.*	1
B. *The joke is so well known that it is no longer funny.*	0

12. Your teacher gives a lesson and you don't understand it.

	PvB
A. *I didn't pay attention to anything that day.*	1
B. *I didn't pay attention when my teacher was talking.*	0

13. You fail a test.

	PmB
A. *My teacher makes hard tests.*	1
B. *The past few weeks, my teacher has made hard tests.*	0

14. You gain a lot of weight and start to look fat.

	PsB
A. *The food I have to eat is fattening.*	0
B. *I like fattening foods.*	1

15. A person steals money from you.

	PvB
A. *That person is dishonest.*	0
B. *People are dishonest.*	1

16. Your parents praise something you make.

	PsG
A. *I am good at making some things.*	1
B. *My parents like some things I make.*	0

17. You play a game and you win money.

	PvG
A. *I am a lucky person.*	1
B. *I am lucky when I play games.*	0

18. You almost drown when swimming in a river.

                                                          PmB

    A. *I am not a very cautious person.*   1

    B. *Some days I am not a cautious person.*   0

19. You are invited to a lot of parties.

                                                            PsG

    A. *A lot of people have been acting friendly toward me lately.*   0

    B. *I have been acting friendly toward a lot of people lately.*   1

20. A grown-up yells at you.

                                                        PvB

    A. *That person yelled at the first person he saw.*   0

    B. *That person yelled at a lot of people he saw that day.*   1

21. You do a project with a group of kids and it turns out badly.

                                                        PvB

    A. *I don't work well with the people in the group.*   0

    B. *I never work well with a group.*   1

22. You make a new friend.

                                                        PsG

    A. *I am a nice person.*   1

    B. *The people that I meet are nice.*   0

23. You have been getting along well with your family.

                                                        PmG

    A. *I am easy to get along with when I am with my family.*   1

    B. *Once in a while I am easy to get along with when I am with my family.*   0

24. You try to sell candy, but no one will buy any.

                                                        PmB

    A. *Lately a lot of children are selling things, so people don't want to buy anything else from children.*   0

    B. *People don't like to buy things from children.*   1

25. You play a game and you win.

                                                                   PvG

    A. *Sometimes I try as hard as I can at games.*   0

    B. *Sometimes I try as hard as I can.*   1

26. You get a bad grade in school.

     PsB

    A. *I am stupid.*   1

    B. *Teachers are unfair graders.*   0

27. You walk into a door and you get a bloody nose.

     PvB

    A. *I wasn't looking where I was going.*   0

    B. *I have been careless lately.*   1

28. You miss the ball and your team loses the game.

     PmB

    A. *I didn't try hard while playing ball that day.*   0

    B. *I usually don't try hard when I am playing ball.*   1

29. You twist your ankle in gym class.

     PsB

    A. *The past few weeks, the sports we played in gym*
       class have been dangerous.   0

    B. *The past few weeks I have been clumsy in gym class.*   1

30. Your parents take you to the beach and you have a good time.

     PvG

    A. *Everything at the beach was nice that day.*   1

    B. *The weather at the beach was nice that day.*   0

31. You take a train which arrives so late that you miss a movie.

     PmB

    A. *The past few days there have been problems with*
       the train being on time.   0

    B. *The trains are almost never on time.*   1

32. Your mother makes your favorite dinner for you.

                                                     PvG

    A. *There are a few things that my mother does to*
       please me.   0
    B. *My mother likes to please me.*   1

33. A team that you are on loses a game.

                                                     PmB

    A. *The team members don't play well together.*   1
    B. *That day the team members didn't play well together.*   0

34. You finish your homework quickly.

                                                     PvG

    A. *Lately I have been doing everything quickly.*   1
    B. *Lately I have been doing schoolwork quickly.*   0

35. Your teacher asks you a question and you give the wrong
answer.

                                                     PmB

    A. *I get nervous when I have to answer questions.*   1
    B. *That day I got nervous when I had to answer questions.*   0

36. You get on the wrong bus and you get lost.

                                                     PmB

    A. *That day I wasn't paying attention to what was going on.*   0
    B. *I usually don't pay attention to what's going on.*   1

37. You go to an amusement park and you have a good time.

                                                     PvG

    A. *I usually enjoy myself at amusement parks.*   0
    B. *I usually enjoy myself.*   1

38. An older kid slaps you in the face.

                                                     PsB

    A. *I teased his younger brother.*   1
    B. *His younger brother told him I had teased him.*   0

39. You get all the toys you want on your birthday.

                                                     PmG

    A. *People always guess what toys to buy me for my*
       birthday.   1
    B. *This birthday people guessed right as to what toys I*
       wanted.   0

40. You take a vacation in the country and you have a wonderful time.

    PmG

    A. *The country is a beautiful place to be.*   1
    B. *The time of the year that we went was beautiful.*   0

41. Your neighbors ask you over for dinner.

    PmG

    A. *Sometimes people are in kind moods.*   0
    B. *People are kind.*   1

42. You have a substitute teacher and she likes you.

    PmG

    A. *I was well behaved during class that day.*   0
    B. *I am almost always well behaved during class.*   1

43. You make your friends happy.

    PmG

    A. *I am a fun person to be with.*   1
    B. *Sometimes I am a fun person to be with.*   0

44. You get a free ice-cream cone.

    PsG

    A. *I was friendly to the ice-cream man that day.*   1
    B. *The ice-cream man was feeling friendly that day.*   0

45. At your friend's party the magician asks you to help him out.

    PsG

    A. *It was just luck that I got picked.*   0
    B. *I looked really interested in what was going on.*   1

46. You try to convince a kid to go to the movies with you, but he won't go.

    PvB

    A. *That day he did not feel like doing anything.*   1
    B. *That day he did not feel like going to the movies.*   0

47. Your parents get a divorce.

                                                               PvB
    A. *It is hard for people to get along well when they are
       married.*   I
    B. *It is hard for my parents to get along well when they
       are married.*   0

48. You have been trying to get into a club and you don't get
    in.

                                                               PvB
    A. *I don't get along well with other people.*   I
    B. *I don't get along well with the people in the club.*   0

SCORING KEY

PmB_____   PmG_____

PvB_____   PvG_____

HoB _____

PsB_____   PsG_____

Total B_____   Total G_____

G – B _____

You can score the test now. You can share your child's scores with him
if you like. If you do tell him what his scores are, also explain what they
mean.

Start with the PmB (Permanent Bad) score. Total the numbers in the
right-hand margin that follow the answers your child chose to questions
13, 18, 24, 28, 31, 33, 35, and 36. Enter that total in the scoring key above,
next to "PmB."

Then add the PmG scores—questions 5, 9, 23, 39, 40, 41, 42, and 43—
and enter the total in the scoring key.

Then do the pervasiveness scores and note them in the key. The PvB
questions are 12, 15, 20, 21, 27, 46, 47, and 48. The PvG questions are 1,
3, 17, 25, 30, 32, 34, and 37.

Total the PmB and PvB scores to get the hope (HoB) score. Record it.

Now score personalization. The PsB questions are 6, 7, 10, 11, 14, 26, 29, and 38.

The PsG questions are 2, 4, 8, 16, 19, 22, 44, and 45.

Compute the total scores for bad events (PmB + PvB + PsB) and record the Total B; then total the scores for good events (PmG + PvG + PsG) and record it.

Finally, compute the overall scale score, G – B, by subtracting the Total B from the Total G. Write it on the bottom line of the key.

Here's what your child's scores mean and how your child compares to the thousands of children who have taken this test.

First, girls and boys score differently. Girls, at least up to puberty, are noticeably more optimistic than boys. The average nine-to-twelve-year-old girl has a G – B score of 7.0. The average nine-to-twelve-year-old boy has a score of 5.0. If your girl scores less than 4.5, she is somewhat pessimistic. If she scores less than 2, she is very pessimistic and at risk for depression. If your boy scores less than 2.5, he is somewhat pessimistic; less than 1, he is very pessimistic and at risk for depression.

As for Total B score, the average nine-to-twelve-year-old girl's is 7.0, and the average boy's is 8.5. Scores of three points *higher* than the average are very pessimistic.

The average Total G score for nine-to-twelve-year-old girls and boys is 13.5. Scores three points lower are very pessimistic. The individual good dimensions (PmG, PsG, and PvG) each average about 4.5, with scores of 3 or below being very pessimistic. The individual bad dimensions (PmB, PvB, PsG) average about 2.5 for girls and 2.8 for boys, with scores of 4 or *higher* being risk markers for depression.

Why Children Can't Be Hopeless

YOU MAY HAVE been surprised about the norms and what the scores mean, particularly compared to your own scores. On the whole, prepubescent children are extremely optimistic, with a capacity for hope and an immunity to hopelessness they will never again possess after puberty, when they lose much of their optimism.

When my son, David, was five, my wife and I divorced. Explaining it to him in euphemisms did not seem to work. He kept asking me, every weekend, if Kerry and I would get married again. The time had come for straight talk. I told him at length that people fall out of love, and that it can be final. Trying to make the point, I asked him: "Did you ever have a friend that you used to like a lot and then stopped liking so much?"

"Yes," he agreed reluctantly, searching his memory.

"Well, that's the way your mother and I feel about each other. We don't love each other anymore, and we never will again. We'll never get married to each other again."

He looked up at me, nodding agreement, and then, having the last word, concluded the discussion: "You might!"

Children's explanatory style is enormously lopsided, much more so than adults'. Good events are going to last forever, are going to help in all ways, and are the child's doing. Bad events just happen along, melt away quickly, and are someone else's fault. So lopsided is the average child that his scores look on average like those of a successful insurance-sales agent for Metropolitan Life. A depressed child's lopsided scores look like those of the average *nondepressed* adult's. No one seems to have the capacity for hope that a young child does, and it is just this fact that makes severe depression in a young child stand out so tragically.

Children do get depressed, and they get depressed as frequently and as profoundly as adults do, but their depression differs from adolescents' and from adults' in one very striking way. They do not become hopeless, and they do not commit suicide. There are between 20,000 and 50,000 suicides among adult Americans each year, almost all of which follow depression. One particular component of depression, hopelessness, is the most accurate predictor of suicide. Potential suicides strongly believe that their present misery is going to last forever and pervade all that they do, and that only death will end their suffering. Childhood suicide is tragic and on the rise now, but the approximately two hundred such suicides a year are hardly a major epidemiological problem. Children below the age of seven *never* commit suicide, even though there are well-documented homicides committed by children as young as five. Children of this age can understand death, they can understand its finality, and they can intend to kill someone; but what they cannot do is sustain a state of hopelessness for very long.

Evolution, I believe, has ensured this. The child carries the seed of the future, and nature's primary interest in children is that they reach puberty safely and produce the next generation of children. Nature has buffered our children not only physically—prepubescent children have the lowest death rate from all causes—but psychologically as well, by endowing them with hope, abundant and irrational.

But for all this buffering against hopelessness, some children are much more predisposed to pessimism and depression than others. The CASQ is a good indicator of who is vulnerable and who is protected. Children who score in the optimistic half—boys above 5.5 and girls above 7.5—will tend to become optimistic teenagers and adults. They will, on average, have less depression, achieve more, and be healthier over their lives than children who score below these averages.

Explanatory style sets in early. We see it in quite crystallized form in children as young as eight. If your child already has an optimistic or pessimistic stance about the world by the third grade, and if it is going to be so important to his future, his health and success, you may wonder where it came from and what you can do to change it.

There are three major hypotheses about the origins of explanatory style. The first concerns the child's mother.

(1) Mother's Explanatory Style:

LISTEN IN as Sylvia reacts to a bad event in the presence of her eight-year-old daughter Marjorie. The scene begins as they get into a car at a shopping-center parking lot. As you listen, try to discern Sylvia's explanatory style.

Marjorie: Mommy, there's a dent on my side of the car.
Sylvia: Damn, Bob will kill me!
Marjorie: Daddy told you to always park his new car far away from the other cars.
Sylvia: Damn, things like this always happen to me. I'm so lazy, I just want to carry groceries a few feet, not a hundred yards. I'm so stupid.

Sylvia is saying some pretty disheartening things about herself, and Marjorie is listening very carefully. It's not only the content that's disheartening but the form. In content, Marjorie hears that Sylvia is in big trouble, and that she's stupid, lazy, and chronically unlucky. Bad enough. But the form of what Sylvia says is even worse.

Marjorie can hear that it's a bad event that is being explained. Sylvia gives Marjorie (quite inadvertently) four explanations:

1. *"Things like this always happen to me."* That explanation is permanent: Sylvia uses *always*. Pervasive, too: "Things like this," not "car dents"; Sylvia doesn't qualify the misfortune or set any boundaries for the troubles that always happen to her. And personal: They "happen to *me*," not to everyone. Sylvia singles herself out as a victim.

2. *"I'm so lazy."* Laziness, as Sylvia has cast it, is a permanent character trait. (Contrast Sylvia's explanation with this one: "I was feeling lazy.")

Laziness hurts in many circumstances, and thus is pervasive. And Sylvia has personalized it.

3. *"I want to carry groceries a few feet"*—personal, permanent (not "I wanted"), but not particularly pervasive since it's just about physical labor.

4. *"I'm so stupid"*—permanent, pervasive, personal.

You weren't the only one who did an analysis of what Sylvia was saying. Marjorie did, too. Marjorie has heard her mother explain a crisis by giving four highly pessimistic causes. She has heard her mother's view that bad events are permanent, pervasive, and her own fault. Marjorie is learning that this is the way the world is.

Every day Marjorie hears her mother make permanent, pervasive, and personal analyses of the untoward events that happen around the house. Marjorie is in the process of learning from the most influential person in her life that bad events are going to last, are going to hurt everything, and are appropriately blamed on the person to whom they happen. Marjorie is forming a theory of the world in which bad events have permanent, pervasive, and personal causes.

Children's antennae are constantly tuned to the way their parents, particularly their mothers, talk about causes of emotionally loaded events. It is no accident that "Why?" is one of the first and most repeated questions that young children ask. Getting explanations for the world around them, particularly the social world, is the prime intellectual task of growing up. Once the parents get impatient and stop answering the never-ending *why* questions, children get their answers in other ways. Mostly they listen closely when you spontaneously explain why things happen—which you do, on average, about once a minute during speech. Your children hang on every word of the explanations you give, particularly when something goes wrong. Not only do they listen for the particulars of what you say, but they listen keenly to its formal properties: whether the cause you cite is permanent or temporary, specific or pervasive, your fault or someone else's.

The way your mother talked about the world to you when you were a child had a marked influence on your explanatory style. We found out about this by giving explanatory-style questionnaires to one hundred children and their parents. The mother's level of optimism and the child's level were very similar. This was true of both sons and daughters. We were surprised to find that neither the children's style nor the mother's style bore any resemblance to the father's style. This tells us that young children listen to what their primary caretaker (usually their mother) says about causes, and they tend to make this style their own. If the child has an optimistic mother, this is great, but it can be a disaster for the child if the child has a pessimistic mother.

These findings raise a question: Is explanatory style genetic? Can we inherit it from our parents, as we seem to inherit a disconcertingly large portion of our intelligence, our politics, and our religious outlook? (Studies of identical twins reared separately show that they both grow up to have uncannily similar political outlooks, belief in God or lack of it, and IQs.) Unlike these psychological traits, the pattern of explanatory style that we find in families suggests that it is *not* heritable: The mother's is similar to both the sons' and the daughters'; the father's is similar to no one's. This is a pattern of results that does not fit any ordinary genetic model.

To be sure, we are now trying to ask the genetic question less indirectly. We will measure the optimism of both the biological and the adoptive parents of children who were adopted when very young. If the children's level of optimism is similar to that of the adoptive parents and dissimilar to that of the biological parents, this will confirm our view that the origins of optimism are learned. If the children's level of optimism resembles the level of the biological parents, whom the children have never met, this would show that optimism can be at least partly inherited.

(2) Adult Criticism: Teachers and Parents

WHEN YOUR CHILDREN do something wrong, what do you say to them? What do their teachers say to them? As noted, children listen carefully not just to content but to form, not just to what adults say to them but *how* adults say it. This is particularly true of criticisms. Children believe the criticisms they get, and use them to form their explanatory style.

Let's look for a minute into a typical third-grade classroom, as Carol Dweck, one of the world's leading researchers into emotional development, has done. Carol's work has illuminated how optimism develops. It may also give us clues about what happens during the childhood of women that makes them far more susceptible to depression than men are.

Once the class gets used to your presence and settles down, the first thing you notice is a striking difference between the demeanor of the girls and that of the boys. The girls are for the most part a pleasure for the teacher: They sit quietly, even fold their hands, and they appear to listen attentively. When they act up, they whisper and giggle, but basically they obey the rules. The boys are a pain. They fidget even when trying to sit still—which they don't try all that often. They don't appear to listen, they don't obey the rules as scrupulously as the girls do. When they act up— which is a lot of the time—they shout and run around.

The class buckles down and takes a test on fractions. What does the teacher say to the children who do badly on the test? What kind of criticisms do boys and girls hear from their teachers in the third grade when they fail?

The boys who fail are typically told: "You weren't paying attention," "You didn't try hard enough," "You were being rowdy when I was teaching fractions." What kinds of explanations are not paying attention, little effort, and rowdiness? They are temporary and specific, not pervasive. Temporary because you can change how much effort you put out, and you can pay attention if you want, and you can stop being rowdy. Boys hear temporary and specific causes invoked to explain why their school performance wasn't up to par.

The girls, Dweck's studies reveal, routinely hear quite a different sort of condemnation. Since they aren't rowdy and they look as if they are paying attention, they can't be criticized on those grounds. For the teacher correcting them, this leaves "You're not very good at arithmetic," "You always hand in sloppy papers," "You never check your work." Most of the temporary causes, such as inattention, not trying, and misbehaving, are ruled out, so girls are barraged with permanent and pervasive criticisms of their failure. What do they distill out of their third-grade experience?

Carol Dweck found out by taking fourth-grade girls and giving them impossible problems to solve. Then she looked at how they explained their failures.

They all got scrambled words to find anagrams for—"ZOLT," "IEOF," "MAPE," and so on—but their effort was in vain, because it was impossible to rearrange the letters to form a real word. All the children tried hard, but before they could exhaust the possible combinations, they were told, "Time's up."

"Why didn't you solve those?" the experimenter asked.

The girls said things like "I'm not very good at word games" and "I guess I'm not very bright."

The boys, when they were given the same test, said things like "I wasn't paying attention"; and "I didn't try very hard"; "Who cares about your lousy puzzles anyway?"

In this test, the girls gave permanent and pervasive explanations for their failures; the boys, on the other hand, gave much more hopeful explanations—temporary, specific, and changeable. What we see here is the impact of the second influence on your child's explanatory style: the criticisms that adults make when the child fails. Again, the child listens attentively, and if what he hears is permanent and pervasive—"You're stupid"; "You're no good"—this finds its way into his theory of himself. If what he hears is temporary and specific—"You didn't try hard enough"; "These puzzles are for sixth-graders"—he sees problems as solvable and local.

(3) Children's Life Crises

IN HEIDELBERG in 1981, I heard Glen Elder, the world's leading sociologist of the family, give a talk to a group of researchers interested in how children grow up under tremendous adversity. He told us about a fascinating study he had been working on his whole adult life. Two generations ago, he said, before the Great Depression, a group of visionary scientists, Glen's predecessors, launched a study about growing up that has gone on for almost sixty years. A group of children from two California cities, Berkeley and Oakland, were interviewed and tested thoroughly for their psychological strengths and weaknesses. These test subjects are now in their seventies and eighties. They have continued to cooperate with this landmark study of life-span development. Not only that but their children, and now their grandchildren, have participated as well.

Glen then talked about who survived the Great Depression intact and who never recovered. He told the spellbound group that middle-class girls whose families lost all their money recovered psychologically by early middle age and then aged well both physically and psychologically. Lower-class girls who were equally deprived during the 1930s never recovered. They fell apart in late middle age, and their old age was tragic, both physically and psychologically.

Glen speculated about the cause.

"I believe that the women who aged well," he said, "learned during their childhood in the Great Depression that adversity would be overcome. After all, most of their families recovered economically during the late 1930s and early 1940s. That recovery taught them optimism, and this crisis and its resolution shaped their explanatory style for bad events, making it temporary, specific, and external. This means that in old age, when their best friend died, they thought, 'I will find friendship elsewhere.' This optimistic outlook . . . helped their health and their aging.

"Contrast the girls from lower-class families. By and large, their families did not recover after the Great Depression. They were poor before it, during it, and after it. They learned pessimism. They learned that when troubles strike, hard times remain forever. Their explanatory style became hopeless. Much later, when their best friend died, they thought, 'I'll never find friendship again.' This pessimism, learned in childhood from the reality of their situation, got imposed on every new crisis, and undermined their health, their achievement, and their sense of well-being.

"These are wild speculations, though," Glen said in closing. "Nobody had thought of the notion of explanatory style fifty years ago, so it wasn't measured. It's too bad we don't have a time machine, so we could go back to 1930 and find out if my speculations are right."

I couldn't sleep that night. "It's too bad we don't have a time machine" kept running through my head. At five in the morning, I was pounding on Glen's door.

"Wake up, Glen, we have to talk. I *do* have a time machine!"

Glen dragged himself out of bed and we went for a walk.

"Last year," I said to Glen, "I got a letter from a remarkable young social psychologist named Chris Peterson. It read like an academic fortune cookie. 'Help,' it said, 'I am trapped at a small college teaching eight courses a year. Have creative ideas, will travel.' I invited him to spend a couple of years working with me at Penn, and he did, indeed, have creative ideas."

The most creative idea Chris had concerned how to determine the explanatory style of people who wouldn't take explanatory-style questionnaires—people like sports heroes, presidents, and movie stars. Chris read the sports pages indefatigably, and every time he found a causal statement made by a football player, he treated it as if it was an item on an explanatory-style questionnaire filled out by the player. So, if a kicker said that he missed the field goal because "The wind was against me," Chris rated that quote for its permanent, pervasive, and personal qualities, on a 1-to-7 scale. "The wind was against me" would get only a *1* for permanent, since nothing is less permanent than wind; about a *1* for pervasive, since the wind being against you only hurts kicking and not your love life; and a *1* for personal, since the wind is not the kicker's fault. "The wind was against me" is a very optimistic explanation of a bad event.

Chris then averaged the ratings over all the causal statements the kicker made and got the kicker's explanatory style, without using a questionnaire. Next we showed that such a profile roughly matches what would have happened if the questionnaire had been taken by the kicker. We called this the CAVE—for content analysis of verbatim explanations—technique.

"Glen," I went on, "the CAVE technique *is* the time machine. We can use it not only on contemporary people who won't take questionnaires, but on people who *can't* take questionnaires, like the dead.

"This brings me to why I woke you up. Did your predecessors save the original interviews with the Berkeley-Oakland children from the 1930s?"

Glen thought for a bit. "That was before the tape recorder was in wide use, but I seem to recall that the interviewers took shorthand notes. I can check it when I get back to my archives."

"If we still have authentic quotes," I said, "we can use the CAVE technique on them. Every time one of the children made a causal statement, we can treat it as an item from an explanatory style questionnaire, and we can have raters—who are blind to the source of the quotes—score them for optimism. At the end of the process, we'd know what each child's explanatory style was fifty years ago. We can travel back in time and test your speculations."

When he got back to the Berkeley archives, Glen checked. There did indeed exist verbatim notes from the early interviews, and complete interviews done at various points later in life, as the young girls became mothers and then grandmothers. We used these notes and interviews to create explanatory-style profiles for these women. We extracted every causal statement from the interviews, gave each statement to raters who did not know its source, and had them rate it on the 1-to-7 scale for pervasiveness, permanence, and personalization.

Glen's speculation was largely correct. The middle-class women, who aged well, tended to be optimists. The lower-class women, who aged badly, tended to be pessimists.

This first use of the time machine accomplished three things.

First, the time machine provided us with an extremely powerful tool. We could now use this tool to ask about the optimism of people who would not take questionnaires, as long as we had verbatim quotes from them. We could "CAVE" an enormous range of material for explanatory style: press conferences, diaries, therapy transcripts, letters home from the battlefront, wills. We could find out the explanatory style of children too young to take the CASQ by listening to them talk, extracting their causal statements and rating them as if they were questionnaire items. We might be able to find out how optimistic long-dead presidents of the United States had been, whether the level of optimism has increased or decreased over historical time in America, and whether some cultures and religions are more pessimistic than others.

Second, the time machine gave us additional evidence that we learn our explanatory style from our mothers. In 1970 the Berkeley-Oakland children, now grandmothers, were interviewed. In addition their children, now mothers themselves, were also interviewed. We "CAVEd" these interviews and found the same results that our questionnaire studies showed. There was marked resemblance between the level of pessimism of the mothers and their daughters. As noted above, this is one of the ways we learn optimism, by listening to our mothers explain the everyday events that happen to them.

Third, the time machine provided our first evidence that the reality of the crises we go through as children shapes our optimism: Girls who went through economic crises that were resolved came to look at bad events as temporary and changeable. But children who experienced the privations of the Great Depression and remained poor afterward came to look at bad events as fixed and immutable. So our major childhood crises may give us a pattern, like a cookie cutter, with which, for the rest of our lives, we produce explanations for new crises.

In addition to the findings of the work with Glen Elder, there is another line of evidence for the proposition that children distill their explanatory style out of major crises in their lives. This evidence has been painstakingly gathered by British professor George Brown. When I first met him, George had spent the last ten years walking around the most poverty-stricken areas of South London, interviewing housewives at great length. He had interviewed more than four hundred, looking for the key to the prevention of depression. The sheer amount of severe depression he uncovered was shocking—over 20 percent of the housewives were depressed, half of those psychotically so. What, he was determined to find out, separated those women who got severely depressed in that trying environment from those who were invulnerable?

He had isolated three protective factors. If any single one of the three was present, depression would not occur, even in the face of severe loss and privation. The first protective factor was an intimate relationship with a spouse or a lover. Such women could fight depression off well. The second was a job outside the home. The third was not having three or more children under the age of fourteen at home to take care of.

In addition to invulnerability factors, Brown had isolated two major risk factors for depression: recent loss (husband dying, son emigrating) and, more important, *death of their own mothers before the women had reached their teens.*

"If your mother dies when you are young," George explained, "you think about later losses in the most hopeless ways. When your son emigrates to New Zealand, you don't say to yourself that he's gone off to make his fortune and he'll be coming back. You see him as dead. All adult losses seem to you to be deaths."

The death of the mother of a young girl is a permanent and pervasive loss. So much of what a girl does depends on her mother. This is true particularly before puberty—before boys and the daughter's teenage crowd become partial substitutes. If the reality of our first major loss shapes how we think about the causes of future losses, George's findings make sense. These unfortunate children learn—just as the lower-class children did during the Great Depression—that loss is permanent and pervasive. Their mother leaves and never comes back, and their whole life is now impoverished. Losses later in life get interpreted this way: He's dead, he's never coming back, I can't go on.

. . .

SO WE HAVE evidence for three kinds of influences on your child's explanatory style. First, the form of the everyday causal analyses he hears from you—especially if you are his mother: If yours are optimistic, his will be too. Second, the form of the criticisms he hears when he fails: If they are permanent and pervasive, his view of himself will turn toward pessimism. Third, the reality of his early losses and traumas: If they remit, he will develop the theory that bad events can be changed and conquered. But if they are, in fact, permanent and pervasive, the seeds of hopelessness have been deeply planted.

8

School

ONE COLD AND windy day in April 1970, when I was still a fairly new professor at the University of Pennsylvania, I found myself waiting in line to check into Haddon Hall, a slightly decaying, once grand hotel that was awaiting the transformation of Atlantic City into the Las Vegas of the East. The occasion was yet another annual convention of the Eastern Psychological Association. Ahead of me was a woman who did not look familiar from behind; but when she turned her head I gaped in astonishment. We'd been friends all during childhood.

"Joan Stern," I exclaimed, "is that you?"

"Marty Seligman! What are you doing here?"

"I'm a psychologist," I said.

"So am I!"

We both burst into laughter. Of course—what other order of being *would* we be, checking into this particular convention hotel on this particular weekend. Joan had gotten a doctorate in psychology from the New School for Social Research and I from Penn, and here we were, both of us professors.

We had gone to kindergarten together ("Do you remember Miss Manville?") and had grown up three blocks apart ("Is Stittig's still there?"). When I was sent off to upper-crust Albany Academy, she had gone off to Saint Agnes, the girls' equivalent. Life had gotten much better for both of us the first day we left Albany and entered college. We discovered that the world contained more than a few people like us, and that Debbie Reynolds's looks and Elvis Presley's music were not universally loved, nor the life of the mind universally scorned. Joan was married now; her married name was Joan Girgus.

I asked her what she was working on.

"Kids," she said, "what they perceive and think, and how this changes as they grow up." She told me about her fascinating work on visual illusions. I told her about learned helplessness.

"Is your father still alive?" she asked. "How difficult that must have been for you," she said when I told her about his death. She understood that kind of loss very well, because her mother had died when Joan was a teenager.

As the meeting continued, we spent more and more time together, trying to connect our common past to what was happening now. By the time we parted, it had occurred to both of us that someday our research interests—hers in childhood and mine in personal control—might merge.

Joan went on to become Dean of Social Sciences at City College in New York and then Dean of the College at Princeton University, and I went on to work on explanatory style. Another decade was to pass before our interests combined. When they did, they coalesced around the question of optimism in the classroom.

HOW DOES a child's explanatory style affect his performance in the classroom?

Let's begin by going back to the basic theory. When we fail at something, we all become helpless and depressed *at least momentarily*. We don't initiate voluntary actions as quickly as we would otherwise, or we may not try at all. If we do try, we will not persist. As you've read, explanatory style is the great modulator of learned helplessness. Optimists recover from their momentary helplessness immediately. Very soon after failing, they pick themselves up, shrug, and start trying again. For them, defeat is a challenge, a mere setback on the road to inevitable victory. They see defeat as temporary and specific, not pervasive.

Pessimists wallow in defeat, which they see as permanent and pervasive. They become depressed and stay helpless for very long periods. A setback is a defeat. And a defeat in one battle is the loss of the war. They don't begin to try again for weeks or months, and if they try, the slightest new setback throws them back into a helpless state.

The theory clearly predicts that in the classroom and, as we shall see in the next chapter, the playing field, success will not necessarily go to the most talented. The prize will go to the adequately talented who are also optimists.

Are these predictions true?

The Classroom

I RECENTLY came across the case of a boy I'll call Alan. At age nine he was what some psychologists would call an omega child—somewhat shy, poorly coordinated, always chosen last in games. He was, however, exceedingly bright and a gifted young artist. His drawings were the best his art teacher had ever seen by a child in elementary school. In Alan's tenth year his parents separated, and he went into a depression. His grades plummeted, he seldom spoke, and he lost all his interest in drawing.

His art teacher refused to give up on him. He got the boy to talk and discovered that Alan thought himself stupid, a failure, a sissy . . . and somehow to blame for his parents' separation. Patiently the art teacher made Alan see how wrong each of those self-assessments was and led Alan to other, more realistic judgments of himself. Alan came to accept that, far from stupid, he was an outstanding success. He now knew that coordination came late to some boys, and the fact that sports weren't easy for him made his pluck all the more admirable. The teacher knew Alan's parents and was able to show him that he had no role whatsoever in their separation.

In effect, he helped Alan change his explanatory style. Within a few months Alan was winning awards in school and beginning to make some progress in sports as well, with spirit and enthusiasm substituting for skill. No longer an omega child, Alan was on the road to becoming an alpha teenager.

When your child is doing poorly at school, it is all too easy for his teachers or even for you to conclude falsely that he is untalented or even stupid. Your child may be depressed, and his depression may be preventing him from trying, from persisting, from taking risks which would let him fulfill his potential. Worse, if you conclude that stupidity or lack of talent is the cause, your child will realize this and incorporate it into his theory of himself. His explanatory style will get even worse, and his poor academic performance will become habitual.

Rate Your Child's Depression

How can you tell if your child is depressed?

Short of a diagnostic interview with a psychologist or psychiatrist, there is no conclusive way to tell. But you can get an approximate answer by asking your child to take the following test. This test, a modification of the depression test you took in chapter four, was devised by Myrna Weissman, Helen Orvaschell, and N. Padian working through the Center for Epidemiological Studies of the National Institute of Mental Health. It is called the CES–DC (Center for Epidemiological Studies–Depression Child) test. Here's how to introduce it to your child:

"I've been reading a book about how kids feel, and I've been wondering how you feel lately. Sometimes it's hard for kids to find the words to describe how they feel. Here's something that gives you different ways to say how you feel. You'll see that there are four choices for each sentence. I'd like you to read each sentence and pick out the choice that describes best how you have been feeling or acting *for the past week*. After you make a choice, go on to the next group. There are no right answers or wrong answers."

During the past week

1. I was bothered by things that don't usually bother me.
   Not at all ____ *A little* ____ *Some* ____ *A lot* ____

2. I did not feel like eating; I wasn't very hungry.
   Not at all ____ *A little* ____ *Some* ____ *A lot* ____

3. I wasn't able to feel happy, even when my family or friends tried to help me feel better.
   Not at all ____ *A little* ____ *Some* ____ *A lot* ____

4. I felt that I was not as good as other kids.
   Not at all ____ *A little* ____ *Some* ____ *A lot* ____

5. I felt like I couldn't pay attention to what I was doing.
   Not at all ____ *A little* ____ *Some* ____ *A lot* ____

6. I felt down.
   Not at all ____ *A little* ____ *Some* ____ *A lot* ____

7. I felt like I was too tired to do things.
   Not at all ____ *A little* ____ *Some* ____ *A lot* ____

8. I felt like something bad was going to happen.
   Not at all ____ *A little* ____ *Some* ____ *A lot* ____

9. I felt like things I did before didn't work out.
   Not at all _____ *A little* _____ *Some* _____ *A lot* _____

10. I felt scared.
    Not at all _____ *A little* _____ *Some* _____ *A lot* _____

11. I didn't sleep as well as I usually sleep.
    Not at all _____ *A little* _____ *Some* _____ *A lot* _____

12. I was unhappy.
    Not at all _____ *A little* _____ *Some* _____ *A lot* _____

13. I was more quiet than usual.
    Not at all _____ *A little* _____ *Some* _____ *A lot* _____

14. I felt lonely, like I didn't have any friends.
    Not at all _____ *A little* _____ *Some* _____ *A lot* _____

15. I felt like kids I know were not friendly or that they didn't want to be with me.
    Not at all _____ *A little* _____ *Some* _____ *A lot* _____

16. I didn't have a good time.
    Not at all _____ *A little* _____ *Some* _____ *A lot* _____

17. I felt like crying.
    Not at all _____ *A little* _____ *Some* _____ *A lot* _____

18. I felt sad.
    Not at all _____ *A little* _____ *Some* _____ *A lot* _____

19. I felt people didn't like me.
    Not at all _____ *A little* _____ *Some* _____ *A lot* _____

20. It was hard to get started doing things.
    Not at all _____ *A little* _____ *Some* _____ *A lot* _____

Scoring the test is simple. Each "Not at all" counts as 0, each "A little" counts 1, each "Some" counts 2, and each "A lot" counts 3. To score the test, total these numbers. If your child checked two boxes for one question, give him the higher of the two scores.

Here's what the scores mean: If your child scored from 0 to 9, he is probably not depressed. If he scored 10 to 15, he is probably mildly depressed. If he scored over 15 he is showing significant levels of depression; 16 to 24 puts him in the moderately depressed range; and, if he scored over 24, he may well be severely depressed. An important caveat is in order, however: No pen-and-paper test is the equivalent of a professional diagnosis. There are two mistakes a test like this can make, and you should watch out for them: First, many children hide their symptoms, particularly from their parents. So some children who score below 10 may actually be depressed. Second, some children with high scores may have problems other than depression, which are producing the high scores.

If your child scored 10 or more and is doing badly in school, depression may be causing the poor schoolwork and not vice versa. We have found that among children in the fourth grade, the higher the depression rating the worse the child does at solving anagrams and on IQ-test items, and the worse his grades. This is true even of children who are very talented and very intelligent.

So, if your child scores over 15 across a two-week span, you should arrange for professional help. If your child scores above 9 and also talks about committing suicide, you should arrange for professional help. A "cognitive-behavioral" child therapist would be ideal. Look in the Yellow Pages under "Psychologists," "Psychiatrists" or "Psychotherapists." If you can't find one who specializes in cognitive or behavioral therapy for children, write a note to me at the University of Pennsylvania or to DART (Depression Awareness, Recognition, Treatment Program) at the National Institute of Mental Health, 5600 Fishers Lane, Rockville, Maryland 20857. Between us we will let you know an appropriate therapist close to where you live.

The Princeton-Penn Longitudinal Study

COULD A pessimistic explanatory style be one root cause of depression and poor achievement among children, as it is among adults? In 1981, when this question emerged from my investigations, I thought of Joan Girgus. Over the years we had stayed in touch and kept abreast of each other's research. Her work with children focused on how perception developed as the child grows. I also knew that at City College of New York she'd been greatly concerned about students' underachievement. I felt she'd be the ideal partner in my inquiry.

"It comes down to this," I said when we met. "I don't think most classroom failure is a matter of lack of talent. Our new data show that if a school kid is depressed, his classroom performance nosedives."

I elaborated a bit and then told Joan about Carol Dweck's latest findings, which pointed to pessimistic explanatory style as the culprit in poor academic performance. "I just heard through the grapevine," I said, "about Carol's latest work. She divided grade-school children into 'helpless' and 'mastery-oriented' groups, depending on their explanatory style. She then gave them a series of failures—unsolvable problems—followed by successes—solvable problems.

"Before the failures, there was no difference at all between the two groups. But once they started to fail, an astonishing difference emerged. The helpless children's problem-solving strategies deteriorated down to the first-grade level. They began to hate the task and to talk about how good they were at baseball or acting in the class play. When the mastery-oriented children failed, they stayed at their fourth-grade level in their strategies, and while acknowledging that they must be making mistakes, they stayed involved. One mastery-oriented child actually rolled up her sleeves and said, 'I love a challenge.' They all expressed confidence that they would soon be back on track, and they kept at it.

"What's more," I went on, "at the end when all the kids were given successes, the helpless kids still discounted their success. They predicted that in the future, they would solve only fifty percent of the kind of problems that they had just solved perfectly. The mastery-oriented kids predicted ninety percent.

"It seems to me," I concluded, "that the basic problem underlying many kids' depression and much poor schoolwork may be pessimism. When a kid believes there is nothing he can do, he stops trying, and his grades plunge. I'd like you to join me in investigating this."

Joan didn't respond to my invitation immediately. She asked more questions, and then she thought for a moment. Finally she said, "I've become convinced that optimism and the ability to bounce back from setbacks are keys to academic success here. But I suspect that the time of life to look at is not college and not even high school. It's in grade school and junior high school that lifelong habits of seeing the world crystallize. Before puberty, not after.

"I've been thinking about changing my research to something that connects more directly to what I've seen as a dean. Finding out about depression, school achievement, and explanatory style in kids sounds like just the right kind of thing."

By one of those lucky coincidences, Susan Nolen-Hoeksema had just arrived at the University of Pennsylvania as a first-year graduate student, and she became the catalyst that made this project happen. Susan was a quietly determined twenty-one-year-old whose mentor at Yale sent me a note saying she was the best undergraduate he had seen in ten years, and he envied the fact that she was determined to study helplessness in children. He also warned me not to mistake her quiet demeanor for either shyness or ordinariness of mind.

I described my conversation with Joan to Susan, and her reaction was immediate: "This is exactly what I want to spend my life doing."

What followed was two years of begging school superintendents near Princeton, New Jersey, then principals, then teachers and parents, then children, and finally the National Institute of Mental Health, to let us undertake a large-scale study to predict who gets depressed and who does poorly in the grade-school classroom. We wanted to find the source of the depression that afflicts so many young children and damages their schoolwork. In the fall of 1985, the Princeton-Penn Longitudinal Study got under way. Four hundred third-grade children, their teachers, and their parents began an investigation that was to go on until these children finished seventh grade, nearly five years later.

We hypothesized that there are two major risk factors for depression and poor achievement among children:

- *Pessimistic explanatory style*. Children who see bad events as permanent, pervasive, and personal will over time get depressed and do badly in school.
- *Bad life events*. Children who suffer the most bad events—parents separating, family deaths, family job loss—will do worst.

The data for the first four years of this five-year study are now in. The greatest risk factor for later depression is, not surprisingly, an earlier bout of depression. Children who have been depressed once tend to get depressed again, and children who are depression-free in third grade tend to be depression-free in the fourth and fifth grades. We didn't need to do a half-million-dollar study to find that out. But over and above this, we established that both explanatory style and bad life events are significant risk factors for depression.

First, Explanatory Style:

CHILDREN WITH pessimistic explanatory style are at a serious disadvantage. If your child starts off in third grade with a pessimistic score on the CASQ, he is at risk for depression. We divided the children into those whose depression scores got worse as time went on and those whose depression got better as time went on. Explanatory style separates these two groups into the following tendencies:

- If you start off the third grade with a pessimistic style and you are not depressed, you become depressed as time goes on.
- If you start off pessimistic and you are also depressed, you stay depressed.
- If you start off optimistic and you are also depressed, you get better.
- If you start off optimistic and you are not depressed, you stay depression-free.

Which comes first—being a pessimist or being depressed? It could be that pessimism makes you depressed, but it could also be that depression makes you see the world pessimistically. Both turn out to be true. Being depressed in the third grade makes you more pessimistic in the fourth grade, and being pessimistic in the third grade makes you more depressed in the fourth grade. The two together form a vicious circle.

One child we encountered, Cindy,* was caught in this vicious circle. In the winter of third grade, Cindy's parents told her that they were separating, and her father moved out. Her explanatory-style scores had been a bit more pessimistic than average before this, but she now became listless and teary. Her depression scores went sky-high. Her schoolwork began to suffer, and she withdrew from her friends, as depressed children often do. She then began to think of herself as unloved and as stupid, and this caused her explanatory style to become more pessimistic. This pessimistic style, in turn, made it harder for her to tolerate disappointment. She interpreted even minor setbacks as meaning "Nobody likes me" or "I'm no good," and she got even more depressed.

Recognizing when this vicious circle has begun in your own child and learning how to break it up is one of the crucial things parents must learn to do. You will see how in chapter thirteen.

Second, Bad Life Events:

THE MORE MISFORTUNES befall a child, the worse his depression. Optimistic children resist the impact of bad events better than pessimistic

---

* The reader is reminded that to protect the confidentiality of the participants in our research I have created composites as my examples both for the children and for patients in therapy.

children do, and popular children resist better than unpopular do. But this does not prevent bad events from having some depressing effects on all children.

Here are some events to watch out for. When these occur, your child can use a lot of your time and all the help and support you can muster. It'a also a good time to put the exercises you will learn about in chapter thirteen into practice.

- A brother or sister leaves home for college or work.
- A pet dies—this may seem trivial, but it is devastating.
- A grandparent whom the child knows well dies.
- The child moves to a new school—loss of friends can be very disruptive.
- You and your spouse are fighting.
- You and your spouse divorce or separate—along with parents' fights, this is the number-one problem.

Divorce and Parental Turmoil

BECAUSE DIVORCE and serious turmoil between parents are increasing and are also the common events most depressing to children, we have focused in the Princeton-Penn Longitudinal Study on children who have experienced them.

When we began the study, sixty of the children—roughly 15 percent—told us their parents were divorced or separated. We have watched these children carefully for the last three years and contrasted them to the rest of the children. What they tell us has important implications for our society at large and for how you should deal with your children if divorce happens to you.

First—and most important—the children of divorce do badly, by and large. Tested twice a year, these children are much more depressed than the children from intact families. We had hoped the difference would diminish over time, but it doesn't. Three years later, the children of divorce are still much more depressed than the other children. Our finding applies to all symptoms of depression: The children of divorce are sadder and they act out more in the classroom; they have less zest, lower self-esteem, and more bodily complaints; and they worry more.

It is important to realize that these are *averaged* findings. Some of the children did not become depressed, and some of the depressed children recovered in time. Divorce does not doom a child to years of depression; it only makes depression much more likely.

Second, many more bad life events continue to happen to children of divorce. This continued disruption could be what keeps depression so high among those children. These events divide into three kinds. First are the events the divorce itself causes, or which are caused by the depression the divorce brings in its wake. These things happen more often to children of divorce:

- Their mother starts a new job.
- Their classmates are less friendly.
- A parent remarries.
- A parent joins a new church.
- A parent is hospitalized.
- The child fails a course at school.

Children of divorce also experience more ongoing events that themselves might have caused the divorce:

- Their parents argue more.
- Their fathers go on more business trips.
- A parent loses a job.

Pretty unsurprising so far. But we were astonished by the last category of bad events that children of divorce suffer more of. We still don't know what to make of these remarkable facts, but we think you should know about them:

- The children of divorce see a sibling hospitalized three and a half times more often than children of intact families do.
- The child's own chance of being hospitalized is three and a half times greater.
- The chance that a friend of the child will die is twice as great.
- The chance that a grandparent will die is also twice as great.

Some of these events may be causes or consequences of divorce. But, in addition, families that divorce seem to be cursed by more kinds of misfortune that seem to have nothing to do with the divorce itself, either as cause or as consequence. We cannot imagine how the death of a good friend of the child's or a grandparent dying could be a consequence of divorce or how it could be a contributing cause. Yet the statistics are there.

This all adds up to a very nasty picture for the children of divorce. It used to be said that it is better for the children to have their unhappy parents divorce than to live with two parents who hate each other. But our findings show a bleak picture for these children: prolonged, unrelieved depression; a much higher rate of disruptive events; and, very strangely, much more apparently unrelated misfortune. It would be irresponsible for me not to advise you to take these dismaying data seriously if you are thinking about divorcing.

But the problem may not be the divorce itself. The root of the problem may be the parents' fighting. We have for three years also followed seventy-five children from the Princeton Longitudinal Study whose parents have not divorced, but who say that their parents fight a lot. The children of fighting families look just as bad as the children of divorce: They are highly depressed, remain depressed long after the parents are said to stop fighting, and suffer more untoward life events than children from intact families whose parents don't fight.

There are two possible ways fighting between parents might hurt children so lastingly. The first is that parents who have grown very unhappy with each other fight and then separate. The fighting and separation directly disturb the child, causing long-term depression. The second possibility is more like traditional wisdom: Parents who fight and separate are very unhappy with each other. The fighting and separation themselves have little direct effect on the child, but the child is aware of his parents' great unhappiness and that so disturbs the child as to produce long-term depression. There is nothing in our data to tell us which of these two theories is right.

What does this mean for you?

Many people are in rocky marriages, filled with strife and conflict. Less dramatic, but more common, is this situation: After several years of marriage, many people don't like their spouses much anymore. This is fertile ground for fighting. But at the same time, both parents are often overwhelmingly concerned with the well-being of the children.

It seems to be a plain fact—at least statistically—that either separation or fighting in response to an unhappy marriage is likely to harm your children in lasting ways. If it turns out that parents' unhappiness rather than overt fighting is the culprit, I would suggest marital counseling aimed at coming to terms with the shortcomings of the marriage.

But if the act of fighting and the choice to separate turn out to be responsible for children's depression, very different advice follows if your children's interest—not your own life satisfaction—is primary for you. Are you willing to forgo separation? An even harder challenge: Are you willing to choose to refrain from fighting?

I am not naïve enough to advise you never to fight. Fighting sometimes works: The problem resolves and the situation improves. But many marital fights are unproductive. I cannot advise you on how to fight productively, since I have no special expertise about this. The only piece of solid research I know about on *how* to fight concerns resolution. Children who watch films of adults fighting are much less disturbed when the fight ends with a clear resolution. This suggests that when you fight, you should go out of your way to resolve the quarrel, unambiguously and in front of your child.

I believe it is important, beyond this, to be aware at the moment you choose to fight that your fighting may harm your children. You may well consider fighting your sacred right. After all, we live in an age when many people consider letting it all hang out healthy and legitimate. It is deemed perfectly all right, if you are angry, to fight, and fight, and fight. This attitude comes out of Freudian views of the negative consequences of bottling up anger. But what happens if you turn the other cheek? On the one hand, unexpressed anger does cause at least momentary rises in blood pressure, and therefore might possibly contribute—in the long run—to psychosomatic problems. On the other hand, letting anger out often causes delicately poised relationships to topple. Anger escalates and, unresolved, begins to take on a life of its own. The couple winds up living in a balance of recriminations.

But these consequences of not fighting affect you and your spouse. As far as your children are concerned, there is very little to be said in favor of parents' fighting. Therefore, I choose to go against the prevailing ethic and recommend that, if it is your children you care most about, you step back and think twice or three times before you fight. Being angry and fighting are *not* a human right. Consider swallowing anger, sacrificing pride, putting up with less than you deserve from your spouse. Step back before provoking your spouse and before answering a provocation. Fighting is a human choice, and it is your child's well-being, more than yours, that may be at stake.

Our research shows the following chain of events to be common: Parental fighting or separation leads to a marked increase in the child's depression. The depression itself then causes school problems to increase and explanatory style to become much more pessimistic. School problems combine with this newly minted pessimism to maintain depression, and a vicious circle has begun. Depression now becomes a permanent way of life for your child.

An escalation of parental fighting, or the decision to separate, marks exactly the point at which your child needs extra help to prevent depression and the shift to pessimism, and to ward off school problems. This is exactly when he will need special help from his teachers and from you.

Go out of your way to be very close to your child. One major loving relationship, undisturbed, may counteract the effects of fighting. This is also
the time to consider professional help. Therapy for you and your spouse
may teach you to fight less and more productively. Therapy for your
child at this stage of your marriage just might prevent a lifetime of
depression for him.

Girls vs. Boys

THE DISASTROUS long-term effects of divorce and fighting were not the
only data that surprised us. We had been very interested in sex differences.
We had strong expectations about which sex should be more depressed
and pessimistic, but when we looked at our data, we found the opposite—
over and over again.

As you know from chapters four and five, adult women are much more
depressed on average than men. Twice as many women are found to suffer
depression—whether the phenomenon is measured by treatment statistics,
by door-to-door surveys, or by number of symptoms. We supposed that
this must begin in childhood and that we would find that girls are more
depressed than boys and have a more pessimistic explanatory style.

Not so. At every point in our study, *the boys are more depressed than
the girls*. The average boy will have many more depressive symptoms and
suffer more severe depression than the average girl. Among the boys in
the third and fourth grades, a whopping 35 percent are found to be severely
depressed at least once in the third and fourth grades. Among the girls
only 21 percent showed severe depression. The difference is confined to
two sets of symptoms: The boys show more behavioral disturbance (e.g.,
"I get in trouble all the time") and more anhedonia (lack of enjoyment,
not enough friends, social withdrawal). In sadness, diminished self-esteem,
and bodily symptoms, the boys do not exceed the girls.

The explanatory-style differences are parallel. To our surprise, the girls
are more optimistic than the boys, at each measuring. They are more optimistic than the boys about good events and less pessimistic about bad ones.

So the Princeton-Penn Longitudinal Study yielded another surprise. Boys
are more pessimistic and more depressed than girls, and boys are more
fragile in their response to bad events, including divorce. This means that
whatever causes the huge difference in depression in adulthood, with
women twice as vulnerable as men, it does not have its roots in childhood.
Something must happen at or shortly after puberty that causes a flip-flop

—and hits girls very hard indeed. We can only guess what this might be. But the children we are following are just approaching puberty now, so in its last year the Princeton-Penn Longitudinal Study may tell us what happens around puberty that shifts the burden of depression from males to females.

College

ONE SPRING DAY in 1983 I listened to Willis Stetson, the University of Pennsylvania's dean of admissions, describe the problems the admissions office had—actually, the errors it made. I had come because I was master of one of Penn's colleges and had seen close up just how poor the results of the selection procedure could be. I volunteered to let the admissions office try my test out, to see if it would help predict academic success better than current methods did.

"After all," Dean Stetson was complaining, "it's just a statistical guess. We have to accept a certain number of mistakes."

I asked him how Penn admits freshmen.

"We take three important academic factors into account," he said. "Grades in high school, College Board scores, and achievement-test results. We have a regression equation—thank God I don't have to explain that to *you*. We plug the three scores into the equation, and we come up with a number, like 3.1. That is in fact the students' predicted average for the freshman year. We call it the PI, or predictive index. If it's high enough, you get admitted."

I knew, indeed, what regression equations are, and how fallible they are. A regression equation takes into account past factors, like your SAT scores and your high-school grades, and relates them to some future criterion, like grade-point average in college. It then jiggers the numbers around in order to assign a weight to each past factor and make it fit the criterion. For example, if you were trying to predict the birth weight of a baby from the weights of its parents, you might look at the last thousand babies born in a certain hospital and note their weights, and then note their parents' weights, and you might find that if you divide the mother's weight by 21.7 and the father's weight by 43.4 and then average those two numbers, the result would correspond to the baby's birth weight. There would be no significance in the number 21.7 or the number 43.4; the weights wouldn't connect to any law of nature; they'd be statistical accidents. Regression equations are what you do when you don't know what else to do.

That's what the admissions committee at the university was up to. They were taking the SATs and high-school grades for several freshman classes running and correlating the data with the grade-point average all these freshmen got. They saw then that roughly—but only roughly—the higher the SATs, the better the college grades, and the higher the high-school grades, the better the college grades.

But it might turn out, for instance, that the SATs were twice as good a predictor of college grades as high-school grades were, and one and a half times better than the achievement tests. So, it might turn out that 5.66 times the grades in high school plus 3.21 times the achievement-test scores plus 2.4 times the SAT total best "fit" later freshman grades, when all the results were averaged over the last ten freshman classes. The weights are arbitrary, chosen because they happen to fit. For this reason, college-grade prediction is very much a statistical guess. You get the majority right, but you make lots of errors. And lots of errors mean disappointed, complaining parents, overworked professors, and undergraduate academic misfits.

"We make two kinds of errors," Dean Stetson continued. "First, some students—a small number, I'm happy to say—do much worse as freshmen than they are expected to do. Second, a much larger number do much better than their PI. Even so, we'd like to decrease our margin of error. Tell me more about this test of yours."

I explained the ASQ and the theory behind it. I told the dean that people determined by the test to be optimists do better than they are expected to do, probably because they try harder in the face of challenge, whereas pessimists give up when they fail. For more than an hour I went over the ASQ and how it worked. I told him what we were doing with the Metropolitan Life Insurance Company and discussed what the consequences of the ASQ for University of Pennsylvania admissions might be: a further reduction in the margin of error, and the ability to predict freshman grades over and above the PI. "You're missing some good kids," I said, "and you're admitting some others who will only crash. Either way, it's a tragedy for the kids and bad for Penn."

Finally Dean Stetson said: "Let's give it a shot. Let's try it on the class of '87."

So the week the class of '87 arrived, over three hundred of them took the ASQ. And then we just waited. We waited for them to suffer through their first midterms and the grueling two weeks of final exams. We waited for these students—many of whom were all-stars in high school—to find out what the competition at a major university was like. We waited for some to go under and some to rise to the challenge.

At the end of the first semester, we saw the errors that the dean worried about. Fully one-third of the students had done either much better or much

worse than their SATs, high-school grades, and achievement tests predicted. Of these hundred freshmen about twenty did much worse and about
eighty did much better.

We saw what we expected by now—the same thing we were seeing with
life-insurance salesmen and with fourth-graders. Freshmen who rose to the
occasion and did much better than their level of "talent" were, on the
average, optimists when they entered. Those who did much worse than
they should have had entered as pessimists.

Beast Barracks

FAILING A midterm exam in college and getting rejected for the lead in
the Easter show in third grade are pretty mild, compared to the whole
range of human failure. But at least one academic setting produces stress
on a more worldly scale: "Beast Barracks" at West Point.

When the nervous eighteen-year-old plebe arrives for the first time at
West Point in early July, he (actually it is now also she) is greeted by an
upper-class cadre whose job is to teach him iron discipline for the rest of
the summer—standing at attention for long periods, ten-mile dawn marches
at double time, shining and reshining brass, memorizing line after line of
fraternal nonsense, and obedience, obedience, obedience. The point is to
mold the character necessary for U.S. Army officers of the future. West
Pointers think it has worked well for over 150 years.

As abused as he is, the plebe is a precious commodity. Plebes are selected
for leadership and academic potential from a huge pool of applicants. West
Point is one of the most elite of all American colleges. Plebes' SATs are
high; their athletic prowess is exceptional; their high-school grades, particularly in engineering-related courses, have been outstanding; and, most
important of all, they have been conspicuously fine members of their community—the eagle scouts. The education of one West Pointer costs around
$250,000 and each empty spot in the graduating class can be reckoned as
a loss to the taxpayer of this magnitude. Yet many cadets are wasted along
the way by the rigors of the program—quite a number before they even
begin it.

I learned all this in February 1987, when I got a call from Richard Butler,
the head of personnel research for West Point. "Dr. Seligman," he began
in a crisp voice that sounded accustomed to command, "I think Uncle Sam
needs you. We have a dropout problem at West Point that you might be
able to do something about. We admit twelve hundred plebes a year. They
arrive for Beast Barracks on July first. Six quit on the first day and by the

end of August—before classes have begun—we've lost a hundred. Will you try to help us predict who drops out?"

I consented eagerly. It sounded like an ideal setting to test the power of optimism to keep people going through the most rigorous academic setting I had ever heard of. In principle, the pessimists should be the quitters—just as at Metropolitan Life and among University of Pennsylvania freshmen.

So on July 2 I drove north with a special research assistant, my fourteen-year-old son, David, to help me pass out the questionnaires. The cadre marched the entire plebe class into the gleaming new Eisenhower Auditorium, and twelve hundred of America's choicest young people stood at attention waiting for our permission to sit down and begin the test. Beast Barracks, we were told, had been "softened" for the first time in decades. Prolonged bracing (standing at extreme attention) and food and water deprivation were now forbidden. In any case I was impressed with the spectacle, and David was awestruck.

Dick Butler's statistics proved accurate. Six plebes quit on the first day, one right in the middle of the test. He got up, vomited, and raced out of the auditorium. One hundred had quit by the end of August.

At this writing we have now followed the class of '91 for two years. Who quits? Once again, the pessimists. Those plebes who explained bad events by saying "It's me, it's going to last forever, it's going to undermine everything I do" are at greatest risk for not making it through the rigors of Beast Barracks. Who gets better grades than the SATs predict? The optimists. And the pessimists get worse grades than their SATs predict.

I cannot yet recommend that a traditional place like West Point change its admission and training policies based on these first findings. But it looks to me as if selecting for optimism among our future officers could produce better leadership in the military. Even more intriguing is the possibility that using techniques of the sort you will learn later in this book to help pessimists become optimists could salvage quite a few dropouts and give them a chance to become the fine officers their talents augur.

Traditional Wisdom About Success at School

FOR ALMOST a hundred years *aptitude* and *talent* have been the code words for academic success. These idols occupy the place of honor on the altars of all admissions and personnel officials. In America you can't even get placed on the track unless your IQ or your SAT score or your MCAT score is high enough, and the situation is even worse in Europe.

I think "talent" is vastly overrated. Not only is talent imperfectly measured, not only is it an imperfect predictor of success, but also the traditional wisdom is wrong. It leaves out a factor that can compensate for low scores or greatly diminish the accomplishments of highly talented people: explanatory style.

Which comes first—optimism or achievement in the classroom? Common sense tells us that people become optimistic as a consequence of being talented or because they do well. But the design of our classroom studies clearly establishes that the causal arrow also points in the opposite direction. In our studies, we hold talent—SAT scores, IQ, life-insurance qualification test scores—constant to begin with and then look at what happens to the optimists and pessimists among the highly talented. Over and above their talent-test scores, we repeatedly find that pessimists drop below their "potential" and optimists exceed it.

I have come to think that the notion of potential, without the notion of optimism, has very little meaning.

9

Sports

I CAN'T ABIDE the eleven o'clock news. It's not just the fact that models read the stuff. It's what they read and the film clips they show. A fire in North Philadelphia was the big story last night. I was treated to thirty seconds of flames shooting out of windows, one minute of interviews with the survivors, who were mostly bewailing their lost possessions, and one minute with the sobbing wife of a fireman overcome by smoke inhalation. Don't misunderstand: It was a tragic event and deserved some coverage. But the producers of the eleven o'clock news seem to believe that the American public consists mostly of morons interested only in tear-jerking anecdotes and incapable of understanding statistics and analysis. So what's really newsworthy about that fire is not reported: the astonishingly high rate of fires in the slums at the start of the heating season; the decrease in the frequency of smoke inhalation among firefighters; the low percentage of full claims on fire damage paid by insurance companies—in short, the statistics that get at the underlying causes of particular sensational events.

Bertrand Russell said that the mark of a civilized human being is the ability to read a column of numbers and then weep. Is the American public as "uncivilized" as the news producers think? Are we incapable of understanding statistical arguments or do we only understand anecdotes?

You only have to spend an afternoon in any baseball park in America to know how badly the general public's capacity to appreciate and enjoy statistics has been underestimated by our tastemakers. Every child over six in the park knows what a .300 hitter is and knows Tony Gwynn is more likely to get a hit than Juan Samuel is. Every beer-guzzling adult in the park knows what an earned run average is, even though this is a more complicated statistic than the basic statistics on fire-insurance claims and the dangers of oil-heater start-ups.

Americans delight in sports statistics. We positively revel in probabilities—when they concern José Canseco or Dwight Gooden or Larry Bird. They are the grist for sports betting, a business now rivaling traditional American industry in gross take. Bill James and the Elias Sports Bureau write massive, ingenious compilations of baseball statistics that sell tens of thousands of copies each year. And it is not just the general public that loves this stuff. It makes for serious scientific reading as well, for professional sports is now one of the best quantitatively documented activities in the world. Theories that make fine-grained predictions about human capacity can use these veritable almanacs of sport to test themselves.

This is true of explanatory-style theory, and my students and I have spent thousands of hours reading the sports pages and testing my theory against sports statistics. What does my view of optimism say about the playing field?

Quite simply, there are three basic predictions for sports. First, everything else being equal, the individual with the more optimistic explanatory style will go on to win. He will win because he will try harder, particularly after defeat or under stiff challenge.

Second, the same thing should hold for teams. If a team can be characterized by its level of optimism, the more optimistic team should win—if talent is equal—and this phenomenon should be most apparent under pressure.

Third, and most exciting, when athletes' explanatory style is changed from pessimistic to optimistic, they should win more, particularly under pressure.

The National League

CONSIDER the great American pastime—baseball. I confess, at the outset, that I love this kind of science. In spite of innumerable hours squinting at microfilm, in spite of too many midnight sessions poring over endless columns of batting averages, in spite of attempts to invent new statistics only to find them worthless or redundant, this research is more fun than any I have ever done. Not just because I love baseball (I can be found in the third row behind home plate at most of the Phillies' home games), but because these findings take us to the very heart of human success and failure. They tell us how the "agony of defeat" and the "thrill of victory" really work.

But stating the predictions of the theory is much easier than seeing if they are right. There are three problems.

First, does a team—a group of individuals—have an explanatory style? All our past work had shown that pessimistic *individuals* do worse, but is there such a thing as a pessimistic *team*? And does a pessimistic team do worse? To answer these questions, we use the CAVE technique and study for an entire season every sports-page quote including a causal statement for each individual on a team. Because sportswriters focus on bad events, such quotes abound in the daily sports section of every newspaper. We use raters blind to who said it and what team they are on, and we compute a profile for each player. We also study the manager. Finally we average all the individuals and get a team explanatory style. We then compare all the teams in the league.

The second problem concerns the sports-page quotes themselves. We don't have the clout or the resources to interview all the leading baseball players ourselves. So we rely on what is reported in the sports pages of hometown newspapers and in that marvelous gold mine, *Sporting News*. Now, what a player says to a reporter is pretty degraded scientific material. The quote itself may be inaccurate, hyped by the reporter to make more exciting copy. The player may not say what he means. He may try to shift or take on the blame. He may try to be overmodest or overmacho for the sake of appearances. So we don't know if the quotes accurately reflect explanatory style. The only way to find out is to "bootstrap": If the study does actually predict how a team goes on to do, the quotes must have had validity. If it doesn't predict, either the theory is wrong or the quotes are not valid indicators of underlying optimism.

That's not the only difficulty with sports-page quotes. There is the sheer volume of material to wade through to discover a team explanatory style. In our National League study, we read all of the sports pages in the hometown papers of each of the twelve National League teams for the whole 1985 baseball season, April through October. Because the results looked so fascinating, we then repeated the study for 1986. All in all we "CAVEd" about fifteen thousand pages of sports reporting.

The third problem is how to show that the causal arrow goes from optimism to victory and not the other way around. The New York Mets, as you will see in a moment, were a very optimistic team in 1985. They were also a very good team in 1985, losing out to the St. Louis Cardinals in a heart-stopping pennant race in the last week. Did they do well because they were optimistic or did their optimism arise because they were doing so well? To untangle this, we must predict from optimism in one season to victory in the next season, correcting of course for personnel changes. Players who leave the team are omitted from the explanatory-style profile.

But even this isn't enough. We must also correct for how well the team did in the first season. Take the Mets. They were the most optimistic team in the National League in 1985. They also had the second-best record (98 wins and 64 losses). They went on, as we would predict, to do even better in 1986. Was this because they were optimistic (as measured by their 1985 quotes) or merely because they had so much talent (as reflected in their 1985 win-loss record)? To find out we have to correct for prior win-loss record—to hold it "statistically constant"—and see if optimism predicts success above and beyond prior success. This is exactly what we did in our study of academic success, when we asked if optimism predicted college grades better than high-school grades and SATs did.

We also wanted to know if optimism works its magic by governing how a team does under pressure, as the theory claims. My son, David, went through the box scores of every game (there are 972 games a season in the National League), and we invented statistic after statistic on pressure situations. After we were done, we found that the "Elias," one of the statistical almanacs of baseball, computed even better statistics on late-inning pressure. So we threw ours away and used theirs. Elias tells us how the hitters on a team do in the last three innings of a close game. So we predicted that teams optimistic in 1985 would in 1986 have higher batting averages under late-inning pressure than would teams that were pessimistic in 1985. Again we needed to show that this was above and beyond their overall batting averages, by correcting statistically for hitting when they were not under pressure.

The 1985 Mets and Cardinals in 1986

TWO GREAT TEAMS battled neck and neck for the Eastern Division pennant in 1985. For the whole season, we grabbed each causal statement that newspapers quoted individual Mets and Cardinals as making, and rated it. When the season was over we took grand totals.

Here's what the Mets had to say as the season went on. I will attach actual CAVE numbers to each quote. They range from 3 (very temporary, specific, and external) to 21 (completely permanent, pervasive, and personalized). Numbers in the 3 to 8 range are very optimistic. Numbers above 13 are very pessimistic.

Start with manager Davey Johnson, asked why his team lost: "We lost because they [the opponents] made the plays tonight" (external—"they"; temporary—"tonight"; specific—tonight's opponent: 7).

Their sluggers: First, left fielder George Foster: "I got a fan pissed off" because "It must have been one of those days" (7).

Right fielder Darryl Strawberry, asked why he missed a fly ball: "The ball really carried. I just about got my glove on it"(6).

Strawberry on why the Mets were shut out: "Sometimes you go through these kinds of days" (8).

First baseman Keith Hernandez, on why the Mets won only two games on the road: "All the time on the road began to tax us" (8).

Hernandez again, on why the Mets' lead had shrunk to half a game: "They [the opponents] made a bad play and came up smelling like a rose" (3).

Star pitcher Dwight Gooden, explaining why a batter hit a home run off him: "He hit well tonight" (7).

Gooden on why the Mets lost: "It was one of those days" (7); "It wasn't my day" (8); "The heat was too much" (8).

Gooden threw a wild pitch because "Some moisture must have gotten on the ball" (3).

You can probably see what all this adds up to. When the Mets do badly, it's just for today, it's just these opponents, and it's not our fault. They hereby become a textbook example of optimistic explanatory style in sports. As a group, they had the most optimistic style of any National League team in 1985. Their average score for bad events was 9.39, optimistic enough for them to be successful life-insurance salesmen.

Listen now to the St. Louis Cardinals, the team that beat them in the stretch and went on to win the playoffs, then lost a heartbreaking World Series to Kansas City on the strength of a bad ruling by an umpire. The Cardinals were loaded with even more raw talent than the Mets. The Mets batted .257 for the year, whereas the Cardinals batted .264; the Cardinal pitchers had a slightly better earned run average than the Mets.

Manager Whitey Herzog (arguably the most brilliant in baseball today): The team lost because "We can't hit. What the Hell, let's face it" (permanent, pervasive, and personalized: 20).

Herzog on why the press talks much more to Pete Rose (then the playing manager of the Cincinnati Reds) than to him: "What do you expect? He has 3800 more hits than I have" (permanent, pervasive, personalized: 14).

Herzog on why the team had trouble all year in games following days off: "It's a mental thing. We were too relaxed" (14).

The 1985 National League batting champion, Willie McGee, said he didn't steal as many bases as he should have because "I don't have the expertise" (16).

McGee played poorly in 1984 because "Mentally, I was bummed out. I didn't know how to accept struggling" (15).

Slugger Jack Clark on dropping a fly ball: "It was a real catchable ball. I just didn't catch it" (12).

Second baseman Tom Herr said his batting average dropped twenty-one points because "I am having a lot of trouble concentrating and keeping my mind on the job" (17).

What we have here is a portrait of a superbly talented team with a pessimistic explanatory style. This is part of what coaches mean when they say an athlete has a "poor attitude"; indeed, it may be the only active ingredient. Statistically, the Cardinals had a below-average explanatory style for bad events, 11.09, ninth out of the twelve teams. Our theory claims that a team that does very well in a given season in spite of a poor explanatory style must be extremely talented to make up for this handicap.

And the theory predicts what should happen in the next season: As far as these two teams were concerned, the Mets should have excelled and the Cardinals should have deteriorated, relative to 1985.

This is just what happened. In 1986, the Mets were a wonder team. Their win percentage went up to .667 (from .605), they won the division pennant and the playoffs, and they came from behind in a historic finish to steal the World Series from the Boston Red Sox. Their overall batting average in 1986 was a respectable .263, but under late-inning pressure it went up to a superb .277.

The Cardinals fell apart in 1986. They won only 49 percent of their games, finishing nowhere. In spite of massive talent, they batted only .236 overall and deteriorated to a miserable .231 under pressure.

Using their quotes, we computed the 1985 explanatory style for the twelve National League teams. Statistically, in 1986, optimistic teams bettered their 1985 win-loss records, and pessimistic teams did worse than they had in 1985. Teams optimistic in 1985 hit well under pressure in 1986, whereas the hitting of teams pessimistic in 1985 fell apart under pressure in 1986, compared to how well both kinds of teams normally hit.

In general I do not become convinced of my own work's validity until I have repeated it. We repeated the whole study the next year to see if explanatory style could again predict how the National League teams would do, taking all the quotes for 1986 in order to predict 1987 performance. The results were basically the same. The optimistic teams do better the next year than their previous win-loss records would suggest, and the pessimistic teams do worse. Under pressure, the optimistic teams hit well and the pessimistic teams hit poorly.

The National Basketball Association

BASKETBALL does two things for us that baseball doesn't. First, there are fewer players, so "CAVEing" becomes a little less labor-intensive. Second, and most important, basketball is exquisitely handicapped. For each and every game, handicappers predict not only who should win but by how much. The "how much" is called the point spread. So, if the New Jersey Nets were playing the Boston Celtics on any evening in the mid-1980s, Boston would have been favored to win. But you couldn't bet on the Celtics just to win, since they were so likely to win that no one was willing to bet against them. So Boston would, in addition, be predicted to win by, say, nine points, and you could bet on the Celtics to "cover" the spread—that is, to win by nine or more points. If the Celtics did so, you doubled your money, but if they won by fewer than nine points (or, freakishly, lost) you lost your money. So exquisitely skilled are the handicappers that half the bettors will pick the Celtics to cover and half will pick the Nets.

I don't bet on sports—in fact, I have made only one substantial bet in my life (you'll read about it in chapter eleven)—so it's not the betting that interests me. Rather, the spread is a terrific scientific convenience because it equates the two teams for all known factors, such as skill, home-court advantage, who is injured, recent slumps, and so on. Explanatory-style theory claims that there is an additional factor which no one takes into account, the optimism of the team, and that this will determine how a team fares under pressure—above and beyond all the known factors. The more optimistic team should do better than handicapping predicts, and the less optimistic team worse. This should only happen under adverse circumstances, however; for example, after a loss in the previous game. This means that the optimistic teams should tend to cover the point spread in the game following a loss while pessimistic teams should tend to fail to cover the point spread after a loss.

The Boston Celtics and the New Jersey Nets

IN THE SECOND most labor-intensive study I ever did, we read the hometown sports pages for the NBA Atlantic Division teams for all of

1982–83, computed the explanatory style for each team, and used the optimism level to predict how the teams would fare under pressure in 1983–84. We then repeated the study, using 1983–84 sports-page explanatory style to predict the 1984–85 season. All in all we read over ten thousand sports pages, and we assembled about a hundred event-explanation quotes for each team.

Let's look at the two extremes. First, some representative quotes from the Boston Celtics explaining bad events:

A loss: "The fans [at the opponents' home court] are by far the noisiest and most outrageous crowd in the NBA" (9).

Another loss: "Strange things just happen to us there [opponents' home court]" (8).

A low-scoring quarter: "The crowd was very dead" (6).

Loss of a playoff game: "They were making good, quick cuts to the basket" (6).

Loss of the first game in the finals: "That's the best I've ever seen a team run" (8) and "They [the opponents] threw caution to the winds" (4).

An opponent's scoring forty points: "The way he played tonight, he was going to get his forty points regardless of who was on him. We were draped on him. We held him. We punched him, kicked him down, the guy was unreal" (5).

The Celtics sound like manic patients. Bad events were always explained away as temporary, specific, and not their fault. The Celtics beat the point spread in 68.4 percent of the games following a loss in 1983–84 and in an amazing 81.3 percent of such games in 1984–85. (Remember that on average a team beats the point spread 50 percent of the time. The Celtics beat the spread in 51.8 percent and 47.3 percent of games following a win in 1983–84 and 1984–85 respectively.) They were an almost uncanny comeback team.

Now listen to the 1982–83 New Jersey Nets explaining bad events:

Loss of a playoff game: "We are all missing everything" (18) and "We botched up things ourselves and blew all our opportunities" (16).

Other losses: "This is one of the physically weakest teams I've ever coached" (18); "Our intelligence was at an all-time low" (15); and "We're passing up shots. We have no confidence at all" (17).

The Nets were not physically a bad team in 1983–84. They won 51.8 percent of their games. But mentally they were shipwrecked. As you heard, they explained losses as permanent, pervasive, and their own fault. How did they do after a loss in 1983–84? They beat the spread a dismal 37.8 percent of the time in games after losses. After wins, however, they beat the spread 48.7 percent of the time. The Nets improved their explanatory style during 1983–8 , largely because of personnel changes, and during 1984–85 they went on to beat the point spread after a loss 62.2 percent of the time.

Overall, here is what we found. A team's explanatory style for bad events strongly predicts how they do against the point spread after a loss in the next season. The optimistic teams cover the spread more often than the pessimistic teams do. This effect of optimism works above and beyond the "quality" of the team. We know this since the point spread itself holds quality constant (teams should beat it, on average, 50 percent of the time regardless of how good or bad they are) and because we partial out the win-loss record from both the current and the previous seasons, as well as how often the team beat the spread after a win.

We also found the same trend we saw in baseball's National League: A team's overall win-loss record in the next season is predicted by their explanatory style in this season, equating for their win-loss record in this season.

Consider the basketball and baseball studies together. They show:

- Teams, and not just individuals, have a meaningful and measurable explanatory style.
- Explanatory style predicts how teams will do above and beyond how "good" a team is.
- Success on the playing field is predicted by optimism.
- Failure on the playing field is predicted by pessimism.
- Explanatory style works by means of how a team does under pressure—after a loss or in the late innings of close games.

The Berkeley Swimmers

THERE WAS A lot of hype in the press about Berkeley swimming star Matt Biondi's chances in the 1988 Seoul Olympics. He was scheduled to swim seven events, and the American press made it sound likely that he would win seven gold medals, duplicating Mark Spitz's unparalleled performance in the 1972 Olympics. To insiders *any* seven medals—gold, silver, or bronze—Biondi won against the competition in Seoul would represent superb swimming.

The first event Biondi swam was the two-hundred-meter freestyle. He finished a disappointing third. The second event was the one-hundred-meter butterfly, not his premier event. Overpowering the field, he led all the way. But in the last two meters, rather than taking one extra stroke and crashing into the finish wall, he appeared to relax and coast the final meter. You could hear the groan in Seoul, and imagine it across America, as he was inched (centimetered?) out by Anthony Nesty of Surinam, who took the extra stroke to win Surinam's first medal ever. The "agony of defeat" interviewers hammered Biondi on the disappointment of a bronze and a silver medal and speculated that he might not be able to rebound. Would Biondi carry home gold in his five remaining events after this embarrassing start?

I sat in my living room confident that he would. I had reason to believe this, because we had tested Matt Biondi in Berkeley four months before to determine his capacity to do just what he had to do now—come back from defeat.

Along with all his teammates, he had taken the Attributional Style Questionnaire, and he had come out in the top quarter of optimism of an optimistic bunch. We had then simulated defeat under controlled conditions in the pool. Nort Thornton, Biondi's coach, had him swim the one-hundred-yard butterfly all out. Biondi swam it in 50.2 seconds, a very respectable time. But Thornton told him that he had swum 51.7, a very slow time for Biondi. Biondi looked disappointed and surprised. Thornton told him to rest up for a few minutes and then swim it again—all out. Biondi did. His actual time got even faster, 50.0. Because his explanatory style was highly optimistic and he had shown us that he got faster—not slower—after defeat, I felt he would bring back gold from Seoul.

In his last five events in Seoul, Biondi won five gold medals.

Our baseball and basketball studies show that teams have an explanatory style that predicts athletic success. But do the explanatory styles of individual athletes predict how they will do, particularly under pressure? This is the question that Biondi and his teammates helped us answer.

I've never met Nort Thornton. I've only seen him on television. But Nort and his wife, Karen Moe Thornton, respectively the men's and women's swimming coaches at the University of California at Berkeley, are two of my most valued collaborators. And collaborators like the Thorntons are among the most precious assets a scientist can have. I've talked to Nort only on the phone, and his first call came in March 1987.

"I've read about your studies on insurance salesmen," he said, "and I wonder if the same thing might work in swimming. Let me tell you why I think it would work."

I did everything I could to restrain myself and not shout back "Yes! Yes! Yes!" before Nort had finished telling me his line of reasoning. "It sounds like you measure something—deeply held positive beliefs—that we, as coaches, can't quite get hold of," Nort continued. "We know attitude is important, but kids can fake attitude and fall flat when it matters. We also don't know how to change a bad attitude very well."

In October 1988, before the season started, all fifty of the men's and women's varsity swimmers took the ASQ. In addition, Nort and Karen rated each of the swimmers on how they thought the swimmers were likely to do over the season, particularly under pressure. We did this because we wanted to see if the ASQ told the Thorntons anything they didn't already know as coaches intimately familiar with their athletes.

I found right away that I knew something the coaches didn't. The optimism scores from the ASQ were totally unrelated to the coaches' ratings of how the swimmers would do under pressure. But did these scores predict actual success in swimming?

To find this out, Nort and Karen rated each swim for each swimmer for the entire season as "worse than expected" or "better than expected." The swimmers also rated themselves for the same thing, and it was clear that the coaches and the swimmers were on the same wavelength, since the ratings coincided perfectly. I merely totaled up the number of "worse than expected" swims for the season. The pessimists on the ASQ had about twice as many unexpectedly poor swims as the optimists did. The optimists lived up to their swimming potential, and the pessimists fell below theirs.

Would explanatory style work once again to predict the way people responded to defeat, as it had in baseball, basketball, and sales?

To test this, we simulated defeat under controlled conditions. At the end of the season, we had each athlete swim one of his or her best events all out. Nort or Karen then told the swimmer that his time was between 1.5 and 5 seconds (depending on the distance) worse than it actually was. So Biondi was told that he swam the one-hundred butterfly in 51.7 seconds, when he actually swam it in 50.2. We chose the amount of "failure" because we knew it would be very disappointing (one swimmer sat and rocked like a baby in a corner for twenty minutes afterwards), but undetectable as false. Each swimmer then rested and swam the event again as fast as he or she could. As we expected, the pessimists got worse. The performance of two stars who are also pessimists deteriorated in their hundred-yard events by a full two seconds, the difference between winning their event and finishing dead last. The optimists either held on or, like Biondi, got even faster. Several of the optimists got faster by between two and five seconds, again enough to be the difference between a lousy race and a win. The swimmers were, of course, debriefed afterwards.

So the Berkeley swimmers make it clear that explanatory style can work to produce success or failure at an individual level, just as the professional-sports data show this at a team level. Moreover, explanatory style works by the same means for both individuals and teams. It makes athletes do better under pressure. If they are optimists, they try harder and come back from defeat.

What Every Coach Should Know

IF YOU ARE a coach or a serious athlete, you must take these findings seriously. They have several immediate, practical implications for you.

- Optimism is not something you know about intuitively. The ASQ measures something you can't. It predicts success beyond experienced coaches' judgments and handicappers' expertise.
- Optimism tells you when to use certain players rather than others. Consider a crucial relay race. You have a fast athlete, but he's a pessimist who lost his last individual race. Substitute. Use pessimists only after they have done well.
- Optimism tells you who to select and recruit. If two prospects are close in raw talent, recruit the optimist. He'll do better in the long run.
- You can train your pessimists to become optimists.

I didn't tell you what else the Thorntons wanted. They asked if I could take their pessimistic swimmers and make them optimists. I told them I wasn't yet sure, but our programs for change were just being developed, and they looked promising. As a way of thanking them I agreed to give them first crack in sports at our training program. As I write this chapter, our trainers are on their way to Berkeley to teach the entire varsity the skills of optimism. You will find these techniques in the last section of this book.

10

Health

DANIEL WAS only nine when the doctors diagnosed him as having Burkitt's lymphoma, a form of abdominal cancer. He was now ten, and in
spite of an agonizing year of radiation and chemotherapy, the cancer was
still spreading. His doctors and almost everyone else had given up hope.
But not Daniel.

Daniel had plans. He was going to grow up to be a researcher, he told
everyone, and discover how to cure diseases like this so other kids would
be safe. Even as his body weakened, Daniel's optimism remained strong.

Daniel lived in Salt Lake City. The main focus of his hope was a doctor
he described as "the famous East Coast specialist." This doctor, an authority on Burkitt's lymphoma, had gotten interested in Daniel's illness
and had been consulting long-distance with Daniel's doctors. He planned
to stop in Salt Lake City on the way to a West Coast pediatrics meeting
to meet Daniel and talk with his doctors.

Daniel had been excited for weeks. There was so much that he wanted
to tell the specialist. He was keeping a diary, and he hoped the diary would
give some clues about what his cure would be. He felt he was participating
in his own treatment now.

On the day the specialist was to arrive, fog blanketed Salt Lake City
and the airport closed down. The control tower sent the specialist's plane
over to Denver, and he decided to go directly on to San Francisco. When
Daniel heard the news, he cried quietly. His parents and nurses told him
to rest, and they promised to get the doctor by phone in San Francisco so
Daniel could talk to him. But by the next morning Daniel was listless; he

had never been listless before. He had a high fever, and pneumonia set in. By evening he was in a coma. He died the next afternoon.

What do you make of a story like this? I'm sure it isn't the first poignant tale you have heard of death following hope dashed, or of remission following hope gained. Such stories are told the world over, frequently enough to inspire the belief that hope is by itself life-sustaining and hopelessness life-destroying.

But there are other plausible interpretations. You might believe some third factor—for example, a well-tuned immune system—both saves life and engenders hope. Or you might believe that we as a species have such a deep desire to believe hope works miracles, we tell and retell the few cases that seem to prove it—but that are really coincidences—while suppressing the all-too-common stories going the other way around, with illness following hope and recovery following despair.

In the spring of 1976 a most unusual application for admission to our graduate program crossed my desk. In it, a woman named Madelon Visintainer, a nurse in Salt Lake City, narrated Daniel's story. She said she had nursed several such cases, both among children with cancer and, in a reference she did not expand upon, during her "time in Vietnam." Such "stories," she said, could no longer be satisfactory evidence for her. She wanted to find out if it was really true that helplessness, by itself, could kill, and, if it could, to discover how. She wanted to come to the University of Pennsylvania and work with me, testing these questions first with animals, then taking the benefits to people.

Visintainer's plain and unpretentious statement, the only one like it we had ever seen, moved one of the members of the admissions committee to tears. Furthermore, Visintainer's grades and her Graduate Record Exam results were exemplary. There were, however, several holes in her application. From the dates she had given, it was hard to figure out where she had been at what time, or what she had done during several periods of her adult life. She just seemed to disappear every so often.

After some fruitless attempts to clear up these mysteries, we admitted Visintainer. I eagerly awaited her arrival in September 1976. She didn't show up. She did call, saying something about needing to stay one more year in Salt Lake City, something about having to direct a grant on cancer. Directing a grant on cancer research was strange doings for a person who had claimed to be "just" a nurse. She asked if we would hold her place for the following September.

In turn, I asked her if she really wanted to come to the University of Pennsylvania and work on such an unfashionable topic. I warned her that few psychologists and almost no medical types believed that psychological states like helplessness actually caused physical illness. She would be walking into an academic mine field, and she could expect one obstacle after another. She replied that she hadn't been born yesterday and she knew what she was in for.

She did arrive in September 1977—as unadorned and plain-spoken as her application, and also as mysterious. She avoided conversation about her past or what she wanted to achieve in the future. But she did superbly in the present. She proved to be a scientific whirlwind. She undertook, as her first-year project, the awesome task of demonstrating that helplessness could cause death.

She was tremendously excited by the new findings of Ellen Langer and Judy Rodin, then young health researchers at Yale. They had worked with elderly people in a nursing home, changing the amount of control the old people had over daily happenings in their lives.

They had divided the home by floors. On the first floor, the residents received extra control in their lives, and extra choice. One day, the director gave a speech to the residents: "I want you to know about all the things that you can do for yourself here at Shady Grove. There are omelettes or scrambled eggs for breakfast, but you have to choose which you want the night before. There are movies on Wednesday or Thursday night, but you have to sign up in advance. Here are some plants; pick one out and take it to your room—but you have to water it yourself."

The director told the second floor: "I want you to know about all the good things we do for you here at Shady Grove. There are omelettes or scrambled eggs for breakfast. We make omelettes on Monday, Wednesday, and Friday, and scrambled eggs the other days. There are movies on Wednesday night and Thursday night. Residents from the left corridor go Wednesday and from the right Thursday. Here are some plants for your rooms. The nurse will pick one out for you and she'll take care of it."

So the extra good things the people on the first floor received were under their own control. The people on the second floor got the same added goodies, but nothing the residents did affected those goodies.

Eighteen months later, Langer and Rodin returned to the nursing home. They found that the group with choice and control was more active and happier, as measured by a variety of scales. They also found that fewer of this group than of the other had died. This amazing fact strongly indicated that choice and control could save lives and, perhaps, that helplessness could kill.

Madelon Visintainer wanted to investigate this phenomenon in the laboratory, where conditions could be finely regulated, and to understand *how* mastery and helplessness could affect health. She took three groups of rats, giving one group mild escapable shock, the second group mild inescapable shock, and the third group no shock at all. But the day before she did this, she implanted a few cells of a sarcoma on each rat's flank. The tumor was of a type that is invariably lethal if it grows and is not rejected by the animal's immune defenses. Visintainer had implanted just the right number of sarcoma cells so that, under normal conditions, 50 percent of the rats would reject the tumor and live.

This was a beautifully designed experiment. Everything physical was controlled: the amount and duration of shock; diet; housing; tumor load. The only thing that differed among the three groups was the psychological state they were in. One group was suffering learned helplessness, the second had experienced mastery, and the third was psychologically unchanged. If these three groups turned out to differ in ability to reject the tumor, only the psychological state could have caused the difference.

Within a month, 50 percent of the rats not shocked had died, and the other 50 percent of the no-shock rats had rejected the tumor; this was the normal ratio. As for the rats that mastered shock by pressing a bar to turn it off, 70 percent rejected the tumor. But only 27 percent of the helpless rats, the rats that had experienced uncontrollable shock, rejected the tumor.

Madelon Visintainer thus became the first person to demonstrate that a psychological state—learned helplessness—could *cause* cancer.

Actually, almost the first. As Madelon was writing up her findings to submit to *Science*, the premier journal for major scientific breakthroughs, I opened up the latest issue. In it two Canadian researchers, Larry Sklar and Hymie Anisman from Ottawa, reported a similar experiment—they used mice rather than rats and measured the rate of tumor growth rather than ability to reject tumors—with the same results: Helplessness produced more rapid growth of tumors.

Another of Madelon's discoveries was about rats' childhood ("weaning-linghood," to purists). Madelon had found that rats who had experienced mastery when young would be immunized against tumors as adults. She had given young rats escapable shock, inescapable shock, or no shock and then waited until they were adults. She then implanted the sarcoma, divided each of the original groups into threes, and gave each new group escapable shock, inescapable shock, or no shock. Most of the rats that had learned helplessness when young failed to reject the tumor as adults, and most of the rats that escaped shock when young rejected the tumor as adults. So childhood experience proved to be crucial in tumor rejection by adults. Childhood mastery immunized, and early helplessness put adult rats at risk for cancer.

When she completed her Ph.D., Madelon applied to various universities for an assistant professorship, and some of those universities had insisted on a complete vita from her. On seeing one I learned to my astonishment that she had already been an assistant professor of nursing at Yale before undertaking graduate training in psychology. I learned, further, that she had earned a Silver Star and sundry other decorations for courage under fire in Vietnam. She had run a hospital in Parrot's Beak, Cambodia, during the 1970 incursion.

More I could not coax out of her. But now I understood something about the sources of the courage and strength of character she had needed back in 1976, to wade into the intellectual battlefield she had picked for herself. When Madelon entered her chosen field—psychological effects on physical health—it was the province of faith healers and hucksters. She wanted to demonstrate scientifically that mind could influence disease, and this ambition had been met through most of her nursing career with the jeers and disbelief of her medical colleagues. According to dogma, only physical processes, not mental processes, could influence disease. She turned to academe for a sympathetic hearing and support. By the time she turned in her landmark doctoral dissertation, she had helped prove that the mind can indeed control illness. And even the medical world was beginning to believe it. Today Madelon is chairperson of the Department of Pediatric Nursing at the Yale School of Medicine.

The Mind-Body Problem

WHY DOES THE possibility that mental life influences physical illness meet with such resistance? The answer reflects the knottiest of all the philosophical problems I know.

There are but two kinds of substance in the universe, argued the great seventeenth-century rationalist René Descartes: physical and mental. How do they act upon each other? We can see how one billiard ball hitting another causes it to move. But how does the mental act of willing your hand to move cause the physical movement of your hand? Descartes had his own quirky answer. He said that the mind runs the body via the pineal gland, a brain organ whose function is still not well understood. Descartes' answer was wrong, and scientists and philosophers ever since have been trying to figure out by what path mental substance might influence physical substance.

Descartes was a dualist. He believed that the mental could affect the physical. In due course an opposing school of thought developed, and it carried the day: materialism, whose adherents believed either that there is only one kind of substance—the physical—or who believed that there is mental substance but that it has no effects of its own. Almost all modern scientists and physicians are materialists. They resist to the death the notion that thought and emotion can affect the body. For them that is spiritualism. All claims that emotional and cognitive states influence illness run afoul of materialism.

I have wrestled for the last twenty years with three questions about health and hope. Each is at the frontier of the attempt to understand physical illness, an attempt that is a modern incarnation of the mind-body problem.

The first question concerns *cause*. Does hope actually sustain life? Do hopelessness and helplessness actually kill?

The second concerns *mechanism*. In this material world, how might hope and helplessness work? By what mechanism do matters so eminently spiritual touch matters so physical?

The third question is that of *therapy*. Can changing the way you think, changing your explanatory style, improve health and prolong life?

Optimism and Good Health

IN THE LAST five years, laboratories around the world have produced a steady flow of scientific evidence that psychological traits, particularly optimism, can produce good health. This evidence makes sense of—and supersedes—the torrent of personal stories in which states ranging from laughter to the will to live appear to help health.

In four ways, the theory of learned helplessness strongly suggests that optimism should benefit health.

The first follows from Madelon Visintainer's findings that learned helplessness in rats made them more susceptible to tumor growth. These findings were soon bolstered by more detailed work on the immune systems of helpless rats. The immune system, the body's cellular defense against illness, contains different kinds of cells whose job is to identify and then kill foreign invaders, such as viruses, bacteria, and tumor cells. One kind, the T-cells, recognize specific invaders such as measles, then greatly multiply and kill the invaders. Another kind, natural killer cells (NK cells), kill anything foreign they happen across.

Researchers looking at the immune systems of helpless rats found that the experience of inescapable shock weakens the immune system. T-cells from the blood of rats that become helpless no longer multiply rapidly when they come across the specific invaders they are supposed to destroy. NK cells from the spleens of helpless rats lose their ability to kill foreign invaders.

These findings show that learned helplessness doesn't just affect behavior; it also reaches down to the cellular level and makes the immune system more passive. This means one of the reasons Visintainer's helpless rats did not fight off tumors might be that their very immune defenses had been weakened by the helplessness experience.

What does this mean in terms of explanatory style? Explanatory style is the great modulator of learned helplessness. As we saw earlier, optimists resist helplessness. They do not become depressed easily when they fail. They do not give up easily. Across a lifetime, an optimistic person will have fewer episodes of learned helplessness than a pessimistic person will. The less learned helplessness experienced, the better shape the immune system should be in. So the first way in which optimism might affect your health across your lifetime is by preventing helplessness and thereby *keeping immune defenses feistier*.

A second way in which optimism should produce good health concerns *sticking to health regimens and seeking medical advice*. Consider a pessimistic person who believes that sickness is permanent, pervasive, and personal. "Nothing I do matters," he believes, "so why do anything?" Such a person is less likely to give up smoking, get flu shots, diet, exercise, go to the doctor when ill, or even follow medical advice. In a thirty-five-year-long study of one hundred Harvard graduates, pessimists were in fact found to be less likely than optimists to give up cigarettes, and more likely to suffer illness. So optimists, who readily take matters into their own hands, are more likely to take action that prevents illness or get it treated once illness strikes.

A third way in which optimism should matter for health concerns the *sheer number of bad life events* encountered. It has been shown statistically that the more bad events a person encounters in any given time period, the more illness he will have. People who in the same six months move, get fired, and get divorced are at greater risk for infectious illness—and even for heart attacks and cancer—than are people who lead uneventful lives. This is why when major change occurs in your life, it is important to have physical checkups more frequently than usual. Even if you are feeling fine, it is particularly important to watch your health carefully when you change jobs, leave a relationship, or retire, or when someone you love dies. Widowers are several times more likely to die in the first six months following the death of their wives than at any other time. If your mother dies, see to it that your father has at least one complete physical checkup soon afterward—it could extend his life.

Who, would you guess, encounters more bad events in life? Pessimists do. Because they are more passive, they are less likely to take steps to avoid bad events and less likely to do anything to stop them once they start. Putting two and two together, if pessimists have more bad events and if more bad events lead to more illness, pessimists should have more illness.

The final reason that optimists should have better health concerns *social support*. The capacity to sustain deep friendships and love seems to be important for physical health. Middle-aged people who have at least one person whom they can call in the middle of the night to tell their troubles to, go on to have better physical health than friendless people. Unmarried people are at higher risk for depression than couples. Even ordinary social contact is a buffer against illness. People who isolate themselves when they are sick tend to get sicker.

When my mother was in her mid-seventies, she had surgery which left her for a few months with a colostomy—an opening in her gut, which was attached to an external bag. Many people are squeamish about colostomies, and my mother was ashamed. She avoided her friends, stopped playing bridge, discouraged us from visiting, and stayed home alone until the colostomy was closed and the bag removed. Unfortunately, during her lonely period she suffered a return of tuberculosis, to which she had been exposed as a small child in Hungary. She experienced what is statistically a regular cost of loneliness: higher risk for disease, particularly the recrudescence of those diseases which never completely go away.

Pessimists have the same problem. They become passive more easily when trouble strikes, and they take fewer steps to get and sustain social support. The connection between lack of social support and illness provides a fourth reason to believe that optimistic explanatory style is likely to produce good health.

Pessimism, Ill Health, and Cancer

THE FIRST SYSTEMATIC study of pessimism's role in causing sickness was carried out by Chris Peterson. In the mid-1980s, when he was teaching abnormal psychology at Virginia Tech, Chris got his class of 150 students to fill out the ASQ. They also reported their health and the number of visits they'd made to doctors in the recent past. Chris then followed the health of his students for the next year. He found that the pessimists went on to have twice as many infectious illnesses and make twice as many visits to doctors as the optimists did.

Was this just because pessimists complain more both on the question-naire and about their aches and pains, rather than actually being physically sick more? No. Chris looked at the number of illnesses and visits to doctors *before* the students filled out the ASQ as well as after. The high rate of illness and visits to doctors among the pessimists occur over and above the earlier level of health.

Other studies looked at breast cancer. In a pioneering British study, sixty-nine women with breast cancer were followed for five years. Women who did not suffer a recurrence tended to be those who responded to cancer with a "fighting spirit," whereas those who died or who suffered a recurrence tended to respond to their initial diagnosis with helplessness and stoic acceptance.

In a later study, thirty-four women visited the National Cancer Institute with their second bout of breast cancer. Each of them was interviewed at length about her life: marriage, children, job, and the disease. Surgery, radiation, and chemotherapy then began. We got these interviews and content-analyzed them for optimism, using the CAVE technique that we used before.

Long survival is unusual after two bouts of breast cancer, and after about a year, the women in the study began to die. Some died in a matter of months; others, a small minority, are alive today. Who survived the longest? Those who felt great joy in living and those with optimistic ex-planatory style.

Could it be merely that those optimistic women were also not as sick to begin with, and therefore lived longer because their cancer was less severe, not because of joy or optimism? No. The National Cancer Institute keeps invaluable, detailed records of severity of illness—Natural Killer cell ac-tivity, number of cancerous lymph nodes, degree of spread. The longevity benefits of joy and optimistic explanatory style occurred over and above the severity of illness.

Such results did not go unchallenged. In 1985, in a widely publicized study of patients with terminal cancer, Barrie Cassileth found that no psychological variable made any difference to length of survival. In a special editorial in the *New England Journal of Medicine*, associate editor Marcia Angell trumpeted this study as evidence that should lead us to "acknowl-edge that our belief in disease as a direct reflection of mental state is largely folklore." Ignoring all the well-designed studies and citing the worst studies she could find, Angell condemned the entire field of health psychology as perpetuating a "myth" that mind could influence disease. The materialists, seizing any straw to support the dogma that psychological states can never influence physical health, had a field day.

How can we reconcile Cassileth's findings with the many studies that show psychological state affecting disease? First, Cassileth's psychological tests were inadequate; she used fragments of well-established tests, rather than the whole tests. Concepts that usually require dozens of questions to measure were measured with one or two brief questions. Second, all of Cassileth's patients were terminally ill. If you are hit by a Mack truck, your level of optimism is not going to make much difference. If you are hit by a bicycle, however, optimism could play a crucial role. I do not believe that when a patient has such a lethal load of cancer as to be deemed "terminal," psychological processes can do much good. At the margin, however, when tumor load is small, when illness is beginning to progress, optimism might spell the difference between life and death. We have seen this in studies of the impact of bereavement and of optimism on the immune system.

The Immune System

MATERIALISTS VIEW the immune system as isolated from the psychology of the person in whom it resides. They believe that psychological variables like optimism and hope are as vaporous as spirit, so they are doubting Thomases about claims that optimism, depression, and bereavement all affect the immune system. They forget that the immune system is connected to the brain, and that states of mind, such as hope, have corresponding brain states that reflect the psychology of the person. These brain states then affect the rest of the body. So there is no mystery and no spiritualism involved in the process by which emotion and thought can affect illness.

The brain and the immune system are connected not through nerves but through hormones, the chemical messengers that drift through the blood and can transmit emotional state from one part of the body to another. It has been well documented that when a person is depressed the brain changes. Neurotransmitters, which are hormones that relay messages from one nerve to another, can become depleted. One set of transmitters, called catecholamines, becomes depleted during depression.

By what chain of physical events might the immune system sense that its host is pessimistic, depressed, or grieving? It turns out that when catecholamines get depleted, other chemicals called endorphins—your body's own morphine—increase activity. Cells of the immune system have receptors that sense the level of endorphins. When catecholamines are low, as in depression, endorphins go up; the immune system detects this and turns itself down.

Is this all just biological fancy or do depression, bereavement, and pessimism actually turn off the immune system?

About a decade ago a pioneering group of Australian researchers rounded up twenty-six men whose wives had just died from fatal injuries or illness. They persuaded each man to give blood twice, first one week and then again six weeks after their wives had died. Thus the researchers were able to look at the immune system during the course of grieving. They found that the immune system turned down during grieving. T-cells did not multiply as rapidly as usual. Over time the immune system began to recover. American research has since confirmed and extended these ground-breaking findings.

Depression also seems to affect the way the immune system responds. Bad life events and depression were examined among thirty-seven women, along with the T-cells and NK cells from their blood. Women undergoing major life changes had lower NK activity than women whose lives were not in upheaval. The more depressed the women became, the worse their immune response.

If depression and grieving temporarily lower immune activity, then pessimism, a more chronic state, should lower immune activity in the longer run. Pessimistic individuals, as we saw in chapter five, get depressed more easily and more often. This might mean that pessimistic people generally have poorer immune activity.

To test this, Leslie Kamen, a graduate student at the University of Pennsylvania, and I worked with Judy Rodin, from Yale. Judy had been following the health of a large number of senior citizens living in and around New Haven, Connecticut. Several times each year these people, whose average age was seventy-one, gave long interviews about their nutrition, their health, and their grandchildren. Once a year they gave blood so their immune systems could be checked. We rated the interviews for pessimism, and then we looked at the next blood draw to see if we could predict immune activity. As we expected, the optimists had better immune activity than the pessimists. In addition, we found that neither their health nor their depression level at the time of the interview predicted immune response. Pessimism itself seemed to lower immune activity, unmediated by health or depression.

Taken together, all this evidence makes it clear that your psychological state can change your immune response. Bereavement, depression, and pessimism all can lower your immune system's activity. Exactly how this works has yet to be precisely determined, but there is one likely path: As mentioned earlier, some of the brain's neurotransmitters get depleted during these states; this turns up the brain's level of internal morphine. The immune system has receptors for these hormones and shuts down when endorphin activity rises.

If your level of pessimism can deplete your immune system, it seems likely that pessimism can impair your physical health over your whole life span.

Optimism and a Healthier Life

Is IT POSSIBLE that optimists live longer than pessimists? Is it more likely that if you have an optimistic explanatory style while you are young, you will be healthier for the rest of your life?

This is not an easy question to answer scientifically. It will not do to point to the legions of very old people and show that the majority are optimists. They may be optimists because they have lived long and been healthy, rather than the other way around.

Before we could answer this question, we had to answer several others. First we needed to find out if explanatory style is stable across a whole lifetime. If optimism while you are young is to affect your health into old age, it should be the case that your level of optimism lasts a lifetime. To investigate this, Melanie Burns, a graduate student at the university, and I advertised in senior citizens' publications for people who still had diaries they kept when they were teenagers. Thirty people answered our ad and turned their diaries over to us. We "CAVEd" them, creating a teenage explanatory-style profile for each person. In addition, each volunteer wrote a long essay for us on his or her life now: his health, his family, his work. We "CAVEd" this as well, and formed a separate old-age explanatory-style profile. How did the two profiles relate?

We found that explanatory style for good events was completely changeable across fifty years. The same person could, for example, at one point in life regard good events as due to blind fate and at another time as due to his own skill. But we found that explanatory style for bad events was highly stable across a period of more than fifty years. The women who as teenagers wrote that the boys were not interested in them because they were "unlovable" wrote fifty years later that they were "unlovable" when their grandchildren didn't visit. The way we look at bad events—our theory of tragedy—remains fixed across our lifetime.

This key finding moved us closer to the point when we could ask if the explanatory style of a young person affects health much later in life. What else did we need before we could ask this question?

We needed a large group of individuals with certain characteristics:

1. While young they had to have made a quantity of causal statements that had survived and could be "CAVEd."
2. We had to be sure they were healthy and successful when they made these youthful pronouncements. This was necessary because if they were already unhealthy, or already failures, it might have made them pessimistic as well as less healthy later. And if that were so, optimism early in life would correlate with longer, healthier lives, but perhaps only because early ill health or early failure produces unhealthier lives. Hardly worth writing home about.
3. We also needed subjects who had had regular physical checkups so we could chart their health across their life span.
4. Finally, we needed subjects who were quite old now, so there would be a lifetime of health to predict.

That was asking quite a lot. Where could we find such people?

The Grant Study Men

GEORGE VAILLANT is a psychoanalyst I admire greatly. In 1978–79, he and I had been "classmates" at a think tank, the Center for Advanced Studies in the Behavioral Sciences, in Stanford, California. From psychoanalysis George had extracted the notion of defense, and he ran with it. What happens to us across our lives, he argued, is not a result of the sheer number of misfortunes that befall us but of how we defend against them mentally. He also thought our habits of explaining misfortunes were among our defenses, and he had tested his theories on a unique sample. George has spent more than a decade tracking down an extraordinary group of men and interviewing them as they grew through middle age into the beginning of old age.

In the mid-1930s, the William T. Grant Foundation decided to study healthy people across the whole adult span of their lives. The originators of the study wanted to follow a group of exceptionally gifted individuals to learn about the determinants of success and good health, and so they winnowed five Harvard freshmen classes, looking for men who were physically very fit and intellectually and socially gifted. On the basis of extensive testing they picked out two hundred men—about 5 percent of the classes of 1939 through 1944—and have followed them ever since. These men, who are now nearing seventy, have for fifty years cooperated fully with this demanding study. They receive extensive physical checkups every five years, are interviewed periodically, and endlessly fill out questionnaires. They have produced a gold mine of information about what makes a person healthy and successful.

When the originators of the Grant study themselves grew too old to continue, they looked for a successor young enough to carry the study on to the end of the subjects' lives. It was the time of the twenty-fifth reunion of the Harvard men. The originators chose George, then in his early thirties and one of America's most promising young research psychiatrists.

George's first important finding from the Grant study was that wealth at age twenty does not guarantee health or success. There is a high rate of failure and poor health among these men: failed marriages, bankruptcy, premature heart attacks, alcoholism, suicide, and other tragedy—indeed, one man was assassinated. These men experienced just about the same rate of heartbreak and mortal shock as men who were born at the same time in the inner city. George's theoretical challenge has been to try to predict and understand who among his subjects would have good lives and whose lives will go sour.

As I have said, his main concern has been what he calls defenses: the characteristic way in which people deal with bad events. Some of the men, while in college, handled failure with "mature defenses"—humor, altruism, sublimation. Others never did: For example, when their girlfriends broke up with them, they used denial, projection, and other "immature defenses." Remarkably, those men who had mature defenses in their early twenties went on to much more successful and healthy lives. By age sixty, none of the men who had deployed mature defenses at twenty were chronically ill; whereas over one-third of the men without mature defenses at twenty were in poor health by sixty.

Here, then, was the group we wanted. They had made documented causal statements while young; they were successful and healthy when they made these statements; their health had been followed religiously for a lifetime; and they were now in late middle age. In addition, a great deal of other information about their personalities and their lives was known. Would the optimists among them lead healthier lives than the pessimists? Would they live longer?

George generously agreed to work with Chris Peterson and me. George believes that he is custodian of a precious and unique sample, and he "lends" it (ever vigilant to protect the anonymity of his men) to other serious scientists who wish to find the predictors of health and success across the life span.

We decided to use the "sealed-envelope" technique. George saw to it that we worked in complete ignorance of who the men were and which ones had turned out to be healthy. First he picked, by random sample, half (ninety-nine) of the men and gave us essays they had written when they returned in 1945–46 from the Second World War. These were rich documents—full of explanations, pessimistic and optimistic:

> "The ship went down because the admiral was so stupid."
> "I could never get along with the men because they resented my privileged Harvard background."

We "CAVEd" all the essays and compiled an explanatory-style portrait of each of the men at the end of their youth.

Then one snowy day, Chris and I flew up to Dartmouth, where George is a professor of psychiatry, to open the so-called sealed envelope—that is, to learn how the lives of the men we had worked on had worked out. What we saw was that health at age sixty was strongly related to optimism at age twenty-five. The pessimistic men had started to come down with the diseases of middle age earlier and more severely than the optimistic men, and the differences in health by age forty-five were already large. Before age forty-five optimism has no effect on health. Until that age the men remained in the same state of health as at age twenty-five. But at age forty-five the male body starts its decline. How fast and how severely it does so is well predicted by pessimism twenty-five years earlier. What's more, when we fed several other factors—the subject's defenses and their physical and mental health at age twenty-five—into the equation, optimism still stood out as a primary determinant of health, beginning at age forty-five and continuing for the next twenty years. These men are just entering the time of mortality, and so in the next decade we will be able to find out if optimism predicts a longer life as well as a healthier one.

The Mind-Body Problem Revisited

THERE IS convincing evidence that psychological states do affect your health. Depression, grieving, pessimism: All seem to worsen health in both the short run and the long term. What's more, it is no longer a complete mystery how this might work. There is a plausible chain of events that starts with bad life events and ends up in poor health.

The chain begins with a particular set of bad events—loss, failure, defeat—those events that make you feel helpless. As we have seen, everyone reacts to such events with at least momentary helplessness, and people with a pessimistic explanatory style become depressed. Depression produces catecholamine depletion and increases in endorphin secretion. Endorphin increases can lower the activity of the immune system. The body is at all times exposed to pathogens—agents of disease—normally held in check by the immune system. When the immune system is partly shut down by the catecholamine–endorphin link, these pathogens can go wild. Disease, sometimes life-threatening, becomes more likely.

Each link of the *loss–pessimism–depression–catecholamine depletion–endorphin secretion depletion–immune suppression–disease* chain is testable, and for each we already have evidence of its operation. This chain of events involves no spirits and no mysterious, unmeasurable processes. What's more, if this is actually the chain, therapy and prevention can work at each link.

Psychological Prevention and Therapy

"THIS IS A once-in-a-lifetime opportunity," Judy Rodin said. "We should not propose to do something safe. We should propose what we have always yearned to do." Judy, with whom I had worked on the New Haven study of the effects of pessimism on the immune system, was vexed. Here was a small group of prominent scientists, the world leaders in health psychology, facing the prospect of at last having enough money to make their scientific dreams come true—but where were the big dreams?

Judy is a prodigy: a chaired professor at Yale, president of the Eastern Psychological Association, and a member of the prestigious National Institute of Medicine, all before her fortieth birthday. Her role this afternoon was as leader of the MacArthur Foundation Network on health and behavior. She had called us together to tell us, that frigid winter morning in New Haven, that she thought the time was ripe to ask the MacArthur Foundation to support the fledgling field of psychoneuroimmunology, the study of how psychological events change health and the immune system. "The MacArthur Foundation is not stodgy," she said. "They are looking for the kind of project to support that could change the face of medicine but is too adventurous for normal funders—like the National Institutes of Health—to take seriously. And we're dredging up the same routine science that we submit every three years to NIH for funding. What do you really—in your heart of hearts—want to do but have been afraid to propose to the establishment?"

The usually shy and soft-spoken Sandra Levy, a young professor of psychological oncology from Pittsburgh, spoke up. "What I'd really like to do," she said with emotion, "is to try therapy and prevention. Judy and Marty have convinced us that pessimistic explanatory style produces lousy immune functioning and poor health. There is a plausible chain by which this might happen. And there is convincing evidence that cognitive therapy changes explanatory style. Let's intervene at the psychological link. Let's change explanatory style, and, yes, read my lips, cure cancer."

There was a long, embarrassed silence. Almost no one outside that room would have believed that a psychological therapy could boost a poorly working immune system. Few people would ever have believed that a psychological therapy could cure cancer. To the rest of the profession, this would be seen as quackery, flying in the face of accepted medical treatment. And nothing can kill a hard-won reputation as a careful scientist quite as quickly as intimations of quackery. Psychotherapy to treat a physical disease, indeed.

I gathered my courage and broke the silence. "I agree with Sandy," I said, not quite certain what I was getting us into. "If Judy wants something visionary, if she wants dreams, okay, let's try to change the immune system by psychological means. If we're wrong, we'll have wasted a couple of years of our time. If we're right, and if we can convince the establishment by doing an impeccable study—a very big *if*—this will revolutionize the health system."

That morning, Judy Rodin, Sandra Levy, and I resolved to try it. First came a request to the foundation to support pilot work on cognitive therapy to boost the immune system. This was quickly approved, and over the next two years, we treated forty patients in the throes of melanoma and colon cancer, two quite severe forms of cancer. These patients continued to get their normal chemotherapy and radiation. In addition, once a week for twelve weeks they got a modified form of cognitive therapy. We designed their therapy not to cure depression but to arm these patients with new ways of thinking about loss: recognizing automatic thoughts; distraction; disputing pessimistic explanations. (See chapter twelve.) We supplemented cognitive therapy with relaxation training for handling stress. We also created a control group of cancer patients who received the same physical therapies but no cognitive therapy or relaxation training.

"Holy cow! You should see these numbers." I have never heard Sandy as excited as she was on the phone that November morning, two years later. "The Natural Killer cell activity is up *very* sharply in the cancer patients who got cognitive therapy. Not at all in the controls. Holy cow!"

In short, cognitive therapy strongly enhanced immune activity—just as we hoped it would.

It is still too early to know if this therapy changed the course of the disease or saved the lives of these cancer patients. The disease runs a much slower course than the immune activity, which can change from day to day. Time will tell. But this pilot study was enough for the MacArthur Foundation. Adventurous souls that they are, they agreed to support the long-range project. Starting in 1990 we will be giving cognitive therapy to cancer patients on a larger scale, trying to boost their immune systems and deflect the disease—and perhaps even lengthening their lives.

Just as exciting, we will be trying prevention. We will be giving the exercises you'll find in chapter twelve to people at high risk for disease: newly divorced or separated individuals and military recruits in Arctic cold. These people ordinarily suffer unusually high rates of illness. Will changing pessimistic explanatory style bolster their immune defenses and prevent physical illness?

We have high hopes.

11

Politics, Religion, and Culture:
A New Psychohistory

MY BOYHOOD READING of Sigmund Freud powerfully influenced the questions that have captivated me since. It left me fascinated by "hot" psychology—motivation, emotion, mental illness—and strangely indifferent to "cold" psychology—perception, information processing, hearing, and vision. But another popular writer from my boyhood, usually less esteemed than Freud, left an even deeper mark: Isaac Asimov, prolific science-fiction writer, novelist, and visionary.

In his impossible-to-put-down *Foundation Trilogy*—I read it in one thirty-hour burst of adolescent excitement—Asimov invents a great hero for pimply, intellectual kids. Hari Selden is the scientist who creates "psychohistory" in order to predict the future. Individuals, Selden believes, are unpredictable, but a mass of individuals, like a mass of atoms, becomes highly predictable. All you need are Hari Selden's statistical equations and his behavioral principles (Asimov never divulges these to us) and you can foresee the course of history, even the outcome of crises. "Wow!" thought this impressionable adolescent. "Predicting the future from psychological principles!"

That "Wow!" has stayed with me all my life. As a young professor in the early 1970s, I was excited to learn that a field called psychohistory actually existed. In due course, with my close friend Alan Kors, then an assistant professor of history at the University of Pennsylvania, I gave a graduate seminar on the topic. The seminar gave us all a chance to look closely at the academic version of Asimov's vision. What a disappointment.

We read Erik Erikson's attempt to apply the principles of Freudian psychoanalysis to Martin Luther. Luther, said Erikson, got his rebellious attitude toward Catholicism from his toilet training. Professor Erikson had drawn that astounding hypothesis from a few scraps of information about Luther's childhood. This sort of farfetched extrapolating was definitely not what Hari Selden had in mind. First, its principles wouldn't accomplish much. They wouldn't even help a therapist clearly explain the rebelliousness of patients lying on his couch, whose childhood he could hear about in as much detail as he could bear, let alone the rebelliousness of someone hundreds of years dead. Second, what passed for "psychohistory" in those days consisted of single case studies, whereas, as Asimov had stressed, to make valid predictions you need a mass of instances, in order to dampen out unpredictable individual variations. Third, and worst, that kind of psychohistory didn't *predict* anything at all. Rather, it took events already long concluded and concocted a story that—with psychoanalytic hindsight—made sense of them.

When I took up Glen Elder's challenge, in 1981, to develop a "time machine," Asimov's vision was still very much with me, and I planned to use the technique of content analysis—the analysis of written or spoken utterances for what they revealed about explanatory style—to find out the optimism level of people who wouldn't take questionnaires: mother-daughter pairs, sports heroes, CEOs locked in a hostile takeover challenge, world leaders. But there is another very large group of people who don't take questionnaires—the dead, the people whose actions make up history. I told Glen that the CAVE technique was the time machine he had been dreaming of. I suggested that it could be used not only on contemporary people who wouldn't take questionnaires but on people who *couldn't*, like dead people. All we needed was their verbatim quotes. As long as we had verbatim quotes, we could CAVE them for explanatory style. I pointed out that we could use an enormous range of material: autobiographies, wills, press-conference transcripts, diaries, therapy transcripts, letters home from the battlefront, nomination-acceptance addresses. "Glen," I said, "we can do psychohistory."

We had, after all, the three essential things that Hari Selden demanded. First, we had a sound psychological principle: Optimistic explanatory style predicts the ability to fight off depression, predicts high achievement, and predicts stick-to-itiveness. Second, we had a valid way of measuring explanatory style in people living or dead. Third, we had large numbers of people to study—numbers large enough to allow us to make statistical predictions.

One morning in spring 1983 I found myself explaining all this to one of the yeastiest twenty-year-old undergraduates I have ever met, Harold Zullow. His ideas, his energy, his originality, and his enthusiasm were remarkable. I explained the CAVE technique to him and described the vistas it might open up, trying to impress him and recruit him for the University of Pennsylvania.

"Have you thought about applying this to politics?" he said. "Maybe we could predict elections. I'll bet the American people want optimists to lead them, people who tell them that their problems will be solved. Not hand-wringers and doubters. You want large numbers? How about the size of the American electorate? You can't predict how individual voters will vote in an election, but we might be able to predict how they'll vote as a mass. We could make an optimism profile of the two candidates from what they say and predict who'll win."

I liked his use of *we*, because it meant Harold was going to come to Penn. Come he did, and what he accomplished over the next five years was unique. With a bit of help from me, he became the first psychologist to predict a major historical event before it happened.

The American Presidential Elections, 1948–1984

WHAT KIND of president do American voters want? Does optimism make a difference to the American voter?

Political science was Harold Zullow's hobby, and he began his graduate research by indulging in his hobby. We reread the nomination-acceptance speeches of the big losers and big winners of recent times. The discrepancies in optimism stuck out. Listen to Adlai Stevenson, twice a big loser, accepting his first nomination before the Democratic convention in 1952:

> When the tumult and the shouting die, when the bands are gone and the lights are dimmed, there is the stark reality of responsibility in an hour of history haunted with those gaunt, grim specters of strife, dissension and materialism at home, and ruthless, inscrutable and hostile power abroad.

Deathless prose, perhaps, but it also consists of one rumination after another. True to his intellectual reputation, Stevenson was dwelling upon bad events and analyzing them, without proposing action to alter them. Listen to his explanatory style:

> *The ordeal of the twentieth century—the bloodiest, most turbulent era of the Christian age—is far from over.* Sacrifice, patience, and implacable purpose may be our lot for years to come. . . .
>   I would not seek your nomination for the Presidency, *because the burdens of that office stagger the imagination.* [italics mine]

These are two vintage Stevensonian explanations. The italic text is the explanation, the roman text the event it explains. Very permanent: The ordeal to come, many years long, will cause sacrifice. Very pervasive: The awesomeness of the burdens cause him not to seek the nomination. Adlai Stevenson, a man of high intelligence, was an emotional black hole. His explanatory style was depressive and so was his rate of ruminating.

The speeches of Dwight D. Eisenhower, twice Stevenson's opponent, were as different from Stevenson's as they could be—low in rumination, optimistic in explanatory style, and replete with reference to action. Listen to Eisenhower ("I will go to Korea"), accepting the Republican nomination in 1952:

> Today is the first day of our battle.
>   The road that leads to November fourth is a fighting road. In that fight I will keep nothing in reserve.
>   I have stood before on the eve of battle. Before every attack it has always been my practice to seek out our men in their camps and along the road and talk with them face to face about their concerns and discuss with them the great mission to which we are all committed.

Eisenhower's speeches lacked the grace and subtlety of Stevenson's prose. Nevertheless, Eisenhower won in landslides both in 1952 and 1956. He was of course a great war hero and his opponent's record by comparison was much more modest. Historians doubt that anyone could have beaten Eisenhower, and indeed the Democrats as well as the Republicans sought him as their nominee. But did Eisenhower's optimism and Stevenson's pessimism play a causal role in the outcome of the elections? We think it did.

What should happen to a presidential candidate who has a more pessimistic and more ruminating style than his opponent? There should be three consequences, all negative.

First, the candidate with the darker style should be more passive, making fewer campaign stops and rising less readily to challenge.

Second, he should be less well liked by the voters; in controlled experiments, depressed people are not as well liked as nondepressed people and are more likely to be avoided. This is not to say that presidential candidates are depressed—usually they are not—but rather that the voter is exquisitely sensitive to the whole dimension of optimism and picks up even small differences between two candidates.

Third, the more pessimistic candidate should engender less hope in the voters. The permanent and pervasive statements that pessimists make about bad events signal hopelessness. The more the candidate ruminates, the more this hopelessness is conveyed. If voters want a president who makes them believe he will solve the country's problems, they will choose the optimist.

These three consequences taken together predict that the more pessimistically ruminating of two candidates is the one who will lose.

To test whether the optimism of candidates actually affects the outcome of elections, we needed a standard setting in which the speeches of the two candidates are comparable with each other and with their predecessors' speeches. There exists a perfect setting—the nomination-acceptance speech, in which the nominee outlines his ideas for the nation's future. Until forty years ago the speech was given to the party faithful assembled in a hall, and did not find its way into most American homes. But since 1948 the speech has reached an enormous audience watching on television. So starting with the year 1948, we extracted every causal statement from every nomination-acceptance speech for the last ten elections, shuffled them randomly, and had raters—blind to who said what—rate them for optimism by the CAVE technique. In addition we rated rumination, by taking the percentage of sentences that evaluate or analyze a bad event without proposing a course of action. We also rated "action-orientation," the percentage of sentences that talk about what the candidate has done or will do. We added the explanatory-style score to the rumination score to yield a total score, which we called pessrum. The higher the pessrum score, the worse the candidate's style.

The first thing we found when we compared the pessrum scores of the two candidates in each election from 1948 to 1984 was that the candidate with the lower score—the more optimistic candidate—won nine of the ten elections. We did better than the polls did, simply by looking at the content of speeches.

We missed one—the Nixon-Humphrey election in 1968. Hubert Humphrey was slightly more optimistic than Richard Nixon in his acceptance speech, and so we picked Humphrey. But something happened on the Happy Warrior's march to what should have been victory at the polls. Humphrey's speech to the Chicago convention was accompanied by riots in the streets of Chicago, featuring police beating hippies. Humphrey's popularity plummeted immediately and he began the campaign—the shortest in modern history—15 percent behind in the polls. But the story did not end there. Humphrey steadily gained ground and on Election Day lost the popular vote by less than 1 percent. If the campaign had lasted another three days, pollsters tell us, the optimistic Humphrey would have won.

How did the size of the victory relate to the difference in the candidates' pessrum? Very strongly. The candidates who were much more optimistic than their opponents won in landslides: Eisenhower (twice) over Stevenson, LBJ over Goldwater, Nixon over McGovern, and Reagan over Carter. The candidates who were just a bit more optimistic than their opponents wound up winning the popular vote by a nose: for example, Carter over Ford.

Wait a minute. What comes first, optimism or being ahead? Does the greater optimism of the winner-to-be make voters vote for him or does it just reflect the fact that he is optimistic because he is already leading? Is optimism causal or is it a mere epiphenomenon of being the favorite?

A good way to look at this is to follow the underdogs who came from behind to win. By definition all of them start behind in the polls, in some cases way behind. Leading cannot be making them more optimistic, because they are not leading. In 1948 Truman began 13 percent behind Thomas E. Dewey, but his pessrum was much more optimistic than Dewey's. Truman won by 4.6 percent, confounding all the pollsters. In 1960 John Kennedy began 6.4 percent behind Richard Nixon. Kennedy's pessrum was considerably more optimistic than Nixon's, and he squeaked through by 0.2 percent, the closest modern election. In 1980 Ronald Reagan started 1.2 percent behind incumbent Jimmy Carter. Reagan's pessrum was more optimistic, and he wound up winning by over 10 percent.

It is possible to control statistically for being ahead in the early polls and also for being an incumbent, two factors that would inflate optimism. When these factors are controlled, optimism still has an effect—in fact, the major effect—on the size of victory, with the differences in pessrum predicting the difference in popular vote much more exactly than any other known factor.

There are three possible reasons why optimism works on voters: more energetic campaigning by the optimist; more voter dislike of the pessimist; and more hope engendered by the optimist. We have no direct measure of the second or the third factor, but in seven of the ten elections we could count the number of campaign stops each candidate made every day—a measure of vigor of campaigning. As predicted, the more optimistic candidate made more campaign stops: he was the more vigorous campaigner.

The nomination-acceptance speech is usually ghosted and highly rewritten. Does it reflect the real optimism level of the candidate, or does it reflect the speechwriter's optimism, or what the candidate thinks the public wants to hear? From one point of view it doesn't matter. This analysis of optimism predicts what voters will do based on the *impression* they have of the candidate, whether that impression is valid or manipulated. But from another point of view it is important to know what the candidate *really* is like. One way to get at this is to compare press conferences and debates, which are more off-the-cuff, with set speeches. We did this in the four elections in which debates took place. In each of them, the candidate whose pessrum was better at nomination was also better in the debates.

Then I rated the set speeches and press conferences of half a dozen world leaders (to whose identity I was kept blind) for explanatory style. Remarkably, I found a "fingerprint," which remains constant from vetted speeches to impromptu remarks at press conferences. The scores for permanence and for pervasiveness are identical across vetted and unvetted speeches, and each leader I looked at had a distinct profile. (I suspect this technique could be used to determine whether a written message really came from the person in question—say, from a hostage or from the group holding him.) The personalization score changed by a constant from speeches to press conferences: In other words, personal explanations, such as taking the blame, are laundered out of formal speeches, but are a bit more frequent in off-the-cuff remarks.

My conclusion is that, ghostwritten or not, the set speech usually reflects the underlying personality of the speaker. Either he rewrites the speech to his level of optimism or he picks ghostwriters who match him on this important trait. But there has been at least one exception—Michael Dukakis.

1900–1944

WE DECIDED to see if our prediction of nine of the ten postwar elections was a fluke, or if, perhaps, voting for optimists is just a phenomenon of the television era. We read all the nomination-acceptance speeches going back to the McKinley-Bryan campaign of 1900. We analyzed them blindly for explanatory style and rumination. This added twelve more elections to our portfolio.

The same thing happened. In nine of the twelve elections, the candidate with the better pessrum score won. The margin of victory was again strongly related to how *much* better the pessrum score of the victor was. The three exceptions—like the Nixon-Humphrey "exception"—were interesting. We missed on all three Franklin D. Roosevelt reelections. In each, FDR won by a healthy margin, even though his pessrum was more downbeat than Alfred M. Landon's, Wendell L. Willkie's, or Thomas E. Dewey's. But we suspect that in these elections the votes were influenced more by FDR's proven record in crisis rather than the hopefulness of his opponent's speeches.

In the twenty-two presidential elections from 1900 through 1984, Americans chose the more optimistic-sounding candidate eighteen times. In all elections in which an underdog pulled off an upset, he was the more optimistic candidate. The margin of victory was very strongly related to the margin in pessrum, with landslides won by candidates who were much more optimistic than their opponents.

Having successfully predicted the past, Harold Zullow and I decided it was time to try to predict the future.

The 1988 Election

PSYCHOHISTORY AS practiced in academia attempts to "postdict" events—to predict the past by studying the even earlier past. So in the notorious *Young Man Luther*, Erik Erikson takes what he can glean about Luther's toilet training and "predicts" that Luther will become a religious revolutionary, bent on the destruction of authority. Not so astonishingly, that's just what Luther becomes. There seems to be lots of room for peeking when the outcome is already known.

So too with our "postdiction" of the last twenty-two presidential elections. We knew who won, and although we tried to keep the analysis pure and the raters blind—they did not know who said what—a skeptical reader would be within bounds to say "Predict something!" Psychohistory becomes practically interesting, and methodologically above suspicion, if it goes on actually to predict the future, as Hari Selden urged.

By the end of 1987, after two years of work, Harold Zullow had completed his analyses of the 1900–1984 elections.

We at last were ready to try to predict what would happen in 1988. No social scientist had ever predicted major historical events before the fact. Economists were forever predicting booms and busts, but when the opposite of what they predicted took place, they never seem to be around to 'fess up. Our findings from the past looked so strong I felt we could stick our necks out.

We decided to predict in three arenas. First, the presidential primaries: Who would be the nominee of each party? Second, who would win the presidental election itself. And third, there would be thirty-three Senate races to predict. We would begin immediately and gather the speeches from as many candidates as we could.

The Presidential Primaries of 1988

IN JANUARY 1988, thirteen contenders were out on the hustings, speaking day after day in New Hampshire, Iowa, and elsewhere. Six Republicans were slugging it out, with Robert Dole and George Bush neck and neck in the polls. Smart money thought Bush would lose; Dole was tough and Bush a wimp. But the evangelist Pat Robertson, the conservative Jack Kemp, and the general Alexander Haig could not be counted out.

The Democratic race was completely up for grabs. Gary Hart seemed to be making a comeback from sexual scandals and was once again leading the polls. Senator Paul Simon, Governor Michael Dukakis, Senator Albert Gore, and Representative Richard Gephardt were all rated as having a chance. The Reverend Jesse Jackson, it was thought, would get only the black vote.

The New York Times published the stump speeches—the basic speeches the candidates gave several times per day with minor variations. We "CAVEd" all thirteen and analyzed them for pessrum. We made our predictions. The weekend before the Iowa caucuses in February, Harold— worried that no one would believe we had predicted the future if we turned out to be correct—insisted we put our predictions in sealed envelopes and send them to *The New York Times* and the administrator of Penn's psychology department. "If we're right," Harold asserted plaintively, "I want to be sure no one says we peeked."

The predictions were unequivocal. Among Democrats, there was a clear winner: the still obscure governor of Massachusetts, Michael Dukakis. In pessrum he was head and shoulders better than the pack. There was a clear loser: Gary Hart, the besmirched senator from Colorado, was at the bottom in pessrum, sounding in fact like a depressed patient. Jesse Jackson was quite good in pessrum, high enough to suggest hidden strength and surprise the pundits. Dukakis, of course, won, and Hart finished last, quitting the race without a delegate. Jackson surprised the world and made a tussle of it.

Among Republicans, there was also a clear winner: George Bush, far and away the most optimistic, with a better pessrum score even than Dukakis. Robert Dole was far down the list, with an even larger gap in pessrum than that betwen Dukakis and Hart. Dole would fade fast by our predictions. Even farther down the list was Robertson and at the bottom, Haig, with the darkest pessrum. Robertson would go nowhere, we predicted, and Haig would bust completely.

Bush, as it turned out, bested Dole more easily than anyone had thought. Robertson's candidacy never took off, to the great distress of the Moral Majority. Haig was the biggest loser, quitting without a delegate won.

I couldn't believe it when Harold and I sat down in early May to review how the predictions he'd sealed into envelopes in early February had fared. Virtually perfect.

The 1988 Presidential Campaign

ONLY HALF THE primaries were over when we got a call from *The New York Times*. The reporter we had sent our predictions to (it was he who actually first suggested we CAVE the stump speeches), seeing how well they were working out, had written a story about it. "We're going to run it on the front page," he said, and asked who would win the election. We tried to be evasive. In the stump speeches, we determined, Bush was noticeably more optimistic than Dukakis. Bush would win the election by 6 percent. But we were unwilling to make a prediction on the basis of just the stump speeches. Not only were there few event-explanation quotes in Bush's speech, but all our previous presidential-election data were based on the nomination-acceptance speech, not on primary speeches.

Harold was worried, but for a different reason. Both campaigns, Republican and Democratic, had contacted us promptly, wanting us to divulge our scoring method. Harold said he didn't mind all the reporters' questions—and I could tell he enjoyed them—but was concerned about the candidates themselves. What if they used our principles to rewrite their speeches to give the voters what they wanted to hear? It would invalidate our predictions for the upcoming elections.

I told him, a bit uneasily, not to worry. American politicians, I said, were too hardheaded to take our research seriously yet. I could barely believe the findings myself, I said, so I thought it unlikely a campaign staff would rely on them to rewrite speeches. I suggested we send both the Republicans and the Democrats the material; our research belonged to the public. The campaigners were just as entitled to it as anyone else.

Late on a sultry evening in July, Harold and I sat in my living room and listened to the live nomination-acceptance speech of Governor Michael Dukakis. It was rumored that Dukakis placed enormous weight on this speech and that Theodore Sorenson—the great speechwriter for John F. Kennedy—had been exhumed to draft it. We sat there with our pencils poised, counting the ruminations and explanations as Dukakis uttered them. I was doing the explanations and Harold was doing the ruminations.

In the middle of it I whispered to Harold, "This is a lulu! If he keeps this up, no one can beat him."

It's time to rekindle the American spirit of invention and of daring; to exchange voodoo economics for can-do economics; to build the best America by bringing out the best in every American.

It *was* a lulu. The pessrum was terrifically optimistic. It was one of the most optimistic of any modern nomination-acceptance speech—exceeded only by Eisenhower's in 1952 and Humphrey's in 1968. It was much better in pessrum than Dukakis's stump speech had been. His optimism seemed to have gone way up since the primaries.

The public liked it too. Dukakis emerged from the convention with a very healthy lead in the polls.

Could George Bush top this performance?

We could hardly wait until the end of August and Bush's speech to the Republican convention in New Orleans. It too was a real roof-raiser. Bush's explanations of our problems were couched in highly specific and highly temporary terms:

There's graft in City Hall; the greed on Wall Street; there's influence peddling in Washington, and the small corruptions of everyday ambition.

From his pessrum numbers, Bush's speech would, in most elections of modern times, have bested the other candidate's. But not against Dukakis's July speech. Bush's address was somewhat more ruminative and somewhat less optimistic than Dukakis's. We put the pessrum for the speeches into our equations (which factor in the effect of incumbency and the influence of the polls) and turned the crank. From the nomination-acceptance speeches we predicted a narrow victory for Dukakis—3 percent.

I have never placed a bet on an event—sporting or otherwise. But this looked like an almost sure thing. I called the gaming parlors of Las Vegas. They refused to quote odds. It is illegal, they told me, to bet on an American presidential election in America. This is to discourage anybody from trying to fix an election. "Try England," I was advised.

It so happened that I was speaking in Scotland in early September. I had saved up some British pounds and was prepared to lay them all on Dukakis. A friend took me to one betting shop after another. Because Bush had overtaken Dukakis in the polls since his convention speech, I was able to negotiate 6 to 5 odds. The bet was made.

When I got back to Philadelphia, I told Harold about my bet and offered him a piece of the action. Harold said he wasn't sure he would take it; his voice climbed an octave, sending a shiver of fear down my spine. He wasn't convinced, he said, that what we heard in July was the real Dukakis. Harold had been reading Dukakis's speeches since Labor Day, and they didn't sound like his convention speech. Neither did the stump speech he used in the primaries. Harold had begun to wonder if the nomination speech was more Sorenson than Dukakis or, worse, if it had been doctored to present very low pessrum. He said he'd like to wait until the first debate before he bet his graduate stipend.

In the other four elections in which the candidates had debated on television, the person who'd had the better pessrum in the nomination speeches also had the better pessrum in each debate. But this time was different. It looked as if Harold's caution was well founded. Dukakis had dropped sharply from his convention pessrum, back down to his stump-speech level. Bush had stayed steady and was once again showing a more optimistic style than Dukakis.

The morning after the first Bush-Dukakis television debate Harold said he still wasn't ready to take a piece of my bet. His hunch was growing stronger: Bush's campaign performance and his acceptance speech were the real Bush—highly optimistic. But Dukakis no longer looked that optimistic, and Harold couldn't help thinking that the July speech was not Dukakis. The polls seemed to reflect this. Bush had pulled ahead, and the gap was widening.

The second debate was a pessrum disaster for Dukakis. When asked about why he couldn't promise a balanced budget, Dukakis said, "I don't think either one of us can; really, there's no way of anticipating what may happen." This suggestion that the problem was permanent and uncontrollable had a much more pessimistic tone than Dukakis's statements in

July or even in September. The tone was becoming typical of him. Meanwhile, Bush was steadily optimistic.

The rest of the campaign displayed the same discrepancy in pessrum: Bush's stump speech was consistently more optimistic than Dukakis's. To Harold and me, as we followed the campaign, it seemed that, sometime in early October, in his heart, Dukakis gave up. In late October, we plugged the values of the debates and the fall stump speech into our equation and produced our final prediction: a Bush victory by 9.2 percent.

In November George Bush beat Michael Dukakis by 8.2 percent.

The Senate Elections of 1988

THIRTY-THREE Senate seats were being contested, too, and for twenty-nine of them we were able to obtain speeches both candidates had given earlier in the year. mostly in the summer and the spring. Most of these were the speeches the would-be senators made when they announced their candidacy—that is, well before the close of the campaign. So pessrum differences—unlike those in the final Bush-Dukakis debate—could hardly stem from being ahead or behind in the polls. The day before the election, Harold ran his final pessrum analysis of the twenty-nine and committed himself, with sealed envelopes sent to various unimpeachable witnesses.

The presidential results were in early, but for us the suspense continued all night long. Not only had we predicted twenty-five of the twenty-nine Senate races correctly; when all the votes were counted, it turned out we had predicted all the upsets and all the close races correctly, save one.

We predicted that in Connecticut Joe Lieberman would upset favorite incumbent Lowell Weicker in a squeaker. Lieberman did, by .5 percent.

We predicted that Connie Mack would upset Buddy MacKay in Florida. An optimistic Connie Mack had explained in this external, temporary, and specific fashion why taxes had been raised: "Lawton Chiles [the former senator] went along with the big spenders and voted himself a pay raise." (Harold scored that explanation a 4.) Mack's opponent, Buddy MacKay, had pessimistically attributed the problems of Florida's development to "Florida's self-perception." (Harold gave that permanent, pervasive, and personalized explanation a 14.) Though he'd started from way behind, Connie Mack won, by less than 1 percent.

But we missed Montana's surprising upset of the incumbent John Melcher by Conrad Burns.

So there we were. Using only the explanatory style of speeches and the degree of rumination they revealed, we had attempted to predict the presidential primary results, the presidential election, and twenty-nine Senate elections. We succeeded completely for the primaries, predicting the winners and the losers for each party long before the polls named a winner. The prediction for the presidential election was mixed. I had lost my bet, but Harold believed that the Dukakis nomination-acceptance speech was not authentic Dukakis. The fall speeches predicted a Bush victory. But so did everyone else. We called 86 percent of the Senate races right, including all but one of the upsets and squeakers. Nobody else did this well.

This then is the first instance I know of in which social scientists have predicted major historical events—before the fact.

Explanatory Style Across Frontiers

IN 1983 I WENT to Munich to attend the Congress of the International Society for the Study of Behavioral Development, and on the second day I fell into conversation with an intense young German graduate student who introduced herself simply as Ele. "Let me tell you the idea I had when you were talking this morning about the CAVE technique," she said. "But first let me ask a question. Do you think that the benefits of optimism and the dangers of pessimism and helplessness and passivity reflect universal laws of human nature, or do they hold true only in our kind of society—Westernized, I mean, like America and West Germany?"

That was a good question. I told her I sometimes wondered myself whether or not our concern with control and with optimism was conditioned by advertising on the one hand and the Puritan ethic on the other. Depression, I said, doesn't seem to occur in non-Western cultures at anything like the epidemic rate it does in Westernized ones. Perhaps cultures that aren't obsessed with achievement don't suffer the effects of helplessness and pessimism the way we do.

Perhaps, I suggested, lessons from the animal kingdom were relevant. It isn't just Westernized men and women who show the signs of depression when they experience loss and helplessness. Both in nature and in the laboratory, animals respond to helplessness with symptoms amazingly parallel to those of Westernized human beings. Chimpanzees reacting to the death of other chimpanzees; rats reacting to inescapable shock; goldfish, dogs, even cockroaches act very much like we do when we fail. I suspect, I said, that when human cultures don't respond to loss and helplessness with depression, it's because the punishment of endless poverty, of thousands of years of having two out of three children die young, has beaten the natural response of depression out of the culture.

"I don't believe that Westernized human beings have been propagandized into depression, brainwashed into the ethic of control," I said. "But to say that the desire for control and the devastating response to helplessness are natural is not to say that optimism works universally." Consider success at work and in politics, for example, I said. Optimism works well for American life-insurance salesmen and for candidates who want to be president of the United States. But it's hard to imagine the understated Englishman reacting well to the never-give-up salesman. Or the dour Swedish voter electing an Eisenhower. Or the Japanese taking kindly to someone who always blames others for his failures.

I said I thought the learned-optimism approach probably would, in fact, provide relief from the torment of depression in these cultures but that optimism would have to be adapted to other styles in the workplace or in politics. The trouble was, though, that not much work had been done yet on examining how optimism works from one culture to the next.

"But tell me," I asked, "what was that idea you had while I was lecturing on the CAVE technique?"

"I think I have found a way," said Ele, "to discover how much hope and despair there is across cultures and across history. For instance, is there such a thing as a *national* explanatory style, one that predicts how a nation or a people will behave in crisis? Does one particular form of government engender more hope than another?"

Ele's questions were great, I replied, but almost unanswerable. Let's say we learned, by "CAVEing" things they wrote or said or sang, that Bulgarians have a better explanatory style than Navajos do. That result would be uninterpretable. It might be more macho to say optimistic things in one culture than in the other. The peoples experience different weather, have different histories and gene pools, live on different continents. Any difference in explanatory style between Bulgarians and Navajos could be explained in a thousand ways other than a difference in the underlying amount of hope or despair.

"If you do the wrong sort of comparison," Ele said, "yes. But I wasn't thinking of Navajos and Bulgarians. I was thinking of a much more similar pair of cultures—East and West Berlin. They are in the same place, they have the same weather, they speak the same dialect, emotional words and gestures mean the same thing, they have the same history up until 1945. They differ only in political system since then. They are like identical twins reared apart for forty years. They seem a perfect way of asking if despair is different across political systems—with everything else held constant."

The next day at the congress, I told a professor from Zurich about this

creative graduate student I'd met the day before. After I described her
and mentioned that she called herself Ele, he told me she was the Princess
Gabriele zu Oettingen-Oettingen und Oettingen-Spielberg, one of Ba-
varia's most promising young scientists.

My conversation with Gabriele continued the next day over tea. I said
I agreed that East versus West Berlin differences in explanatory style—if
found—could be meaningfully interpreted as stemming only from com-
munism versus capitalism. But how, I asked, could she actually get the
material to compare? She couldn't just cross the Wall and hand out optimism questionnaires to a random sample of East Berliners.

"Not in the present political climate," she agreed. (Andropov was then
premier of the Soviet Union.) "But all I need is writings from both cities,
writings that are exactly comparable. They have to be about the same
events, occurring at the same time. And they should be neutral events—
not politics or economics or mental health. And I've thought of just the
thing," she said. "In about four months, the winter Olympics will take
place in Yugoslavia. They will be reported in great detail in both East and
West Berlin newspapers. Like most sports reporting, they will be filled
with causal statements from athletes and reporters, about victories and
about defeats. I want to CAVE them in their entirety and see which culture
is more pessimistic. This will be a demonstration that the quantity of hope
can be compared across cultures."

I asked what her predictions were. She expected that East German
explanatory style, at least in the sports pages, would be more optimistic.
The East Germans, after all, were an outstanding Olympic nation, and the
newspapers were emphatically organs of the state. Part of their job was to
keep morale up.

This wasn't my prediction, but I kept my silence.

Over the next three months I had several trans-Atlantic phone conversations with Gabriele and received a number of letters from her. She was
worried about the mechanics of getting the newspapers from East Berlin,
since it was sometimes difficult to take written material across the Wall.
She had arranged to have a mechanic friend in East Berlin send her worthless kitchen objects, broken cups and bent forks, by mail—wrapped in
newspaper, the sports pages of course. But this proved to be unnecessary.
During the Olympics, she was able to walk through the Berlin checkpoints
unchallenged, carrying as many East Berlin newspapers as she wanted.

Next came the labor, combing through the three West Berlin and three
East Berlin newspapers for the entire duration of the Olympics, extracting
and rating the event-explanation quotes. Gabriele found 381 quotes. Here
are some of the athletes' and reporters' optimistic explanations.

An ice racer could not stand the pace because "on this day there was no morning sun to cover the ice with a mirrorlike ice film" Negative event (4); a skier fell because "an avalanche of snow from nearby trees covered the visor of her helmet" Negative event (4); athletes were not afraid because "we just know that we will be stronger than our competitors" Positive event (16).

These were among the pessimistic explanations: A disaster came because "she is in such bad shape" Negative event (17); "He had to hold back tears. His hope for a medal had gone" Negative event (17); an athlete succeeded because "our competitors had been drinking all night before" Positive event (3).

But who made the optimistic statements and who made the pessimistic ones? The answers were a complete surprise to Gabriele. The East German statements were much more pessimistic than the West German ones. What made this finding even more remarkable was how well the East Germans did in the games. The East Germans won twenty-four medals and the West Germans only four. So the East Berlin papers had many more good events to report: Indeed, 61 percent of the East's explanations were about good events for the East and only 47 percent of the West's were about good events for the West. Nevertheless, the tone of East Berlin's reportage was much bleaker than that of West Berlin's.

"I'm astonished by my results," Gabriele told me. "As strong as they are, I'm not going to believe them until I find some other way to see if East Berliners are more pessimistic and depressed than West Berliners. I've tried getting accurate suicide and hospital statistics from East Berlin to compare to West Berlin, but of course, I can't get them."

Gabriele's Ph.D. was not in psychology but in human ethology, a branch of biology that deals with observing people in the natural environment and noting in great detail what they do. It started with Konrad Lorenz's observations of ducklings that had "imprinted" on him and then followed him around—they had formed the conviction that he was their mother. His careful observations of nature soon branched out to systematic people-watching. Gabriele had earned her degree under the two leading successors of Lorenz. I knew Gabriele had done a lot of minute observations in classrooms full of kids, but I was apprehensive when she told me what she was going to do in the bars of East and West Berlin.

"The only way I can think of to get converging support for my CAVE findings," she wrote, "is to go to East Berlin and rigorously count the signs of despair and then compare them to the same settings in West Berlin. I don't want to arouse police suspicions, so I'm going to do it in bars."

This is exactly what she did. In the winter of 1985, she went to thirty-one bars in industrial areas. She chose fourteen in West Berlin and seventeen in East Berlin. These bars, called *Kneipen*, are where workmen go to drink after work. They were located near each other, separated only by the Wall. She did all the observations in the five weekdays of one week.

She would enter a bar and take a seat in a far corner, as inconspicuously as she could. She then focused on groups of patrons and counted what they were doing in five-minute blocks. She counted everything observable that the literature considers related to depression: smiles, laughs, posture, vigorous hand movements, small movements like biting one's nails.

Measured this way, the East Berliners were once again much more depressed than the West Berliners. Sixty-nine percent of West Berliners smiled, but only 23 percent of East Berliners. Fifty percent of West Berliners sat or stood upright, but only 4 percent (!) of East Berliners. Eighty percent of West Berlin workmen had their bodies in an open posture—turned toward others—but only 7 percent (!) of the East Berliners did. West Berliners laughed two and a half times as often as East Berliners.

These large effects show that East Berliners display much more despair—as measured both by words and by body language—than West Berliners do. The findings do not show, however, exactly what causes this difference. Clearly, since the two cultures were one until 1945, the findings say something about the amount of hope engendered by two different political systems. But they do not isolate which aspect of the two systems is responsible for increased or decreased hope. It could be the difference in standard of living, or the difference in freedom of expression or of travel. It could even be the difference in books, music, or food.

These findings also fail to tell us whether East Berliners became less hopeful with the advent of the Communist regime and the building of the Wall, or West Berliners have become more hopeful since 1945. All we know is that there is now a difference, with the East showing more despair than the West. But we are working on "CAVEing" the newspaper reporting of every winter Olympics since World War II. That will tell us how hope in East and West Berlin has changed over time.*

These findings also show us something else: that there exists a new method for measuring the quantity of hope and despair across cultures. This method allowed Gabriele Oettingen to compare what other scientists thought were incomparable.

---

* As I edit this manuscript (April 1990), I find myself wondering to what extent the explanatory style of the East Germans over the last few momentous months has changed. The theory asserts that rebuilding and prosperity will depend in part on explanatory style. If it has now become optimistic, the future of East Germany will be bright. If it has remained as dark as it was in 1984, economic and spiritual recovery will be much slower than generally expected. A forecast: the changes in explanatory style of East Germany, Czechoslovakia, Romania, Poland, Hungary, and Bulgaria should predict how successfully these nations will exploit their newly won freedom.

Religion and Optimism

IT IS OFTEN thought that religion produces hope and allows troubled people to better face the trials of this world. Organized religion provides a belief that there is more good to life than meets the eye. Failures of individuals are buffered by belief in being part of a much larger whole: Buffering takes place whether the hope is as concrete as a golden afterlife or as abstract as being part of God's plan or just part of the continuity of evolution. Findings on depression bear this out. Conducting studies in the Outer Hebrides, George Brown, the London sociologist who has made a life's work out of interviewing depressed housewives, has shown that staunch churchgoers experience less depression than nonchurchgoers.

But do certain religions provide more hope than others? This question arose in 1986, when Gabriele came to the University of Pennsylvania as a postdoctoral fellow of the MacArthur Foundation and of the German National Science Foundation. Comparing two religions should in principle be just like comparing hope and despair across two cultures, Gabriele argued. The trick would be to find two religions as closely related in time and place as East and West Berlin.

This is where the question hung until we encountered the fiery Eva Morawska, a young sociologist-historian. I invited her to speak to my graduate seminar on the topic of helplessness among Russian Jews and Russian Slavs in the nineteenth century. Eva presented evidence that the Jews were much less helpless in the face of oppression than the Slavs were. She posed the question of why, when things got intolerable, the Jews got up and left and the Slavs did not. "Both groups," Eva contended, were terribly oppressed. "The peasant Slavs lived under unrelieved, crushing poverty, poverty of a degree unknown in this country. The Jews lived in poverty and under religious persecution and the threat of pogroms. Yet the Jews emigrated and the Slavs stayed.

"Perhaps the Russian Orthodox Slavs felt more helpless and hopeless than the Jews," said Eva. "Maybe the two religions inculcated different levels of optimism. Could it be that Russian Orthodoxy is a more pessimistic religion than Judaism?"

The two cultures sat side by side in many villages in Russia, so it is possible directly to compare the explanatory style of their prayers, their fairy tales, and the stories they told. Do the materials that the Slavs and the Jews heard every day differ in tone?

Soon Gabriele and Eva were collaborating. With the help of Russian Orthodox priests Eva picked out large samples of religious and secular material from the two cultures: the daily liturgy, the high-holy-day liturgy, religious stories, folk stories and songs, and proverbs. These were narrated, sung, and spontaneously uttered in the daily life of each culture. They should have been powerful shapers of explanatory style. Gabriele then "CAVEd" all this material. The secular material did not distinguish the two cultures, but the religious material did. The religious material of the Russian Jews was noticeably more optimistic than the Russian Orthodox material, particularly in the permanence dimension. In Jewish material positive events were projected further in time—nice things would last longer—and negative events were more curtailed.

Eva and Gabriele showed that Russian Judaism was more optimistic than Russian Orthodoxy in its stories and prayers. It remains speculation to claim that the cause of the Jews' emigrating and the Slavic peasants' staying stemmed from the greater hopefulness absorbed drop by drop from the religious messages they heard every day. The causes of a people's emigration are highly complex. But Judaism's relative optimism is a plausible cause, and one never before proposed. Testing the theory will require ingenious historical and psychological investigation. But at least in the process of their investigation Gabriele and Eva created a new method for comparing the degree of hope that two religions engender.

Psychohistory Revisited

WHAT USED TO PASS for psychohistory was a far cry from anything Hari Selden would have respected. It didn't predict, it "postdicted," and in doing so it peeked. It reconstructed single lives, not the actions of groups of humans. It used questionable psychological principles and no statistical tools.

In our hands, this has changed. We try to predict events—major ones—before they occur. When we postdict, we don't peek. We do it blindly. We try to predict the actions of large groups—the votes of an electorate, the emigration of a people. We have built on sound psychological principles, and we use well-validated statistical tools.

But it is only a beginning. It does suggest that psychologists of the future need not confine themselves to questionable laboratory studies or expensive studies of groups over time to test their theories. Historical documents can provide a rich testing ground, and predicting the future can offer an even more convincing test of theories.

Hari Selden, we like to think, would have been proud.

Part Three

Changing:
From Pessimism
to Optimism

An aged man is but a paltry thing,
A tattered coat upon a stick, unless
Soul clap its hands and sing, and louder sing
For every tatter in its mortal dress . . .

> W. B. Yeats
> *The Tower* (1928)
> "Sailing to Byzantium"

12

The Optimistic Life

LIFE INFLICTS the same setbacks and tragedies on the optimist as on the pessimist, but the optimist weathers them better. As we have seen, the optimist bounces back from defeat, and, with his life somewhat poorer, he picks up and starts again. The pessimist gives up and falls into depression. Because of his resilience, the optimist achieves more at work, at school, and on the playing field. The optimist has better physical health and may even live longer. Americans want optimists to lead them. Even when things go well for the pessimist, he is haunted by forebodings of catastrophe.

For pessimists, that is the bad news. The good news is that pessimists can learn the skills of optimism and permanently improve the quality of their lives. Even optimists can benefit from learning how to change. Almost all optimists have periods of at least mild pessimism, and the techniques that benefit pessimists can be used by optimists when they are down.

Giving up pessimism and becoming more optimistic may seem undesirable to some of you. Your image of an optimist may be the crashing bore, the self-aggrandizing braggart, the chronic blamer of others, never taking responsibility for his own mistakes. But neither optimism nor pessimism has a corner on bad manners. As you will see from this chapter, becoming an optimist consists not of learning to be more selfish and self-assertive, and to present yourself to others in overbearing ways, but simply of learning a set of skills about how to talk to *yourself* when you suffer a personal defeat. You will learn to speak to yourself about your setbacks from a more encouraging viewpoint.

There is one other reason why learning the skills of optimism may seem undesirable to you. In chapter six we looked at a balance sheet that weighed optimism against pessimism. While optimism had the virtues recapped in the opening of this chapter, pessimism had one virtue: supporting a keener sense of reality. Does learning the skills of optimism mean sacrificing realism?

This is a deep question which puts the goal of these "changing" chapters into sharper focus. They don't purvey an absolute, unconditional optimism for you to apply blindly in all situations; they offer a *flexible optimism*. They aim to increase your control over the way you think about adversity. If you have a negative explanatory style, you no longer need to live under the tyranny of pessimism. When bad events strike, you don't have to look at them in their most permanent, pervasive, and personal light, with the crippling results that pessimistic explanatory style entails. These chapters will give you a choice about how to look at your misfortunes—and an alternative that doesn't require you to become a slave to blind optimism.

Guidelines for Using Optimism

YOUR SCORE on the test in chapter three is the main way to tell whether or not you need to acquire these skills. If your G−B score (your total score) was less than 8, you will benefit from these chapters. The lower it was, the more benefit you will derive. Even if your score was 8 or above, you should ask yourself the following questions; if the answer to any of them is yes, you too can make good use of these chapters.

- "Do I get discouraged easily?"
- "Do I get depressed more than I want to?"
- "Do I fail more than I think I should?"

In what situations should you deploy the explanatory style–changing skills these chapters provide? First, ask yourself what you are trying to accomplish.

- If you are in an achievement situation (getting a promotion, selling a product, writing a difficult report, winning a game), use optimism.
- If you are concerned about how you will feel (fighting off depression, keeping up your morale), use optimism.

- If the situation is apt to be protracted and your physical health is an issue, use optimism.
- If you want to lead, if you want to inspire others, if you want people to vote for you, use optimism.

On the other hand, there are times not to use these techniques.

- If your goal is to plan for a risky and uncertain future, do not use optimism.
- If your goal is to counsel others whose future is dim, do not use optimism initially.
- If you want to appear sympathetic to the troubles of others, do not begin with optimism, although using it later, once confidence and empathy are established, may help.

The fundamental guideline for *not* deploying optimism is to ask what the cost of failure is in the particular situation. If the cost of failure is high, optimism is the wrong strategy. The pilot in the cockpit deciding whether to de-ice the plane one more time, the partygoer deciding whether to drive home after drinking, the frustrated spouse deciding whether to start an affair that, should it come to light, would break up the marriage should not use optimism. Here the costs of failure are, respectively, death, an auto accident, and a divorce. Using techniques that minimize those costs is inappropriate. On the other hand, if the cost of failure is low, use optimism. The sales agent deciding whether to make one more call loses only his time if he fails. The shy person deciding whether to attempt to open a conversation risks only rejection. The teenager contemplating learning a new sport risks only frustration. The disgruntled executive, passed over for promotion, risks only some refusals if he quietly puts out feelers for a new position. All should use optimism.

This chapter teaches you the basic principles of changing from pessimism to optimism in your daily life. Unlike the techniques of almost all other self-help formulas—which consist of a gallon of clinical lore but only a teaspoonful of research—these have been thoroughly researched, and thousands of adults have used them to change their explanatory style permanently.

I have organized the three "changing" chapters so that each stands on its own. This one is for use in all the realms of adult life, except the office. The second is for your children. The third is for your work. Each uses essentially the same techniques of learned optimism in a different setting, and so the chapters may seem to repeat each other somewhat. If you are interested in only one of these topics, it is not absolutely necessary to read the other two chapters.

The ABCs

KATIE HAS BEEN on a strict diet for two weeks. Tonight after work she goes out for drinks with some friends and eats some of the nachos and chicken wings the others ordered. Immediately afterward she feels she has "ruined" her diet.

She thinks to herself, "Way to go, Katie. You sure blew your diet tonight. I am so unbelievably weak. I can't even go to a bar with some friends without making a total glutton of myself. They must think I'm such a fool. Well, all my dieting over the last two weeks is blown now, so I might as well *really* make a pig of myself and eat the cake in the freezer."

Katie breaks out the Sara Lee and eats a whole chocolate fudge brownie delight. Her diet, followed scrupulously until tonight, begins to unravel.

The connection between Katie's eating some nachos and chicken wings and then really overindulging is *not* a necessary one. What links the two is how she explains to herself why she ate the nachos. Her explanation is very pessimistic: "I am so weak." So is the conclusion she drew: "All my dieting is blown." In fact, her diet wasn't blown until she came up with a permanent, pervasive, and personal explanation. Then she gave up.

The consequences of the nacho episode would have been very different if Katie had merely disputed her own automatic first explanation.

"Slow down, Katie," she might have said to herself. "First of all, I did *not* make a *total glutton* of myself at the bar. I drank two Lite Beers and ate a couple of chicken wings and a couple of nachos. I didn't have dinner, so I think on balance I probably consumed only a few more calories than my diet allows. And letting my diet slip a bit for just one night does not mean I am weak. Think how strong I am in sticking to it so strictly for two weeks. Furthermore, no one thinks I'm a fool. I doubt anyone was keeping tabs on what I was eating, and in fact, a couple of people mentioned I looked slimmer. Most important, even if I did eat some things I shouldn't have, that doesn't mean that I should continue to break my diet and set myself back even further. That makes no sense. The best thing to do is cut my losses, let myself off the hook for making a minor mistake, and continue dieting as strictly as I have been for the last two weeks."

. . . .

It's a matter of ABC*: When we encounter *a*dversity, we react by thinking about it. Our thoughts rapidly congeal into *b*eliefs. These beliefs may become so habitual we don't even realize we have them unless we stop and focus on them. And they don't just sit there idly; they have *c*onsequences. The beliefs are the direct causes of what we feel and what we do next. They can spell the difference between dejection and giving up, on the one hand, and well-being and constructive action on the other.

We have seen throughout this book that certain kinds of beliefs set off the giving-up response. I am now going to teach you how to interrupt this vicious circle. The first step is to see the connection between adversity, belief, and consequence. The second step is to see how the ABCs operate every day in your own life. These techniques are part of a course developed by two of the world's leading cognitive therapists—Dr. Steven Hollon, professor of psychology at Vanderbilt University and editor of the major journal in the field, and Dr. Arthur Freeman, professor of psychiatry at the University of Medicine and Dentistry of New Jersey—along with myself, to change explanatory style among normal people.

I want you now to identify some ABCs so you can see how they work. I'll supply the adversity, along with either the belief or the consequence. You fill in the missing component.

Identifying ABCs

1. A. Someone zips into the parking space you had your eye on.

   B. You think _____ .

   C. You get angry, roll down your window, and shout at the other driver.

2. A. You yell at your children for not doing their homework.

   B. You think "I'm a lousy mother."

   C. You feel (or do) _____ .

* In the "changing" chapters, I use the schema of the ABC model developed by pioneering psychologist Albert Ellis.

3. A. Your best friend hasn't returned your phone calls.

   B. You think _____ .

   C. You're depressed all day.

4. A. Your best friend hasn't returned your phone calls.

   B. You think _____ .

   C. You don't feel bad about it, and go about your day.

5. A. You and your spouse have a fight.

   B. You think "I never do anything right."

   C. You feel (or do) _____ .

6. A. You and your spouse have a fight.

   B. You think, "She [He] was in an awful mood."

   C. You feel (or do) _____ .

7. A. You and your spouse have a fight.

   B. You think, "I can always clear up misunderstandings."

   C. You feel (or do) _____ .

Now, let's take a look at these seven situations and see how the elements interact.

1. In the first example, thoughts of trespass set off your anger. "That driver stole my place." "That was a rude and selfish thing to do."

2. When you explained your treatment of your children with "I'm a lousy mother," sadness and a reluctance to try to get them to do their homework followed. When we explain bad events as the result of permanent, pervasive, and personal traits like being a lousy mother, dejection and giving up follow. The more permanent the trait, the longer dejection will last.

3 and 4. You can see this when your best friend doesn't return your phone calls. If, as in the third example, you thought something permanent and pervasive—such as "I'm always selfish and inconsiderate. No wonder"—depression would follow. But if, as in the fourth example, your explanation was temporary, specific, and external, you wouldn't be disturbed. "She's working overtime this week," you might say to yourself, or "She's in a funk."

5, 6, and 7. How about when you and your spouse have a fight? If, as in example 5, you think "I never do anything right" (permanent, pervasive, personal), you will be depressed and not try to do anything to heal the breach. If, as in example 6, you think "She was in an awful mood" (temporary and external), you will feel some anger, a little dejection, and only temporary immobility. When the mood clears, you'll probably do something to make up. If, as in example 7, you think "I can always clear up misunderstandings," you will act to make up and you soon will feel pretty good and full of energy.

Your ABC Record

To find out how these ABCs operate in daily existence, keep an ABC diary for the next day or two, just long enough for you to record five ABCs from your own life.

To do this, tune in on the perpetual dialogue that takes place in your mind and that you are usually unaware of. It's a matter of picking up the connection between a certain adversity—even a very minor one—and a consequent feeling. So, for example, you are talking to a friend on the phone. She seems very eager to get off the phone (a distressing minor adversity for you), and you then find yourself sad (the consequent feeling). This little episode will become an ABC entry for you.

There are three parts to your record.

The first section, "Adversity," can be almost anything—a leaky faucet, a frown from a friend, a baby that won't stop crying, a large bill, inattentiveness from your spouse. Be objective about the situation. Record your description of what happened, not your evaluation of it. So if you had an argument with your spouse, you might write down that she was unhappy with something you said or did. Record that. But do not record "She was unfair" under "Adversity." That's an inference, and you may want to record that in the second section: "Belief."

Your beliefs are how you interpret the adversity. Be sure to separate thoughts from feelings. (Feelings will go under "Consequences.") "I just blew my diet" and "I feel incompetent" are beliefs. Their accuracy can be evaluated. "I feel sad," however, expresses a feeling. It doesn't make sense to check the accuracy of "I feel sad"; if you feel sad, you are sad.

"Consequences." In this section, record your feelings and what you did. Did you feel sad, anxious, joyful, guilty, or whatever? Often you will feel more than one thing. Write down as many feelings and actions as you were aware of. What did you then do? "I had no energy," "I made a plan to get her to apologize," "I went back to bed" are all consequent actions.

Before you start, here are some helpful examples of the sort of thing you may experience.

Adversity: My husband was supposed to give the kids their bath and put them to bed, but when I got home from my meeting they were all glued to the TV.

Belief: Why can't he do what I ask him? Is it such a hard thing to give them their bath and put them to bed? Now I'm going to look like the heavy when I break up their little party.

Consequences: I was really angry with Jack and started yelling without first giving him a chance to explain. I walked into the room and snapped off the set without even a "hello" first. I looked like the heavy.

Adversity: I came home early from work and found my son and his friends in the garage smoking pot.

Belief: What does he think he's doing? I'm going to strangle him! This just goes to show how irresponsible he is. I can't trust him at all. Everything out of his mouth is just one lie after another. Well, I'm not going to listen to any of it.

Consequences: I was out-of-my-mind angry at him. I refused even to discuss the situation. I told him he was "an untrustworthy little delinquent," and I spent the rest of the evening fuming.

Adversity: I called up a man I was interested in and invited him to a show. He said he would have to take a rain check because he needed to prepare for a meeting.

Belief: Right, what an excuse. He was just trying to spare my feelings. The truth is he doesn't want to have anything to do with me. What did I expect? I'm too assertive for him. That's the last time I'll ever ask someone out.

Consequences: I felt stupid, embarrassed and ugly. Instead of inviting someone else to go to the show with me, I decided to give the tickets to friends.

Adversity: I decided to join a gym, and when I walked into the place I saw nothing but firm, toned bodies all around me.

Belief: What am I doing here? I look like a beached whale compared

to these people! I should get out of here while I still have my dignity.
   Consequences: I felt totally self-conscious and ended up leaving after
fifteen minutes.

It's your turn now. Over the next couple of days, record five ABC
sequences from your life.

Adversity:

Belief:

Consequences:

Adversity:

Belief:

Consequences:

Adversity:

Belief:

Consequences:

Adversity:

Belief:

Consequences:

Adversity:

Belief:

Consequences:

When you have recorded your five ABC episodes, read them over carefully. Look for the link between your belief and the consequences. What you will see is that pessimistic explanations set off passivity and dejection, whereas optimistic explanations energize.

The next step follows immediately: If you change the habitual beliefs that follow adversity for you, your reaction to adversity will change in lockstep. There are highly reliable ways to change.

Disputation and Distraction

THERE ARE TWO general ways for you to deal with your pessimistic beliefs once you are aware of them. The first is simply to distract yourself when they occur—try to think of something else. The second is to dispute them. Disputing is more effective in the long run, because successfully disputed beliefs are less likely to recur when the same situation presents itself again.

Human beings are wired to think about things, bad and good, that attract our attention and place demands on us. This makes a great deal of evolutionary sense. We wouldn't live very long if we didn't recognize dangers and needs straight off and if we weren't primed to worry about how to deal with them. Habitual pessimistic thoughts merely carry this useful process one detrimental step further. They not only grab our attention; they circle unceasingly through our minds. By their very nature they will not allow themselves to be forgotten. They are primitive, biological reminders of needs and of dangers. While evolution seems to have made prepubescent children irrepressible optimists, it has also assured that adults who worried and planned were more likely to survive and have children and have these children survive. But in modern life, these primitive reminders can get in our way, subverting our performance and spoiling the quality of our emotional life.

Let's examine the difference between distraction and disputation.

Distraction

I WANT YOU now *not* to think about a piece of apple pie with vanilla ice cream. The pie is heated and the ice cream forms a delightful contrast in taste and temperature.

You probably find that you have almost no capacity to refrain from thinking about the pie. But you do have the capacity to redeploy your attention.

Think about the pie again. Got it. Mouth-watering? Now stand up and slam the palm of your hand against the wall and shout "STOP!"

The image of the pie disappeared, didn't it?

This is one of several simple but highly effective thought-stopping techniques used by people who are trying to interrupt habitual thought patterns. Some people ring a loud bell, others carry a three-by-five card with the word *STOP* in enormous red letters. Many people find it works well to wear a rubber band around their wrists and snap it hard to stop their ruminating.

If you combine one of these physical techniques with a technique called attention shifting, you will get longer-lasting results. To keep your thoughts from returning to a negative belief after interruption (by snapping a rubber band or whatever), now direct your attention elsewhere. Actors do this when they must suddenly switch from one emotion to another. Try this: Pick up a small object and study it intently for a few seconds. Handle it, put it in your mouth and taste it, smell it, tap it to see how it sounds. You'll find that concentrating on the object this way will have strengthened your shift in attention.

Finally, you can undercut ruminations by taking advantage of their very nature. Their nature is to circle around in your mind, so that you will not forget them, so that you will act on them. When adversity strikes, *schedule some time—later—for thinking things over* . . . say, this evening at six P.M. Now, when something disturbing happens and you find the thoughts hard to stop, you can say to yourself, "Stop. I'll think this over later . . . at [such and such a time]."

Also, *write the troublesome thoughts down the moment they occur.* The combination of jotting them down—which acts to ventilate them and dispose of them—and setting a later time to think about them works well; it takes advantage of the reason ruminations exist—to remind you of themselves—and so undercuts them. If you write them down and set a time to think about them, they no longer have any purpose, and purposelessness lessens their strength.

Disputation

DUCKING our disturbing beliefs can be good first aid, but a deeper, more lasting remedy is to dispute them: Give them an argument. Go on the attack. By effectively disputing the beliefs that follow adversity, you can change your customary reaction from dejection and giving up to activity and good cheer.

> *Adversity:* I recently started taking night classes after work for a master's degree. I got my first set of exams back and I didn't do nearly as well as I wanted.

Belief: What awful grades, Judy. I no doubt did the worst in the class. I'm just stupid. That's all. I might as well face facts. I'm also just too old to be competing with these kids. Even if I stick with it, who is going to hire a forty-year-old woman when they can hire a twenty-three-year-old instead? What was I thinking when I enrolled? It's just too late for me.

Consequences: I felt totally dejected and useless. I was embarrassed I even gave it a try, and decided I should withdraw from my courses and be satisfied with the job I have.

Disputation: I'm blowing things out of proportion. I hoped to get all As, but I got a B, a B+, and a B−. Those aren't awful grades. I may not have done the best in the class, but I didn't do the worst in the class either. I checked. The guy next to me had two Cs and a D+. The reason I didn't do as well as I hoped isn't because of my age. The fact that I am forty doesn't make me any less intelligent than anyone else in the class. One reason I may not have done as well is because I have a lot of other things going on in my life that take time away from my studies. I have a full-time job. I have a family. I think that given my situation I did a good job on my exams. Now that I took this set of exams I know how much work I need to put into my studies in the future in order to do even better. Now is not the time to worry about who will hire me. Almost everyone who graduates from this program gets a decent job. For now I need to concern myself with learning the material and earning my degree. Then when I graduate I can focus on finding a better job.

Outcome: I felt much better about myself and my exams. I'm not going to withdraw from my courses, and I am not going to let my age stand in the way of getting what I want. I'm still concerned that my age may be a disadvantage, but I will cross that bridge if and when I come to it.

Judy effectively disputed her beliefs about her grades. By doing so she changed her feelings from despair into hope and her course of action from withdrawal into plunging ahead. Judy knows some techniques that you are about to learn.

Distancing

IT IS ESSENTIAL to realize your beliefs are just that—beliefs. They may or may not be facts. If a jealous rival shrieked at you in a rage, "You are a terrible mother. You are selfish, inconsiderate, and stupid," how would you react? You probably wouldn't take the accusations much into account. If they got under your skin, you would dispute them (either to her face or to yourself). "My kids love me," you might say. "I spend ungodly amounts of time with them. I teach them algebra, football, and how to get on in a tough world. Anyway she's just jealous because her kids have turned out so poorly."

We can more or less easily distance ourselves from the unfounded accusations of others. But we are much worse at distancing ourselves from the accusations that we launch—daily—at ourselves. After all, if *we* think them about ourselves, they must be true.

Wrong!

What we say to ourselves when we face a setback can be just as baseless as the ravings of a jealous rival. Our reflexive explanations are usually distortions. They are mere bad habits of thought produced by unpleasant experiences in the past—by childhood conflicts, by strict parents, by an overly critical Little League coach, by a big sister's jealousy. But because they seem to issue from ourselves, we treat them as gospel.

They are merely beliefs, however. And just believing something doesn't make it so. Just because a person fears that he is unemployable, unlovable, or inadequate doesn't mean it's true. It is essential to stand back and suspend belief for a moment, to distance yourself from our pessimistic explanations at least long enough to verify their accuracy. Checking out the accuracy of our reflexive beliefs is what disputation is all about.

The first step is just knowing your beliefs warrant dispute. The next step is putting disputation into practice.

Learning to Argue with Yourself

FORTUNATELY, you already have a lifetime of experience in disputation. You use this skill whenever you argue with other people. Once you get started disputing your own unfounded accusations about yourself, your old skills will kick in for use in this new project.

There are four important ways to make your disputations convincing.

- Evidence?
- Alternatives?
- Implications?
- Usefulness?

Evidence

THE MOST CONVINCING way of disputing a negative belief is to show that it is factually incorrect. Much of the time you will have facts on your side, since pessimistic reactions to adversity are so often overreactions. You adopt the role of a detective and ask, "What is the evidence for this belief?"

Judy did this. She believed that her "awful" grades were the "worst in the class." She checked the evidence. The person sitting next to her had much lower grades.

Katie, who allegedly "blew" her diet, could count up the calories in the nachos, the chicken wings, and the Lite Beers and find that they came to little more than the dinner she skipped to go out with her friends.

It is important to see the difference between this approach and the so-called "power of positive thinking." Positive thinking often involves trying to believe upbeat statements such as "Every day, in every way, I'm getting better and better" in the absence of evidence, or even in the face of contrary evidence. If you can actually believe such statements, more power to you. Many educated people, trained in skeptical thinking, cannot manage this kind of boosterism. Learned optimism, in contrast, is about accuracy.

We have found that merely repeating positive statements to yourself does not raise mood or achievement very much, if at all. It is how you cope with negative statements that has an effect. Usually the negative beliefs that follow adversity are inaccurate. Most people catastrophize: From all the potential causes, they select the one with the direst implications. One of your most effective techniques in disputation will be to search for evidence pointing to the distortions in your catastrophic explanations. Most of the time you will have reality on your side.

Learned optimism works not through an unjustifiable positivity about the world but through the power of "non-negative" thinking.

Alternatives

ALMOST NOTHING that happens to you has just one cause; most events have many causes. If you did poorly on a test, all of the following might have contributed: how hard the test was, how much you studied, how smart you are, how fair the professor is, how the other students did, how tired you were. Pessimists have a way of latching onto the worst of all these possible causes—the most permanent, pervasive, and personal one. Judy picked "I'm too old to be competing with these kids."

Here again, disputation usually has reality on its side. There are multiple causes, so why latch onto the most insidious one? Ask yourself, "Is there any less destructive way to look at this?" Judy, an experienced self-disputer, easily found that there was: "I have a full-time job and I have a family." Katie, who also became an ace self-disputer, could change "weakness" into "Look at how strong I am in keeping at this diet so strictly for two whole weeks."

To dispute your own beliefs, scan for all possible contributing causes. *Focus on the changeable* (not enough time spent studying), *the specific* (this particular exam was uncharacteristically hard) *and the nonpersonal* (the professor graded unfairly) *causes.* You may have to push hard at generating alternative beliefs, latching onto possibilities you are not fully convinced are true. Remember that much of pessimistic thinking consists in just the reverse, latching onto the most dire possible belief, not because the evidence supports it, but precisely because it is so dire. Your job is to undo this destructive habit by becoming skilled at generating alternatives.

Implications

BUT THE WAY things go in this world, the facts won't always be on your side. The negative belief you hold about yourself may be correct. In this situation, the technique to use is *decatastrophizing.*

Even if my belief *is* correct, you say to yourself, what are its implications? Judy was older than the rest of the students. But what does that imply? It doesn't mean that Judy is any less intelligent than they are, and it doesn't mean that nobody would want to hire her. Katie's breaking her diet doesn't imply she's a total glutton, it doesn't imply she's a fool, and it certainly doesn't mean she should let her diet unravel completely.

How likely, you should ask yourself, are those awful implications? How likely is it that three Bs mean no one will ever hire Judy? Do a couple of chicken wings and nachos really mean Katie is a total glutton? Once you ask if the implications are really that awful, repeat the search for evidence. Katie remembered the evidence that she had stuck to a strict diet for two whole weeks—so she was hardly a total glutton. Judy remembered that almost everyone who got a master's degree from her program got a decent job.

Usefulness

SOMETIMES the consequences of holding a belief matter more than the truth of the belief. Is the belief destructive? Katie's belief in her gluttony, even if true, is destructive. It is a recipe for letting go of her diet completely.

Some people get very upset when the world shows itself not to be fair. We can sympathize with that sentiment, but the belief that the world should be fair may cause more grief than it's worth. What good will it do me to dwell on that? At times it is very useful, instead, to get on with your day, without taking the time to examine the accuracy of your beliefs and then disputing them. For example, a technician doing bomb demolition might find himself thinking, "This could go off and I might be killed"—with the result that his hands start to shake. In this case I would recommend distraction over disputation. Whenever you simply have to perform *now*, you will find distraction the tool of choice. At this moment the question to ask yourself is not "Is the belief true?" but "Is it functional for me to think it right now?" If the answer is no, use the distraction techniques. (Stop! Assign a later worry time. Make a written note of the thought.)

Another tactic is to detail all the ways you can change the situation in the future. Even if the belief is true now, is the situation changeable? How can you go about changing it?

Your Disputation Record

Now I want you to practice the ABCDE model. You already know what ABC stands for. *D* is for disputation; *E* is for energization.

During the next five adverse events you face, listen closely for your beliefs, observe the consequences, and dispute your beliefs vigorously. Then observe the energization that occurs as you succeed in dealing with the negative beliefs, and record all of this. These five adverse events can be minor: The mail is late; your call isn't returned; the kid pumping gas doesn't wash the windshield. In each of these, use the four techniques of effective self-disputation.

Before you start, study the examples below.

Adversity: I borrowed a pair of really expensive earrings from my friend, and I lost one of them while I was out dancing.

Belief: I am so irresponsible. They were Kay's favorite earrings, and of course I go and lose one. She is going to be so absolutely furious at me. Not that she doesn't have every reason. If I were her, I'd hate me too. I just can't believe how much of a klutz I am. I wouldn't be surprised if she told me she didn't want to have anything to do with me anymore.

Consequences: I felt totally sick. I was ashamed and embarrassed, and I didn't want to call and tell her what happened. Basically, I just sat around feeling stupid for a while, trying to muster up the guts to call her.

Disputation: Well, it is really unfortunate that I lost the earring. They were Kay's favorites [evidence] and she probably will be very disappointed [implication]. However, she will realize it was an accident [alternative], and I seriously doubt she will hate me because of this [implication]. I don't think it's accurate to label myself as totally irresponsible just because I lost an earring [implication].

Energization: I still felt bad about losing her earring, but I didn't feel nearly as ashamed, and I wasn't worried that she would end the friendship over it. I was able to relax and call her to explain.

Here's one you saw the first half of before.

Adversity: I came home early from work and found my son and his friends hanging out in the garage smoking pot.

Belief: What does he think he's doing? I'm going to strangle him! This just goes to show how irresponsible he is. I can't trust him at all. Everything out of his mouth is just one lie after another. Well, I'm not going to listen to any of it.

Consequences: I was out-of-my-mind angry at him. I refused even to discuss the situation. I told him he was "an untrustworthy little delinquent," and I spent the rest of the evening fuming.

But here's how an ace disputer would conclude this internal dialogue:

Disputation: Okay, it is definitely true Joshua is irresponsible to smoke pot, but this doesn't mean he is totally irresponsible and untrustworthy [implications]. He has never cut school or stayed out late without calling, and he has been good about doing his share around the house [evidence]. This is a very serious situation, but it is not helpful to assume that everything he says is a lie [usefulness]. Our communication in the past has been okay, and I think if I remain calm now, things will go better [usefulness]. If I am not willing to discuss the situation with Joshua, things cannot be resolved [usefulness].

Energization: I was able to settle down and begin to handle the situation. I began by apologizing for calling him "untrustworthy," and I told him we needed to talk about his smoking pot. The conversation did get fairly heated at times, but at least we were talking.

Adversity: I threw a dinner party for a group of friends, and the person I was trying to impress barely touched her food.

Belief: The food tastes putrid. I am such a lousy cook. I might as well forget getting to know her any better. I'm lucky she didn't get up and leave in the middle of dinner.

Consequences: I felt really disappointed and angry at myself. I was so embarrassed about my cooking that I wanted to avoid her for the rest of the night. Obviously, things weren't going as I had hoped.

Disputation: This is ridiculous. I know the food doesn't taste putrid [evidence]. She may not have eaten very much but everyone else did [evidence]. There could be a hundred reasons why she didn't eat much [alternatives]. She could be on a diet, she might not have been feeling great, she might just have a small appetite [alternatives]. Even though she didn't eat much, she did seem to enjoy the dinner [evidence]. She told some funny stories, and she seemed to be relaxed [evidence]. She even offered to help me with the dishes [evidence]. She wouldn't have done that if she was repulsed by me [alternative].

Energization: I didn't feel nearly as embarrassed or angry, and I realized that if I avoided her, then I really would hurt my chances of getting to know her better. Basically, I was able to relax and not let my imagination ruin the evening for me.

Now you do it, in your daily life over the next week. Don't search out adversity, but as it comes along, tune in carefully to your internal dialogue. When you hear the negative beliefs, dispute them. Beat them into the ground. Then record the ABCDE.

Adversity:

Belief:

Consequences:

Disputation:

Energization:

Adversity:

Belief:

Consequences:

Disputation:

Energization:

Adversity:

Belief:

Consequences:

Disputation:

Energization:

Adversity:

Belief:

Consequences:

Disputation:

Energization:

Adversity:

Belief:

Consequences:

Disputation:

Energization:

The Externalization of Voices

IN ORDER to practice disputation, you don't have to wait for adversity to strike. You can have a friend provide the negative beliefs for you out loud, and then you dispute his accusations, also out loud. This exercise is called "externalization of voices." To do it, choose a friend (your spouse might do fine) and set aside twenty minutes. Your friend's job is to criticize you. For this reason, you have to choose your friend carefully. Choose someone you trust with your feelings and around whom you don't get defensive.

Explain to your friend that in this situation it is all right to criticize you: You won't take it personally because this is an exercise to strengthen the way you dispute such criticisms when you make them to yourself. Help your friend choose the right kinds of criticisms by going over your ABC record with him, pointing out the negative beliefs that afflict you repeatedly. With these understandings reached, you'll find that you don't, in fact, take the criticisms personally when your friend makes them, and that the exercise can actually strengthen the bond of sympathy between you and your friend.

Your job is to dispute the criticisms out loud, with all the armaments you have. Marshal all the contrary evidence you can find, spell out all the alternative explanations, decatastrophize by arguing that the implications are not nearly as dire as your friend charges. If you believe the accusation is true now, detail all the things you can do to change the situation. Your friend can interrupt to dispute your disputing. Then you should reply.

Before you start, you and your friend should read the following examples. Each contains a situation that the friend exploits in order to make some nasty accusations. (Your friend must be rough on you, because in your own explanatory style you've been rough on yourself.)

Situation: While Carol is putting away some clothes in her fifteen-year-old daughter's bedroom, she finds a packet of birth-control pills hidden under some clothes.

Accusation (by friend): How could this be going on without your knowing it? She's only fifteen years old. You weren't even dating when you were fifteen years old. How could you be so blind to what your daughter is up to? Your relationship must be completely awful if you weren't even aware that Susan is sexually active. What kind of mother are you?

Disputation: Well, it doesn't help to compare when I was a teenager to Susan's experiences [usefulness]. Times have changed. It's a different world these days [alternative]. It's true that I had no idea that Susan was sleeping with someone [evidence], but this doesn't mean our relationship is totally awful [implications]. My discussions with her about birth control must have gotten through, because she is on the pill [evidence]. That's a good sign at least.

Friend interrupts: You're so caught up in your own life and so busy with work that you have no idea what is going on in your own daughter's life. You're a rotten mother.

Disputation continues: I have been preoccupied lately with my work, and maybe I haven't been as in tune with her as I'd like [alternatives], but I can change that [usefulness]. Instead of flying off the handle about this, or getting down on myself, I can use this situation to reopen the lines of communication between us and discuss sex and any concerns she may have [usefulness]. It won't be easy at first. I expect she'll be a bit defensive, but we can make it work.

Situation: The pessimist in this case is a man named Doug. He and his girlfriend, Barbara, go to a dinner party at a friend's house. Barbara spends part of the evening talking to Nick, a man Doug has never met before. In the car on the way home, Doug can't keep himself from remarking bitingly, "You and that guy seemed to have a lot in common. I haven't seen you so excited in a long time. I hope you got his number—it would be a shame to let that friendship die." Barbara is surprised by Doug's reaction and laughingly tells him he needn't be so insecure; Nick is just a friend from work.

Accusation (by friend): It was really rude of Barbara to spend the whole night talking and laughing with someone else. These were a group of her friends, and she knew you'd be the odd man out.

Disputation: I think I'm overreacting a bit. She didn't spend the entire night talking with Nick [evidence]. We were at the party for four hours and she probably spoke to him for forty-five minutes or so [evidence]. Just because I had never met a lot of the people before doesn't mean she's responsible for baby-sitting me [alternative]. She did spend the first hour introducing me to her friends, and it wasn't until after dinner that she spent some time alone with Nick [evidence]. I guess she feels secure enough about us that she doesn't have to cling to me all the time [alternative]. She knows I can mingle and meet people on my own [evidence].

Friend interrupts: If she really cared for you, she wouldn't have spent the night flirting with that guy. You obviously care for her more than she cares for you. If that's how she feels, you might as well call it quits.

Disputation continues: I know Barbara loves me [evidence]. We've been together for a long time, and she has never once mentioned splitting up or seeing other people [evidence]. She's right, I was probably just feeling a little nervous about meeting so many new people at one time [alternative]. I ought to apologize for being so sarcastic with her and explain to her why I reacted as I did [usefulness].

Situation: Andrew's wife, Lori, is an alcoholic. For three years she did not touch any alcohol, but recently she has started drinking again. Andrew has been trying everything he can to get her to stop: He's tried to reason with her, he's threatened her, he's pleaded with her. But each night when he comes home from work, Lori is drunk.

Accusation (by friend): This is awful. You should be able to make Lori stop drinking. You should have realized something was bothering her way before things got as far as they have. How could you have been so blind? Why can't you make her see what she is doing to herself?

Disputation: It would be great if I could make Lori stop drinking, but that isn't realistic [evidence]. Last time I went through this with her I learned there's absolutely nothing I can do to make her stop [evidence]. Until she decides she wants to get off the bottle, there is nothing I can do to make her see what she doesn't want to see [alternative]. This doesn't mean I'm helpless in terms of dealing with my own feelings about this [implication]. I can start going to a support group so that I don't fall into the trap of blaming myself again [usefulness].

Friend interrupts: You thought things were good between the two of you. I guess you've been deluding yourself for the last three years. Your marriage must mean nothing to her.

Disputation continues: Just because Lori has started to drink again, that doesn't totally discount the last three years of our marriage [alternative]. Things were good between us [evidence], and they will get better again. This is *her* problem [alternative], and I just have to keep telling myself that, over and over again [usefulness]. She's not drinking because of anything I did or didn't do [alternative]. The best thing I can do right now for both of us is to talk to someone about how this is affecting me and what my concerns and worries are [usefulness]. It's going to be a bitch to get through this, but I am willing to give it a try.

Situation: Brenda and her sister Andrea have always been very close. They went to the same schools, traveled in the same circles, settled down in the same neighborhood. Andrea's son is a freshman at Dartmouth, and both Andrea and Brenda are excited about helping Joey, Brenda's son, start researching the colleges he wants to attend. At the beginning of his senior year in high school, Joey tells his parents he doesn't want to go to college; instead he wants to restore houses and work in construction. When Andrea asks Brenda why Joey doesn't want to go to college, Brenda loses control and snaps, "Not that it is any of your business, but not everyone has to follow in your son's footsteps."

Accusation (by friend): You ought to be sick and tired of everything in your life being an open book to Andrea. She has her own family. There is no reason for her to be constantly nosing around in your life.

Disputation: I think you are overreacting just a wee bit. All Andrea did was ask why Joey has decided not to go to college [evidence]. That's a fair question [alternative]. I would feel I could ask her that question if the situation were the other way around and it was her son, not mine, who'd decided not to go to college [evidence].

Friend interrupts: She thinks she is superior to you because her son is going to Dartmouth and Joey isn't. Well, you most certainly don't need that kind of attitude from your sister, so she can just buzz off.

Disputation continues: She wasn't acting superior or rubbing my face in it; she's just concerned because she cares about Joey a great deal [alternative]. I guess I am feeling defensive about Joey's decision and envious of where Brenda's son is [alternative]. Actually, I am proud of how close Andrea and I are. Sure, every once in a while things get competitive, but I wouldn't trade our closeness for the world [usefulness].

Situation: Donald is a senior in college. His father died four years ago after a long illness. While Donald is home for Christmas, his mother tells him she is going to marry Geoff, a man she has been seeing for a few months. Donald knew she was involved with Geoff, but he is totally surprised by her plans for marriage. When Donald does not respond to her announcement, his mother asks him what he thinks. Donald explodes with "It is absolutely disgusting that you are going to marry that creep" and storms out of the house.

Accusation (by friend): I can't believe your mom is going to marry that guy. She barely knows him, he's way too old, and he's totally wrong for her. How could she do this to you?

Disputation: Hold on a second. Are things really as bad as that? First of all, I don't know how well she knows Geoff [evidence]. I've been away at school all year [evidence]. They've only known each other a few months, but for all I know they may spend every minute together [alternative]. And the stuff about him being too old is silly [evidence]. He's only ten years older; my dad was thirteen years older than Mom [evidence].

Friend interrupts: How could she do this to your dad? Your dad just died, and already she's replacing him with someone else. That makes me sick. What kind of woman is she that she could do such a lousy thing?

Disputation continues: Mom does seem happier than she has in a very long time [evidence]. I guess what's really bothering me is I still miss Dad so much, and I can't understand how Mom could have gotten over him enough to have fallen in love again [alternative]. Maybe I'll talk to her about that. The fact is, Dad has been dead for four years [evidence], and whether I like it or not, Mom has to move on [alternative]. I don't want to see her alone. In a way, it's kind of a relief [implications]. Now I don't have to worry about her being lonely. I mean, it's not that she's replacing Dad, she's just found someone else who makes her happy [alternative]. I bet Dad would be glad [evidence]. He wouldn't want her to never feel love again [evidence]. It's just that this came as such a surprise to me [alternative]. I think I'll feel a little better about this once I get to know Geoff [usefulness]. I sure hope he's a good guy.

Okay. You do it now.

Review

YOU SHOULD NOW be well on your way to using disputation, the prime technique for learned optimism, in your daily life. You first saw the ABC link—that specific beliefs lead to dejection and passivity. Emotions and actions do not usually follow adversity directly. Rather they issue directly from your beliefs about adversity. This means that if you change your mental response to adversity, you can cope with setbacks much better.

The main tool for changing your interpretations of adversity is disputation. Practice disputing your automatic interpretations all the time from now on. Anytime you find yourself down or anxious or angry, ask what you are saying to yourself. Sometimes the beliefs will turn out to be accurate; when this is so, concentrate on the ways you can alter the situation and prevent adversity from becoming disaster. But usually your negative beliefs are distortions. Challenge them. Don't let them run your emotional life. Unlike dieting, learned optimism is easy to maintain once you start. Once you get into the habit of disputing negative beliefs, your daily life will run much better, and you will feel much happier.

13

Helping Your Child Escape Pessimism

WE LIKE to think of childhood as an idyllic time free of the burdens of responsibility that descend upon us with age, a sheltered interval before life begins in earnest. But, as we have seen in earlier chapters, there is no shelter from pessimism and its grim offspring, depression. Many children suffer terribly from pessimism, a condition that torments them through the years to come, ruining their education and livelihoods, spoiling their happiness. School-age children have the same rate and intensity of depression as adults. Worst of all, pessimism embeds itself as a way of looking at the world, and childhood pessimism is the father and mother of adult pessimism.

As we noted, some studies indicate children actually learn much of their pessimism from their mothers. They also learn pessimism from the criticisms adults make of them. But if children can learn it, they can unlearn it, and they do this exactly the same way adults do: by developing more sanguine ways of explaining life's setbacks to themselves. Although the ABC techniques have been thoroughly researched and learned by thousands of adults, less research has been done with children, but enough is now known to recommend them for your child. It might be said that teaching optimism to your children is as important as teaching them to work hard or be truthful, for it can have just as profound an impact on their later lives. Does your child need to learn the skills of optimism?

Some parents are a bit reluctant to intervene in the natural course of their children's emotional growth. Your child will probably benefit from acquiring these skills, but there are three guidelines for determining if they are especially important for your child.

First, what was your child's score on the CASQ in chapter seven? If your girl scored less than 7.0 or your boy scored less than 5.0, she or he is twice as likely to experience depression as more optimistic children are, and will probably benefit substantially from this chapter. The lower your child's score, the greater the benefit is likely to be.

Second, what did your child score on the depression test in chapter eight? If he scored 10 or higher, he can use these skills. If he scored 16 or higher, I believe that his learning these skills is essential.

Finally, have you and your spouse been fighting, or, more drastic, is separation or divorce a possibility? If so, your child is going to need these skills urgently. We find that children often become massively depressed at such times, and stay depressed for years, with poor school performance and a permanent change toward pessimistic explanatory style. Intervention right now can be crucial.

With this chapter you can take your child through the ABC system you learned in the previous chapter. If you haven't yet read that chapter, or haven't read it recently, you should; familiarity with that material will make you a better instructor.

ABCs for Your Child

SEEING THE CONNECTION between adversity, belief, and consequences is the first step for your child to take in learning optimism. The exercises below attempt to teach that connection. They are designed for children between the ages of eight and fourteen. Younger children may find them difficult, but if you are patient with them and if your child is cerebral enough, you can do this with a child as young as seven. Older children, full-blown teenagers, should do the adult exercises; they will feel patronized by the child examples.

Teaching optimism to your child benefits both of you. The benefit to your child is obvious. But teaching is also the best way of learning something well yourself. Through teaching these skills to your child, your own grasp of them will improve enormously.

Here's how to start. Once you have read the previous chapter and done the adult exercises, set aside half an hour with your child. First explain the ABC model to him. The point you want to get across is that how he feels doesn't just come out of nowhere. Make it clear that what he *thinks* when things go badly actually changes how he feels. When he suddenly feels sad or angry or afraid or embarrassed, a thought has always triggered the feeling. If he can learn to find that thought, he can change it.

Once the child gets the general drift, work through each of the following three examples with him. After each example, have him explain it to you in his own words, concentrating on the connection between the beliefs and the consequences. After he explains it in his own words, go over the questions at the end of each example.

Adversity: My teacher, Mr. Minner, yelled at me in front of the whole class, and everybody laughed.
Belief: He hates me and now the whole class thinks I'm a jerk.
Consequences: I felt really sad and I wished that I could just disappear under my desk.

Ask your child why the boy felt sad. Why did he want to disappear? If he had a different belief about Mr. Minner—for example, if he thought, "The whole class knows Mr. Minner is unfair"—how would the consequences have been different? Would the class think the boy was a jerk?

The beliefs are the crucial step to the consequences; when they change, the consequences do too.

Adversity: My best friend, Susan, told me that Joannie was her new best friend and from now on she was going to sit with Joannie in the cafeteria and not with me.
Belief: Susan doesn't like me anymore because I'm not cool enough. Joannie tells really funny jokes, and whenever I tell a joke *nobody* laughs. And Joannie has really cool clothes, and I dress like a dweeb. I bet if I was more popular Susan would still want to be best friends with me. Now I'm never going to have anybody to sit with at lunch, and everybody is going to know that Joannie is Susan's new best friend.
Consequences: I was really scared to go to lunch because I didn't want to get laughed at and have to eat by myself, so I pretended to have a stomachache, and I asked Miss Frankel to send me to the nurse. I also felt really ugly, and I wanted to change schools.

Why did this girl want to change schools? Was it the fact that Susan was going to sit with Joannie? Or was it the belief that she would never have anyone to sit with? Why did she feel ugly? What role did her beliefs about dressing like a dweeb play? How would the consequences have changed if this child believed Susan was a fickle twit?

Adversity: While I was waiting at the bus stop with my friends a bunch of ninth-graders came by and started calling me "Fatso" and "Blubber" right in front of all my friends.

Belief: There's nothing I can say back, because they're right, I *am* a fatso. Now all my friends are going to laugh at me, and nobody will want to sit with me on the bus. Everybody is going to start teasing me and calling me names, and I'm just going to have to take it.

Consequences: I felt like dying, I was so embarrassed. I wanted to run away from my friends, but I didn't because it was the last bus. So I just put my head down and decided to sit by myself in the very first seat right by the driver.

Why did this boy want to run away from his friends? Was it because of the fact he was called "Fatso" or the belief that all his friends were now going to reject him? Were there other, more constructive beliefs he might have entertained—"My friends are loyal," for example, or "My friends all think those ninth-graders are jerks"? What would have happened then?

ONCE YOU see your child grasps the ABC concept, you should end the session. When you do, set aside half an hour for tomorrow, in which your child will learn to put ABC into practice in his own life.

In the next session, start by reviewing the adversity–belief–consequences link, and work over one of the examples again if necessary. Next, ask him for an example from his own life, and write it down. If he needs prompting, use one or two ABCs from your own record.

Now tell him it's his turn to find ABCs in his daily life. His assignment for the next few days is to bring home one example and discuss it with you. Each day after school, record and discuss the example. Emphasize how sadness, anger, fear, and giving up are all produced by his beliefs, and hint broadly that these beliefs are not inevitable or unchangeable. He may well come home with all five examples in the first day or two. When he has found his five examples, you are ready to go on to the next phase, disputation.

Your Child's ABC Record

Adversity:

Belief:

Consequences:

Adversity:

Belief:

Consequences:

Adversity:

Belief:

Consequences:

Adversity:

Belief:

Consequences:

Adversity:

Belief:

Consequences:

ABCDE for Your Child

DISPUTATION for children is the same process as disputation for adults. Once your child grasps the ABC link, you can explain the disputation–energization link. Set aside forty minutes; begin by reviewing the ABC link. Use two of the child's own examples from his ABC record to review. Explain to your child that just because he has those thoughts does not mean the thoughts are true. They can be disputed, just as if some other child, who hated him, said those things about him.

Taking one of his own examples, ask your child to imagine his worst enemy had said that about him. How would your child respond? When he gives one good response ask him to give another and another, until he can't think of any more. Now explain that he can dispute his own negative thoughts in just the same way he can dispute the accusations of others—but with better effect: When the negatives he says to himself are disputed, he will stop believing them, and will become more cheerful and able to do more.

Now you will need to use some examples and work each one through completely with your child. Here are four examples to use—two old ones and two new ones:

Adversity: My teacher, Mr. Minner, yelled at me in front of the whole class, and everybody laughed.

Belief: He hates me and now the whole class thinks I'm a jerk.

Consequences: I felt really sad and I wished that I could just disappear under my desk.

Disputation: Just because Mr. Minner yelled at me, it doesn't mean he hates me. Mr. Minner yells at just about everybody, and he told our class we were his favorite class. I guess I was goofing around a little, so I don't blame him for getting mad. Everyone in the class, well everyone except for maybe Linda but she's a goody-goody, but everybody else has been yelled at by Mr. Minner at *least* once, so I doubt they think I'm a jerk.

Energization: I still felt a little sad about being yelled at, but not nearly as much, and I didn't feel like disappearing under my desk anymore.

Reread the belief aloud. Ask your child to dispute it in his own words. Ask your child to explain how each point in his dispute works: How does realizing that Mr. Minner yells at everybody counteract "Mr. Minner hates me"?

Adversity: My best friend, Susan, told me Joannie was her new best friend and from now on she was going to sit with Joannie in the cafeteria and not me.

Belief: Susan doesn't like me anymore because I'm not cool enough. Joannie tells really funny jokes, and whenever I tell a joke *nobody* laughs. And Joannie has really cool clothes, and I dress like a dweeb.

I bet if I was more popular, Susan would still want to be best friends with me. Now I'm never going to have anybody to sit with at lunch, and everybody is going to know that Joannie is Susan's new best friend.

Consequences: I was really scared to go to lunch because I didn't want to get laughed at and have to eat by myself, so I pretended to have a stomachache, and I asked Miss Frankel to send me to the nurse. I also felt really ugly, and I wanted to change schools.

Disputation: Susan is really nice and all, but this isn't the first time she has told me she had a new best friend. I remember a while ago she told me that Connie was going to be her best friend and before she told me that Jacklyn was her new best friend. I don't think it matters how funny my jokes are, and it can't be my clothes because Susan and I bought the exact same outfits last time we went to the mall. I guess she just likes to keep switching best friends. Oh well, she's not my only friend; I can sit with Jessica and Latanya at lunch.

Energization: I wasn't as worried about who to eat with, and I didn't feel ugly anymore.

Reread the belief and the consequences out loud. Ask your child to dispute the belief in his own words. Prompt him if necessary. Ask him to explain how each of his points counters the belief: How does realizing that Susan picks a new best friend every few weeks provide evidence against "Susan doesn't like me anymore"? What is the evidence against "I dress like a dweeb"?

Adversity: Today in gym class Mr. Riley picked two kids to be captains for kickball, and the rest of us had to line up and get picked by one of the kids to be on their team. I was the third-to-last kid picked.

Belief: Chrissy and Seth hate me. They don't want me on their teams. Now everyone in the whole entire class thinks I'm a spaz, and no one is ever going to want me on their team again. I really am a spaz; no wonder no one wants to play with me.

Consequences: I felt so stupid and I almost started crying, but I knew if I did cry everyone would laugh at me even worse. So I just kinda stood by myself and prayed the ball wouldn't come to me.

Disputation: The truth is I'm really not so good at sports. But calling myself a spaz only makes me feel worse about it. So I'm not so good at gym, there are other things I'm the best at. Like whenever the teacher tells us to break up into study groups, all the kids want to be in my group. And the essay I wrote about the American Revolution won first prize. I don't think Chrissy and Seth really hate me. They just wanted to have the best kickball players on their team. It's not like they are ever mean to me or anything. Oh well, some kids are good at gym and some kids are good at other things. I just happen to be good at other things like math and reading and social studies.

Energization: After I said those things to myself I felt a lot better. I still wish I was good at *everything*, and I still hate being the last to be picked for teams, but at least I know that in some things I'm the first to be picked and that Chrissy and Seth don't hate me.

Ask your child to do the disputation in his own words and to explain in his own words all the evidence against "Chrissy and Seth hate me." What other evidence might he have looked for to counter this belief?

Adversity: Yesterday was my brother's birthday and my mom and stepdad gave him all sorts of toys and a huge cake and they didn't even look at me.

Belief: Temple has always been their favorite. Whatever Temple wants, Temple gets. They don't even know I exist. I know why they like him better than me—because he gets better grades than me, and on his report card his teacher said he was "super" and on my report card Ms. Crisanti said my penmanship "needs improvement."

Consequences: I felt really sad and lonely, and I was scared that my mom was going to tell me she didn't want me around anymore.

Disputation: Of course Mom and Troy are giving Temple all sorts of toys and things—it's his birthday. When it was my birthday, they gave me lots of presents too. They may be paying more attention to him today, but that doesn't mean they like him better. They're just trying to make him feel special because it's his birthday. I guess I do wish my teacher called me "super" like Temple's teacher did, but my teacher said good things about me under Class Participation and also Science. Anyway, Mom and Troy always say they don't compare my grades to Temple's, that they compare us only to ourselves, and that as long as we try our hardest they will be happy.

Energization: I wasn't scared my mom was going to tell me to leave anymore, and I didn't feel so bad about the attention Temple was getting because I know when *my* birthday comes around again, he'll be feeling the same way.

When your child has the hang of the examples, you can end the session. The next night, hold another forty-minute session. Begin by reviewing the link between disputation and energization, using the example he did best with during the last session.

Now it's his turn. Turn back to his own ABC record. Take each of the five instances and get him to dispute the beliefs. Help him by using the evidence, alternatives, implications, and usefulness techniques, but it is not necessary to teach him these four categories. Just use them to teach him.

Then give him his assignment: Once a day for the next five days, he is actually to dispute a negative belief that occurs in his life. Each evening you and he will write it down and review it. At the end of each session, prime him by reminding him of various adversities he is likely to run into the next day and how to use disputation with them.

Your Child's ABCDE Record

Adversity:

Belief:

Consequences:

Disputation:

Energization:

Adversity:

Belief:

Consequences:

Disputation:

Energization:

Adversity:

Belief:

Consequences:

Disputation:

Energization:

Adversity:

Belief:

Consequences:

Disputation:

Energization:

Adversity:

Belief: —

Consequences:

Disputation:

Energization:

Externalization of Voices for Your Child

THE FINAL EXERCISE to do with your child is the externalization of voices. This psychological technique takes advantage of the fact that we can examine and dispute criticisms about ourselves more easily when they issue from a neutral third party than we can when they come from a biased party. In this application, we are going to take the harsh, threatening things that run through your child's mind and put them into the mouth of a third party: a parent helping him practice, or a hand puppet.

With your child's help, you will provide the criticism, and he will respond. Ask him to help you by telling you what sort of criticisms you should make of him. Help him do that by going over his ABC record with him to extract criticisms that he frequently makes of himself.

Explain to him that this exercise will give him practice toward becoming an ace disputer. You will help by serving as the source of negative beliefs.

Remind him frequently that you don't believe these criticisms are true, and that you are using them only because these are thoughts he himself might often have. Be very careful: You are his parent, after all, and are saying things that, since they are based upon intimate knowledge of him, are bound to be close to the mark, possibly too close. The last thing you want to do is to express serious criticisms that your child will take to heart and be wounded by.

If your child is still young enough to enjoy puppets, one good way of putting some distance between you, as loving parent, and the more difficult criticisms is to play the "Mr. Puppet game." Use any hand puppet to do the talking. Here is how to introduce it:

"Everybody knows that sometimes kids say mean things about other kids. When other kids say mean, unfair things about *you*, you usually talk back to them and set them straight. That's the right thing to do. But you and I know, from the work we've been doing together on the ABC reports, that sometimes people say mean, unfair things about themselves. As a matter of fact, we even know that you sometimes say things about yourself that really are wrong. You've got to learn how to talk back to those unfair things that you sometimes say about yourself, right? Okay. Now we're going to use Mr. Puppet to teach you how to talk back to yourself. Mr. Puppet has read your ABC record. He knows what you say to yourself. But he's also a mean bully, and your job is to talk back to him, to show him that his criticisms are wrong and unfair."

Before you begin, read through these examples aloud so your child can see the sorts of beliefs to be countered and can observe some ace disputers in action. Use Mr. Puppet to make some of the criticisms.

Situation: Ken is in seventh grade. He is bused to a very good school in a middle-class neighborhood. Ken is a good student, he likes the school, and he has a great bunch of friends. Every day after school he and his friends decide whose house they are going to hang out at. Ken would love to invite them all back to his house but he is painfully ashamed of his parents and where he lives. One day someone suggests they go to Ken's house, and Ken becomes very embarrassed and tells them they can't go to his house because, he says, "My dad is a doctor and has his office in the house." Ken, feeling sad and ashamed because he has told his friends a lie, tells them he's not feeling well and heads home by himself.

Accusation (by Mom, but using Mr. Puppet, especially for the nastiest criticisms): You're such a liar [Mr. Puppet]. Your dad, a doctor? That's a joke. You'll never be able to have the gang over to your place. It's only a matter of time before one of them realizes no one has ever been to your house or met your parents.

Disputation: I really do wish my parents and my house were like Ricky's. I hate feeling ashamed of my parents and where I live. But I guess there's not much I can do about that. Anyway, I'm not the only one whose house we've never been to. Actually, most of the time we just go to Henry's since it's the closest.

Mom (sometimes speaking as Mr. Puppet) interrupts: They're going to find out that you live in a dump, that your father's a drunk, and that your mom is a maid. And when they do, there is no way they're going to want to hang out with you anymore. You'll be the laughing-stock of the entire school [Mr. Puppet]."

Disputation continues: I'd definitely feel like a jerk if the guys found out my dad is a bum, but I don't think they'd stop being my friends because of it. They're not hanging out with me because they think I'm some rich kid. I mean, if I found out Stewie's dad didn't have a job, I'd probably feel bad for Stewie but I wouldn't drop him. Gosh, I don't know what everyone else's parents do for a living or where they all live. For all I know, some of the guys' parents might be as bad off as mine. Oh well, I'm not going to invite the gang home with me any time soon, but I'm going to try to stop lying about things.

Read the accusations aloud again. Ask your child to dispute them now, in his own words. Interrupt with more accusations and have him dispute these.

Situation: Lynn is invited to a slumber party by a girl she really thinks is neat. When her mom drops her off, Lynn realizes Betsy's parents aren't home and that the girls are planning to drink some of her parents' liquor. Lynn feels really uncomfortable and pretends to be sick and calls her mom to come get her.

Accusation (by parent): If you didn't want to drink, at least you should have told the truth instead of pretending to be sick. But instead you took the easy way out. You don't have any guts [Mr. Puppet].

Disputation: I do too have guts. The *real* easy way would be to go with the gang and drink just because they were drinking. Faking being sick was smart because it got me out of the situation without being called names or being pressured.

Parent (as Mr. Puppet) interrupts: You're such a baby. The first time you get invited to hang out with Betsy, and what do you do? You go and wreck it by being a Goody Two-Shoes.

Disputation continues: I didn't wreck the slumber party. I wouldn't have had fun if I stayed because I would have been too scared Betsy's

parents would come home. Oh well, maybe Betsy wouldn't make such
a great friend.

Now read the accusation aloud again and have your child dispute it in
his own words. Interrupt if necessary. Can your child add anything to this
dispute to make it more convincing?

Situation: After much pleading, Anita's parents bought her the
puppy she's been wanting. But after only a few weeks, Anita has lost
interest in Hogan and has been very forgetful about feeding and walking him. Finally, Anita's parents tell her they are going to give Hogan
away unless Anita acts more responsibly. Anita screams, "You guys
are sooooo mean. You never wanted me to have a puppy in the first
place. You're just looking for an excuse to take him away from me!"
Accusation (by parent): You've got the meanest parents in the whole
world!
Disputation: Okay, I guess I don't have the meanest parents in the
world. They're okay. They did get me Hogan in the first place, and
for my birthday my dad took me and Deb into New York City for the
day. That was really great of him.
Parent (as Mr. Puppet) interrupts: He's your dog. They bought him
for you, and now they're trying to get rid of him. They just don't want
you to have any fun.
Disputation continues: Maybe the reason they're so mad is 'cause
I haven't been walking and feeding Hogan as much as I said I would.
I did tell them that if they let me get a puppy, I would take full
responsibility. But I didn't realize it would be this much work.
Maybe if I tried harder to walk him and feed him every day, they'd
be willing to help me a little. I guess I ought to talk to Mom and Dad
about this.

Reread the accusation aloud and ask your child to dispute it himself in
his own words.
Now do a few of your child's own criticisms of himself from his ABC
record, using Mr. Puppet. Afterward, praise him and then, if his attention
is still fresh, switch to this last example. In this example, three people are
all accusing themselves and all disputing their own accusations. It is therefore a somewhat complex example and better suited to children aged ten
and older. If you think your child is too young for it, omit it and turn to
the material that follows it.

Situation: Hope is fourteen years old, and her sister Meagan is fifteen. A few months ago their parents separated. Hope and Meagan live with their mother, but they see their father all day Sundays and on Thursday nights for dinner. Every Sunday the same pattern is followed. Their father picks them up at the house. Hope sits in the front of the car, Meagan sits in the back. Hope turns on the radio, her father turns it down. Their father asks, "How are things going?" Hope mutters "Fine" and turns up the radio. Meagan, hating the way Hope acts, takes responsibility for carrying the conversation. Finally, angry and frustrated, their father snaps off the radio, Hope mutters something sarcastic under her breath, and Meagan is silent.

Hope's Accusation: Okay, here we go again. Another fun-filled, action-packed Sunday. Dad thinks he can just waltz into our lives for one day and one dinner a week and everything is going to be swell. How can he ask "How are things going?" and expect me to be able to answer? Of course things aren't going well. He and Mom are separated, and I have to give up my Sundays to spend time with someone who I should be seeing every day. If he really cared about how I'm doing, he would call more often and not just spend time with me because it happens to be a particular day of the week.

Hope's Disputation: Sundays are such a drag. Maybe part of the reason they're so miserable is because we're all so tense. I mean, it shouldn't have to be this way. I guess I could try to relax a little and stop bothering Dad by turning up the radio real loud and giving one-word answers. Maybe Dad doesn't realize it's hard to respond to a question like that. Maybe he's just saying "How are things going?" the way my friends and I say "What's up?" I mean, granted it's not an ideal situation, but I'm lucky he lives close by and that we can see each other. Some of my friends whose parents have split up don't even get to see their fathers at all. I don't like spending every Sunday with him. Sometimes I want to hang out with my friends on Sunday. I'd like it better if we decided each week which day would suit us best. That way it wouldn't feel like another thing I *had* to do. I ought to tell him that. I really don't understand why he doesn't call us more, but I shouldn't automatically assume it's because he doesn't care. I can start calling him, after all, whenever I feel like talking, instead of waiting for him to call me. It bothers me that he doesn't call more often, but I guess it makes more sense to ask him why he doesn't call instead of jumping to conclusions. Maybe I'll bring some of this up later today.

Meagan's Accusation: Here we go again. We've been in the car for all of five minutes and already Dad and Hope are at it. I should be able to keep things running smoothly. What's wrong with me? All I needed to do was keep the conversation going and things would have been fine. If I can't do a simple thing like that, how are things ever going to be good again? I've really ruined things now.

Meagan's Disputation: Maybe I'm being a little too hard on myself. I mean, it does take two people to have a conversation. I can talk and talk until I'm blue in the face but if neither of them responds, then it won't do any good. I just want so desperately for things to be calm and easy again that I guess I'm trying to control things that just aren't possible for me to control. I can be relaxed and pleasant and talkative, but I can't make things be the same. This really stinks. Well, at least I know it isn't my fault that the two of them are bickering.

Dad's Accusation: What the hell is going on? Every Sunday it's the same thing. The second we're in the car, Hope flips on the radio and all but drowns out what I say. I just don't understand her. Doesn't she want to see me? I mean, I know the kids would rather their mother and I were still together, but they have to accept the way things are and make the best of it. Meagan is handling things fine. Why does Hope have to spoil things? The two of them probably think the separation is all my fault. They get to see their mother all day, every day, and instead of having a good time when we're together, I'm treated like a total stranger. I deserve to be treated better than that.

Dad's Disputation: Things really are rough right now. I have to try and slow down and think them through. First of all, Hope has never said she doesn't want to see me. Maybe the reason she's so hostile is because she's still really confused by the separation. I guess I'm forgetting they're just kids and the separation has really shaken up their whole world. It probably doesn't help to compare the way Hope is handling things to the way Meagan is. Meagan is older and she has always been the quieter one. Actually, I shouldn't assume that just because Meagan isn't hostile that she is totally fine with the way things are either. With Hope, at least I know she is upset. I really have no idea about what is going through Meagan's mind. Maybe part of the reason I get so angry so quickly is because I feel frustrated by the situation. I want things to be better, but it's difficult for me to talk about the separation with them. Well, I guess I'd better work at that, because they're just kids and it's my responsibility as their father to bring up the subject, even if it is painful to talk about.

Now continue with some more of your child's ABCs. If you're using Mr. Puppet, use him to read each accusation aloud to your child. Ask your child to take the role of the accused and dispute it in his own words.

. . .

DISPUTING YOUR OWN negative thoughts is a life skill that any child can learn. Like any acquired skill, it will seem a little awkward when first employed. Remember how unnatural the backhand grip felt when you first learned it in tennis. Disputing your own thoughts is like that. But with practice the backhand became natural, and so will disputing your own thoughts. The earlier in life this skill is learned the more grief will be avoided.

When the skills of optimism are learned early, they become fundamental. Like habits of cleanliness and kindness, they are so rewarding in themselves that practice is automatic rather than a burden. But optimism is a habit much more important than cleanliness, particularly if your child scored poorly on the depression test or the CASQ, or if you and your spouse are not getting along. In these cases, a child is at high risk for depression and lowered achievement in school if he does not acquire these skills. If he does acquire them, he may become all but immune from the protracted feelings of hopelessness and helplessness that otherwise could afflict him.

14

The Optimistic Organization

THINK ABOUT the most difficult thing you encounter at work, that time when your job gets really discouraging and you feel you have run up against a brick wall. What do you do when you hit that wall?

Steve Prosper is a life-insurance salesman, and between five-thirty and nine-thirty most evenings he has to make cold calls—phone calls to people he has never met. He hates this part of his job. He gets the names of the people to call from a list of all the couples in Chicago who have had babies recently. A typical evening goes like this:

The first prospect hangs up on him after fifteen seconds. The second one tells him she already has all the insurance she needs. The third one is lonely: He lets Steve talk and gets Steve to listen at length to his version of last night's Cubs game. After thirty minutes, Steve finds out the man is on welfare and has no interest in buying insurance. The fourth hangs up with "Stop bothering me, you creep." At this point, Steve hits the wall. He stares gloomily at the phone, at the list, at the phone. He pages through the newspaper. He stares at the phone some more. He pours himself a Coors and flips on the TV.

Unfortunately for Steve, he has been in direct competition with Naomi Sargent. She has the same list of calls and the same tough job, for another company. But when she meets the wall she doesn't get discouraged. She is able to make the fifth and sixth and tenth calls briskly. On the twelfth call, she gets an appointment. When Steve finally reaches this client three nights later, the man politely tells Steve that his insurance needs have already been taken care of.

Naomi is a success and Steve is courting failure, so it should be no surprise that Naomi is optimistic and enthusiastic about her job, and that Steve is pessimistic and depressed about his. Common sense tells us that success makes people optimistic. But in this book we have seen repeatedly that the arrow goes in the opposite direction as well. Optimistic people become successes. In school, on the playing field, and at work, the optimistic individual makes the most of his talent.

And we now know why. The optimistic individual perseveres. In the face of routine setbacks, and even of major failures, he persists. When he comes to the wall at work, he keeps going, particularly at the crucial juncture when his competition is also hitting the wall and starting to wilt.

Naomi operates on this principle. She knows that in her business only one call out of ten—on the average—results in a face-to-face appointment, and that in turn only one out of three of these appointments results in a sale. Her whole psychology is geared to getting herself over the cold-calling wall, and she has some optimism-supporting techniques she uses on herself to maintain that psychology. These are techniques Steve does not have.

Optimism helps at work, and not just in competitive jobs. It can help every time your work gets very hard. It can make the difference between getting the job done well or poorly or not at all. Take a job that is not at all competitive—writing. Writing this chapter, for example.

Unlike Naomi Sargent, I was not born an optimist. I've had to learn (and sometimes invent) techniques for getting over the wall. The hardest part of writing, for me, is supplying examples, juicy examples that put flesh on the abstract principles I write about. Writing about the principles has always come easily, since I've spent twenty-five years doing research on them. But for many years, when I got to the parts that needed examples, I would get a headache, which told me I'd hit the wall. I'd fidget. I'd do anything other than write: make phone calls; analyze data sheets. If the wall was really high, I'd go out and play bridge. This pattern could go on for hours, even days. Not only would I not get my work done, but as the hours turned to days I'd be stricken with guilt and depression.

All this has changed. I still hit the wall more often than I'd like, but I've found some techniques that always help me. In this chapter you will learn two of these techniques, which you can use at work: listening in on your own internal dialogue and disputing your negative dialogue.

Everyone has his own point of discouragement, his own wall. What you do when you hit this wall can spell the difference between helplessness and mastery, between failure and success. Failure, once the wall looms, does not stem from laziness, although not getting over the wall is commonly mistaken for laziness. Nor is it lack of talent, or lack of imagination. It's simply ignorance of some very important skills not taught in any school.

In your work, when do you hit the wall? Bring to mind the recurrent situation in your work that most blocks and discourages you. It could be making phone calls to clients. It could be writing dialogue. It could be arguing with a customer about a bill. It could be closing a deal. It could be doing the careful profit-and-loss calculations before making a purchase. It could be seeing that glazed look of apathy in your students' eyes. It could be exerting patience when a slow colleague takes longer than you think he should. It could be trying to motivate an unmotivated employee whom you supervise. Hold on to your own example, since much of this chapter will be devoted to getting you over your own personal wall at work.

The Three Edges of Optimism

LEARNED OPTIMISM gets people over the wall—and not just as individuals. The explanatory style of a whole team, as we saw in chapter nine, can produce victory or defeat. And organizations, large and small, need optimism; they need people with talent and drive who are also optimistic. An organization filled with optimistic individuals—or studded with optimistic individuals in the crucial niches—has an edge. There are three ways an organization can use the optimism edge.

The first, selection, was the subject of chapter six, "Success at Work." Your company can select optimistic individuals to fill its ranks, as Metropolitan Life did. Optimistic individuals produce more, particularly under pressure, than do pessimists. Talent and drive alone are not enough. As we have seen, without an unshakable belief that you can succeed, high talent and relentless drive can come to nothing. Over fifty companies now use optimism questionnaires in their selection procedures to identify people who have not just talent and drive but also the optimism needed for success. This ability to select for optimism has been proven especially important in jobs that have high recruitment and training costs and a high turnover rate. Selecting for optimism reduces costly manpower waste and improves the productivity and job satisfaction of the whole team. But the use of optimism does not end here.

The second way a company can use optimism is placement. Strong optimism is an obvious virtue for "high-defeat" and "high-stress" jobs that require initiative, persistence, and bold dreaming. Just as obviously, extreme pessimism is an asset to no one. But some jobs call for a large dollop of pessimism. As we saw in chapter six, there is considerable evidence that pessimists see reality more accurately than optimists do. Every successful company, every successful life for that matter, requires both accurate appreciation of reality and the ability to dream beyond the present reality. These two qualities of mind, it turns out, do not always come in the same body, and few people have the skills you will learn in this chapter, which allow you to use optimism or pessimism when you need them. In any large company, different individuals will perform different tasks. How can you place the right people in the right jobs?

In order to decide what psychological profile best fits a particular job, you must ask two questions about the job. First, to what extent does the job require persistence and initiative and bring with it frequent frustration, rejection, and even defeat? These are the fields in which optimistic explanatory style is a must:

- Sales
- Brokering
- Public relations
- Presenting and Acting
- Fund-raising
- Creative jobs
- Highly competitive jobs
- High-burnout jobs

At the other extreme are the jobs that require a pronounced sense of reality. These are usually "low-defeat" jobs, jobs with low turnover, jobs that call for specific technical skills in low-pressure settings. These jobs call for reflective realists rather than the hard-charging individuals who populate the ranks of the "million dollar–seller" clubs. There are also more senior managerial and professional jobs that require an extremely keen sense of reality, jobs where optimism must be restrained and where mild pessimism can be a virtue. These jobs need people who know when *not* to charge ahead, and when to err on the side of caution. Mild pessimists do well in these fields:

- Design and safety engineering
- Technical and cost estimating
- Contract negotiation
- Financial control and accounting
- Law (but not litigation)
- Business administration
- Statistics
- Technical writing

- Quality control
- Personnel and industrial-relations management

So, with the exception of extreme pessimism, the full range of optimism finds its place in an optimistic organization. It is crucial to learn an applicant's optimism level and fit him into the niche in which he can be most effective.

But every organization has in its ranks individuals who are too pessimistic for the jobs they hold. These individuals often have the right talent and drive for their jobs, and it would be costly and even inhumane to replace them. Happily, these people can learn optimism.

Learning Optimism

THE THIRD EDGE that optimism gives an organization is the main topic of this chapter: learning optimism at work.

Only two groups of people don't need to learn optimism in their work settings: those who were lucky enough to be born optimists and those who occupy the low-defeat jobs I just listed. The rest of us can benefit, some of us greatly, from learning optimism.

Take Steve Prosper. He liked being an insurance agent. He loved the independence: No one looked over his shoulder, he set his own hours, he took time off whenever he wanted. He had excellent aptitude for selling insurance, and he was strongly motivated. Only one thing stood between him and striking success: getting over the wall.

Steve took a four-day course on optimism. The two leading cognitive therapists I mentioned in chapter twelve, Dr. Steven Hollon of Vanderbilt University and Dr. Arthur Freeman of the University of Medicine and Dentistry of New Jersey, and I developed this course for Foresight, Inc. Foresight is a Falls Church, Virginia, company headed by Dr. Dan Oran; it administers our optimism questionnaires to industry and gives workshops for optimism training at work. Unlike most courses for sales agents, which teach you what to say to your clients, this course and the exercises that follow focus on what you say to yourself when your client says no. That is a radical difference. Steve Prosper, for example, learned a set of skills that has made all the difference to him. This chapter is designed to teach you the most basic of these skills as they apply to your line of work.

Changing Your Internal Dialogue at Work: The ABCDE Model

WHAT YOU THINK when things go wrong, what you say to yourself when you come to the wall, will determine what happens next: whether you give up or whether you start to make things go right. Our schema for thinking about this is Albert Ellis's ABCDE model, which will be familiar to you from chapter twelve.

ABC

A STANDS for adversity. For some people adversity is an end point. They say to themselves, "What's the use? I can't go on. Why continue doing this? I'm just screwing up." And they give up. For others adversity is just the beginning of a challenging sequence that often leads to success. Adversity can be almost anything: pressure to earn more money, feelings of rejection, criticism by your boss, a bored yawn from a student, a spouse who refuses to let you out of his or her sight.

Encountering adversity always sets off your beliefs, your explanation and interpretation of why things have gone wrong. The first thing we do when we encounter adversity is try to explain it. As we have seen throughout this book, the explanations with which we interpret adversity to ourselves critically affect what we do next.

What are the consequences of the different beliefs that come into play? When our explanatory beliefs take the form of personal, permanent, and pervasive factors ("It's my fault . . . it's always going to be like this . . . it's going to affect everything I do"), we give up and become paralyzed. When our explanations take the opposite form, we become energized. The consequences of our beliefs are not just actions but feelings as well.

I want you now to identify some ABCs. Some of these examples will apply to your life, others will not. In each of these examples, I'll provide the adversity, along with either the belief or the consequence. You supply the missing component in a way that fits sensibly with the ABC model.

Identifying ABCs

1. A. Someone cuts you off while you are driving.

   B. You think _____ .

   C. You get angry and honk your horn.

2. A. You lose an easy sale.

   B. You think, "I'm a lousy sales agent."

   C. You feel (or do) _____ .

3. A. Your boss criticizes you.

   B. You think _____ .

   C. You're depressed all day.

4. A. Your boss criticizes you.

   B. You think _____ .

   C. You feel pretty good about what happened.

5. A. Your spouse asks that you be home every evening.

   B. You think _____ .

   C. You feel angry and frustrated.

6. A. Your spouse asks that you be home in the evenings.

   B. You think _____ .

   C. You feel sad.

For the next three, imagine you're a sales agent:

7. A. You haven't gotten an appointment all week.

   B. You think, "I never do anything right."

   C. You feel (or do) _____

8. A. You haven't gotten an appointment all week.

 B. You think, "I had a good week last week."

 C. You feel (or do) _____ .

9. A. You haven't gotten an appointment all week.

 B. You think, "My boss gave me lousy leads this week."

 C. You feel (or do) _____ .

The point of this exercise is to bring home how the ways you think about adversity change how you then feel and what you then do.

In the first example, you probably filled in something like "What a jerk," "What's he in such a hurry about?" or "What an inconsiderate bastard." In the fifth example, you might have said "She never thinks about my needs." When our explanation of adversity is external and when we believe that the adversity is a trespass against our domain, we feel anger.

In the second example, you should feel sad, deflated, listless. The explanation "I'm a lousy sales agent" is personal, permanent, and pervasive— the recipe for depression. Similarly, in the sixth example, when your spouse's asking you to stay home every every evening made you sad, you probably said something like "I'm inconsiderate" or "I'm a lousy husband."

What intervening explanation would get you depressed all day when your boss criticizes you in number 3? Something permanent, pervasive, and personal: "I don't know how to write well" or "I'm always screwing up." But how did you change the explanation to come out feeling pretty good after your boss criticized you? What you had to do was, first, to make the reason for the criticism something you could change, something unstable: "I know where I can get help at effective writing" or "I should have proofread it." Second, you had to make your thinking less pervasive: "It was only this report that was poor." Third, you had to shift the blame away from yourself: "My boss was in a terrible mood." "There was too much time pressure on me." If you can habitually make these three moves at the point of belief, adversity can become a springboard to success.

In the last three examples, you can see that if you thought, as in number 7, "I never do anything right"—permanent, pervasive, personal—you felt sad and did nothing. If you thought "I had a good week last week," as in number 8, you held sadness at bay and kept at the job. If you thought, as in number 9, "My boss gave me lousy leads this week"—temporary, local, and external—you would be annoyed at your boss but would also hope that next week would be better.

ABC*DE*

THE ABC LINK, between what you believe about adversity and what you then feel, should be clear to you. If you still need convincing, do the ABC record exercises in chapter twelve (pages 213–17) using ABCs from your workday. Each time you find yourself suddenly deflated, sad, angry, anxious, or frustrated at work, write down the thought that came right before. You will find these thoughts look much like your answers to the ABC exercises.

This means that if you can change B, your beliefs and explanations about adversity, C will change too. You can change from a passive, sad, or angry response to adversity to an invigorated, cheerful response. This depends crucially on D.

D stands for disputing your beliefs.

Disputing Your Beliefs

LET ME REUSE an earlier example. If a drunk, reeling in the street, shouted at you, "You always screw up! You have no talent! Quit your job!" how would you react? You wouldn't take the accusations very seriously. You'd either dismiss them out of hand and go about your business or, if they happened to strike a nerve, you'd dispute them to yourself: "I just wrote a report that turned around our red-ink situation"; "I was just promoted to vice-president"; "Anyway, he doesn't know the first thing about me. He's just a drunk."

But what happens when you shout equally damning things to yourself? You believe them. You do not dispute them. After all, if *you* say them about yourself, you reason, they must be indisputably true.

That is a bad mistake.

As we saw in previous chapters, the things we say to ourselves when trouble strikes can be just as baseless as the ravings of a drunk on the street. Our reflexive explanations are usually not based on reality. They are bad habits that emerge from the mists of the past, from ancient conflicts, from parental strictures, from an influential teacher's unquestioned criticisms, from a lover's jealousy. But because they seem to issue from ourselves—could there be a source with higher credibility?—we treat them like royalty. We let them run our lives without even shouting back at them.

Much of the skill of dealing with setbacks, of getting over the wall, consists of learning how to dispute your own first thoughts in reaction to a setback. So ingrained are these habits of explanation that learning to dispute them effectively takes a good bit of practice. To learn how to dispute your automatic thoughts, you first have to learn to listen to your own internal dialogue at work. Here's a game that will teach you how.

The Wall-Vaulting Game

The focus of this game is your own personal wall, the part of your work that most makes you want to give the whole thing up. In our workshops with insurance-sales agents this part is easy to isolate. It's cold calling, making calls to total strangers to get personal appointments. You have to keep plugging at the cold calls. Agents who are easily discouraged, who can't bounce back briskly from rejection, fall by the wayside. Those who can make their twenty calls every evening succeed.

We use cold calling as a tool to get agents to identify the ABCs in their work. They bring their cold-calling list to the workshop. For homework, the first evening, they make ten cold calls. After each one, they write down the adversity, the belief, and the consequences. Here's what they hear themselves saying:

Adversity: About to start making cold calls.
Belief: I hate doing this. I shouldn't have to make these calls.
Consequences: I felt angry and tense and had a hard time picking up the receiver.

Adversity: My first call of the night hung up on me.
Belief: That was rude. He didn't even given me a chance. He shouldn't treat me like that.
Consequences: I felt sore and had to take a break before making my second call.

Adversity: My first call of the night hung up on me.

Belief: Oh well, that's one no out of the way. It brings me closer to the yes.

Consequences: I felt relaxed and energetic.

Adversity: I kept the woman on the phone for close to ten minutes and then she told me she didn't want to set an appointment.

Belief: I really blew that one. What's wrong with me? If I can't get an appointment from a call like that, I must be really lousy.

Consequences: I felt dejected and frustrated and apprehensive about the next call.

You can see that when adversity is followed by permanent, pervasive, and personal explanations ("I must be really lousy"), dejection and giving up follow. When adversity is followed by the opposite kinds of explanations ("That's one 'no' out of the way"), the consequences are energy and good cheer.

Now it's your turn to play the wall-vaulting game. Tune in on your internal dialogue when you face your own wall at work, and see how these beliefs can determine what you then feel and what you do next. The game has three variants. Pick the one that fits your work.

1. If your work involves making phone calls to strangers, take out your list. Make five calls. After each one, write down the adversity, then the thoughts that went through your head and how you felt and what you then did. Record this below, on page 266.

2. If your work does not involve cold calling, I want you to identify a wall you face each day at work, so that you can carry out your personal ABCs while you are at work. If you're stuck, here are a couple of examples to help you do this.

One of the walls in teaching is dealing with the apathy of the students; it just feels as if no matter what I do, no matter how creative I try to be, there is a group of kids who just don't want to learn. I hate the feeling of cramming knowledge down their throats. Knowing that I'm not going to reach these kids makes it harder and harder for me to be creative because in the back of my head I am thinking, "What's the use?"

In nursing one of the major things that leads to burnout is the treatment many nurses get from both above and below. Patients are often demanding, hostile, and cranky, and doctors are often demanding, hostile and cranky. This can leave the nurse feeling overworked and underappreciated. A typical complaint is this: "I tell myself at the beginning of each shift that I am not going to let the pressure get to me. Of course the patients are demanding and cranky—they are sick in a hospital. Who wouldn't be? It's not so easy to explain away the treatment I get from the doctors. Instead of treating me like a teammate they act as if the work I do isn't as important and I'm not as intelligent. After a while, no matter how many times I pump myself up in the morning, it gets to me and I start to dread my next shift. I start feeling lethargic and moody, and I'm constantly counting the hours until I'm off."

Now identify your own daily wall at work. Next week go right up to that wall every day. Except this time, listen to what you are saying to yourself. As soon as you get a couple of free minutes, write down the adversity, your beliefs, and the consequences. Record them in the spaces provided below (pages 266–7).

3. The third variant is for those of you who face your wall less than once a day. Being unable to get started on major reports or projects is a wall that usually comes up only a few times a year. Another job in which the wall usually looms less than once a day is supervising other people.

One of the walls managers face is to keep the level of incentive high among the people they supervise. As one manager put it: "Managing people can be very frustrating at times . . . at least periodically. The hardest part, the part I really dread, is to keep people motivated and productive. I try to be positive, I try to lead by example, but sometimes I just don't understand what is going through their heads. And then of course, after I have gotten on someone's case, I end up feeling like such a nag. I don't want to be too easy on them, I don't want to be too tough on them, so in the end I feel as if I'm totally ineffectual. As I said, it gets really frustrating."

If you're in this third category, take twenty minutes out this evening at home and go to a quiet room. Imagine as vividly as you can the situation that constitutes your wall. Use props if you have them. If your wall is writing reports, sit down in front of a blank sheet of paper and get into a fantasy about the report's being due tomorrow. Allow yourself to feel the desperation; work up a sweat. If you're a manager, conjure up the face of your surliest employee. Play out the dialogue to yourself. Write down the adversity, your beliefs, and the consequences. Do this five times, trying a different twist in the adversity each time. Record it in the blanks provided below.

Adversity:

Belief:

Consequences:

Adversity:

Belief:

Consequences:

Adversity:

Belief:

Consequences:

Adversity:

Belief:

Consequences:

Adversity:

Belief:

Consequences:

When you have recorded your five ABC episodes, look over your beliefs carefully. You will see that in your own internal dialogue, pessimistic explanations set off passivity and dejection, whereas optimistic explanations set off activity. So the next step is to change those habitual pessimistic explanations that adversity sets off. To do this you must now play the second round of the game: disputation.

Disputation

The second round of the wall-vaulting game consists of repeating what you just did, but now disputing your pessimistic explanations each time you make them. Fortunately, mastering the skill of disputing doesn't take much training. You do this daily, either in reality or in your head, when you disagree with what others say and do. You have had a lifetime of practice disputing other people's negative beliefs. But what you have missed is treating your own negative beliefs as if they emanated not from yourself but from a jealous coworker or a misguided student or your worst enemy.

At home tonight, choose the same scenario you used in the first phase—get out your cold-calling list or, in a quiet room, imagine yourself up against your wall at work. Now, for each of the five encounters with adversity, focus on your own negative thoughts and then dispute them. After each single encounter is over, write down the ABC along with your disputation (D) and the energization and feelings that ensue (E). Before you start, read these examples to help your own disputation:

Cold Calling:

Adversity: The person hung up on me after listening to me for a long time.

Belief: He should have let me finish since he let me get that far. I must have done something wrong to blow it so late in the game.

Consequences: I felt angry at the prospect and real disappointed in myself. I wanted to throw in the towel for the evening.

Disputation: Maybe he was in the middle of something and was feeling antsy to get back to it. I must have been doing pretty well if I kept a busy person on the phone for as long as I did. I can't control what he does. All I can do is present my material as well as I can and hope the person on the other end has an open mind and the time to listen. Obviously, he didn't. That's his loss.

Energization: I was ready to go on to the next call. I was happy with my presentation and confident my work would pay off in the long run.

Adversity: The man was interested but he wouldn't make an appointment until I first talked to his wife.

Belief: What a waste of time. Now I have to take time away from other possibilities to resell this couple. Why can't he just make a decision for himself?

Consequences: I felt very impatient and a bit angry also.

Disputation: Hey, at least it wasn't a no. It wasn't a waste of time because it may very well turn into an appointment. If I sold him, I can sell his wife. So I'm halfway there.

Energization: I felt confident and optimistic that with a little more work I could have a sale.

Adversity: I made my twentieth call and had only six contacts.

Belief: This is a waste of time. I don't have the energy to succeed. I'm so disorganized.

Consequences: I felt frustrated, tired, depressed, and overwhelmed.

Disputation: Six contacts in an hour isn't bad. It's only seven-thirty and I can still do another hour and a half of calling. I can take ten minutes now to get better organized so I can make more calls this hour than I did in the last hour.

Energization: I felt less overwhelmed and depressed and I had more energy, since I'd planned out a course of action.

Adversity: My husband phoned me when I was right in the middle of doing my calling.

Belief: Why is he calling me now? He's throwing off my pace and wasting my time.

Consequences: I felt irritated and I was curt with him on the phone.

Disputation: Don't be so hard on him. He didn't realize his call would distract me. He probably thought it would be a nice break. It's sweet that he thinks about me when we're apart. I'm glad I have such a kind and supportive husband.

Energization: I relaxed and felt good about my husband and our marriage. I called him back and explained why I had been curt.

Adversity: I made forty calls and got no appointments.

Belief: I'm not getting anywhere. This is stupid. I'm not getting any results. It's a total waste of effort and time.

Consequences: I felt frustrated and angry about having spent my time doing this.

Disputation: It was only one night and only forty calls. Everyone has difficulty with cold calling, and nights like this are going to happen from time to time. Anyway, it was a learning experience: I got to practice my presentation. So tomorrow night I'll be even better.

Energization: I still felt a little frustrated but not nearly as much, and I didn't feel angry anymore. Tomorrow night I'll get some results.

Teaching:

Adversity: I haven't been able to break through the apathy some of my students feel toward learning.

Belief: Why can't I reach these kids? If I were more dynamic or more creative or more intelligent, I would be able to excite them about learning. If I can't reach the kids who need the most help, then I am not doing my job. I must not be cut out for teaching.

Consequences: I don't feel like being creative. I have little energy and I feel depressed and dejected.

Disputation: It doesn't make sense to base my worth as a teacher on a small percentage of my students. The truth is that I do excite the majority of my students, and I spend a great deal of time planning lessons that are creative and allow the students as much individualization as possible. At the end of the term, when I have a little more time, I can organize a meeting with other teachers in the school who face this same problem. Maybe as a group we will be able to come up with some ideas that will help us reach the apathetic students.

Energization: I feel better about the work I do as a teacher and hopeful that new ideas can be generated through a discussion with other teachers.

Nursing:

Adversity: I have six hours left of my shift, we're short-staffed, and a doctor just told me I was too slow.

Belief: She's right. I *am* too slow. I should be able to keep things running smoothly at all times, and I don't. The other nurses would be able to keep up. I guess I'm just not right for the job.

Consequences: I feel really down on myself, and I feel guilty that I am not doing as good a job as I ought to. I feel like running out of the hospital in the middle of my shift.

Disputation: It would be ideal if things ran smoothly all the time, but that's not realistic, especially around a hospital. Anyway, it is not my responsibility alone to make sure everything is taken care of. I'm doing just as well as the other nurses on the shift. I may have been a little slower than usual, but we're short-staffed today so I am taking on extra responsibility, which means things take a little longer. I can feel good about taking on the extra work instead of feeling bad about the slight inconvenience it causes the doctor.

Energization: I feel a lot better about myself and much, much less guilty about any inconvenience to the doctor. The prospect of six more hours doesn't seem so overwhelming.

Management:

Adversity: My section is falling behind its production schedules and my boss is beginning to complain about it.

Belief: Why can't the crew I've got do what they're supposed to do? I've shown them all they need to know, but they keep screwing it up. Why can't I get them to work better? That's why I was hired. Now my boss is complaining. He thinks it's all my fault and I'm a lousy manager.

Consequences: I feel really angry and annoyed at my whole section, and I want to call them all into my office and bawl them out. I also feel bad about myself and nervous about my job. I want to avoid my boss until we get back on schedule.

Disputation: First of all, it is true my section is falling behind. But I've got several new recruits, and it will take time for them to learn to do it right and work up to speed. I've had this before, but never with as many new guys. I've given them all the right instruction, but it still takes time. Some are quicker than others, and one is coming along really fast. I haven't done anything that's basically wrong. Also, the old hands are performing well, so it's just a matter of patience, and especially attention to the recruits. I've explained all this to my boss, and he knows it's true—he hasn't told me to try anything different. I'll bet he's under pressure from the production managers. They're not going to let up, so neither is he. I'll talk to him again and ask him directly if there's anything I've missed. At the same time, I'll keep working on the crew, motivating, encouraging, and pushing, and see if there's any way I can get the old hands to help.

Energization: I no longer feel like bawling them out. In fact, now I can discuss the situation with them calmly and with an open mind. I feel a lot less nervous about my job because I know I have a good record with the company. Also, instead of avoiding my boss, I will meet with him to give him a progress report and answer any questions he may have.

Now it's your turn to record your disputations. Do it five times.

Adversity:

Belief:

Consequences:

Disputation:

Energization:

Adversity:

Belief:

Consequences:

Disputation:

Energization:

Adversity:

Belief:

Consequences:

Disputation:

Energization:

Adversity:

Belief:

Consequences:

Disputation:

Energization:

Adversity:

Belief:

Consequences:

Disputation:

Energization:

You should have found that when you began to dispute your negative beliefs, the consequences changed from dejection and lethargy to invigoration and feeling better.

At this point, you probably need some practice in disputing your automatic pessimistic thoughts. We will now turn to an exercise that will make you better at quashing them.

Externalization of Voices

YOUR BOSS FROWNS at you when you walk into the office. You think, "I must have messed up that report. He might fire me." Feeling dejected, you slip into your office and stare glumly at your report. You can't even bring yourself to reread it. You spend the next minutes brooding and your mood gets bleaker.

When something like this happens to you, you must break off your bleak mood by disputing your pessimistic explanations of the boss's frown or whatever it was that caused the mood. As we saw in the last two chapters, there are usually four tacks to take in effective disputation with yourself.

- Evidence?
- Alternatives?
- Implications?
- Usefulness?

Evidence:

Shift to the role of detective and ask yourself, "What is the evidence both for and against the belief?"

For example: On what grounds did you think it was your report that made your boss frown? Do you know of anything wrong with your report, something that might have displeased him? Did it take all the obvious factors into account? Did its conclusion follow from the premises? Has your boss even read the report yet, or is it still lying on his secretary's desk?

Often you will find you have catastrophized, jumped to the worst possible conclusion in the absence of solid evidence—sometimes just on the thinnest hunch.

Alternatives:

Is there any other way to look at the adversity?

For example: What are some alternative explanations for the boss's frown? These may not come readily to mind, because your automatic pessimistic explanations, unchallenged for years, can be very ingrained. You must consciously search for any plausible alternative explanations. "Is he just in one of his black moods?" "Was he up most of the night preparing for the IRS audit?" "If it *was* me, was it my report or my wearing a loud bow tie?"

Once you generate several alternatives, you can go back to the first step and scan the evidence for each one.

Implications:

What if your dark explanation is right? Is it the end of the world?

Suppose it *was* your report that angered the boss. Does this mean he's going to fire you? It's your first slip-up, after all. If he is starting to form a negative impression of your ability, what can you do to turn it around? Again go back to step one: What is the evidence that he would fire you even if he didn't like your report?

Just because a situation is unfavorable doesn't mean it's necessarily a catastrophe. Master the important skill of decatastrophizing by examining the situation's most realistic implications.

Usefulness:

Sometimes the accuracy of your explanation is not what really matters. What matters is whether thinking about the problem *now* will do any good.

If you were a tightrope walker, it would be a poor idea, while you were up on the high wire, to focus on what might happen if you fell. It might be very useful to think about this some other time, but not when you need all your wits about you just to keep from falling.

Will brooding about the worst implications of the boss's frown just get you into hotter water now? Or will brooding throw off the important presentation you are scheduled to make this afternoon? If so, you should distract yourself from your negative beliefs.

There are three reliable ways to accomplish that. Each is simplistic but effective:

• Do something physically distracting, like snapping a rubber band on your wrist, or dashing cold water on your face while saying "Stop!" to yourself.

• Schedule a specific time for thinking things over. It might be a half hour this evening or any other time that fits into your day. When you find yourself ruminating, you can say to yourself, "Stop! I'll tackle that at seven-thirty this evening." The tormenting process of worrisome thoughts going round and round, coming back again and again, has a purpose: to make sure we don't forget or neglect an issue we should deal with. But if we set aside a specific time for thinking the issue over, we undercut the very reason for brooding now, so the brooding is no longer psychologically necessary.

• Write the troublesome thoughts down at the moment they occur. Now you can return to them not helplessly but deliberately, when the time is right for you. Like the second technique for distraction, this one also robs brooding of its very reason for existence.

ARMED WITH THESE four ways of disputing your pessimistic explanations—evidence? alternatives? implications? usefulness?—you now can get some practice at *externalizing* your disputation: bringing your thoughts out into the open where they can be dealt with. Here's a technique that has worked well in optimism seminars: Choose a trusted coworker to practice with. If there is no one appropriate from work, your spouse or any patient friend will do fine. Their job is to throw at you the sort of pessimistic criticism that you heap on yourself. Go over your ABCDE record with them, so they can see what kinds of criticisms you routinely attack yourself with. Your job is to sit on the hot seat and dispute the criticisms out loud, to beat them down. Use every argument you can think of. Here are some examples to study before you start.

Coworker (attacking you the way you attack yourself): The manager didn't make eye contact with you when you spoke. She must not think what you have to say is important.

You (on the hot seat): It's true that most of the time while I was speaking my manager wasn't looking at me. It didn't seem as if she was listening very attentively to my ideas [evidence].

This doesn't mean, however, that my ideas aren't important or that she thinks they're not important [implications]. Maybe she's got a lot on her mind right now [alternatives]. I know in the past she has listened to my ideas and has even sought my opinion on a couple of occasions [evidence].

Coworker (interrupting): You must be stupid.

You (continuing the dispute): Even if she didn't like my ideas, that doesn't mean I'm stupid [implications]. I have a good head on my shoulders and I usually contribute something intelligent to most conversations [evidence]. In the future, I'll be sure to ask whether it's a good time to share some ideas with her before I begin speaking [implications]. This way I won't make the mistake of confusing her distraction for lack of interest in my ideas [alternatives].

Fellow teacher (making criticisms like the ones you usually make of yourself): You aren't reaching your students. They'd rather shoot spitballs than listen to you.

You (on the hot seat): The truth is I am not reaching a group of my students [evidence]. But that doesn't mean I'm not a good teacher [implications]. I'm able to interest most of my students, and I take pride in the creative lesson plans I've developed [evidence]. It would be nice if all my students were interested in this subject, but that's not realistic [alternatives]. I'm continually trying to draw these students into the lesson and to encourage them to get involved in some scholastic activity [evidence].

Fellow teacher (breaking in): You mustn't be a very good teacher if you can't even hold their attention for fifty minutes.

You (continuing the dispute): Just because I haven't yet been successful with this small percentage of my students doesn't erase the fact that I actually am very successful with the majority of the kids I teach [implications].

Coworker: You let her walk all over you. You have no backbone. You must be a real coward.

You (on the hot seat): Discussing problems with superiors is difficult for a lot of people [alternatives]. I don't think I was as assertive with her as I am with my colleagues, but I did express my concerns in a clear, nonemotional way [evidence]. Being cautious doesn't make me a coward. She is my manager and has power over me [alternatives]. It was a delicate situation, and by erring on the side of caution I did not threaten or offend her—which would have closed the door of communication [implications]. This way, before I continue the discussion with her, I can take some time and practice saying what I want to say in an assertive but noncombative style [usefulness].

Coworker: The reason the person you phoned hung up on you is that your presentation is all wrong.

You (on the hot seat): I may not have made a stellar presentation, but it was good and I spoke clearly and with authority [evidence]. The presentation I made was pretty consistent with others I made today, and this was the first hang-up I've had in over twenty cold calls [evidence].

I don't think my presentation had anything to do with the fact that he hung up on me. He may have been in the middle of something important, or perhaps as a rule he doesn't listen to soliciting on the phone [alternatives]. Either way, it was unfortunate he hung up on me, but it's not really a reflection on my ability [implications].

If you have ideas about phone presentations you'd like to share, I'd be interested in hearing them later today, when I'm taking a break [usefulness].

Fellow nurse: Nothing you do is ever enough. The patients always want your attention, and the doctors are continually criticizing you. If you were a better nurse you could make the patients *and* the doctors happy.

You (on the hot seat): It's true—no matter how hard I work there will still be things that need my attention [evidence]. That's just part of the job. It doesn't mean I'm not a good nurse [implications].

Fellow nurse (interrupting): This is a high-pressure job, and you just don't have the drive to make it.

You (responding): It's not realistic to think I have the responsibility or the power to make either the patients or the doctors happy. I can keep the patients as comfortable as possible, and I can help the doctors manage their workload, but I am not responsible for their happiness [alternatives].

It's a high-pressure job, and I'd like to learn some ways of handling the pressure. I'll set aside some time to talk to the more experienced nurses about how they manage the pressure [usefulness].

It's your turn now. Take twenty minutes and sit on the hot seat while your friend throws criticisms at you of the sort you say to yourself. Dispute them with everything you have. Once you have convinced yourself and your friend that you have a plausible way out, go on to the next criticism. After twenty minutes switch roles.

Review

THIS CHAPTER was designed to give you two basic skills to use at work.

First, you learned to tune into your own negative dialogue by writing down the beliefs you have when adversity strikes. You saw that when these beliefs were pessimistic, dejection and passivity usually followed. If you could change those automatic explanations of adversity, you could change the consequent feelings to invigoration and good cheer.

To do this, you practiced disputing your pessimistic beliefs. You did this by writing down your disputations when they arose at work and in imagination. Then you used the externalization of voices to give you more practice.

This is the beginning. The next part is up to you. Now, each time you face adversity listen carefully to your explanations of it. When they are pessimistic, actively dispute them. Use evidence, alternatives, implications, and usefulness as guideposts when you dispute yourself. Use distraction if necessary. Let this become the new habit to supplant the automatic pessimistic explanations you used to make all the time.

15

Flexible Optimism

> "Hope" is the thing with feathers—
> That perches in the soul—
> And sings the tune without the words—
> And never stops—at all—
>
> Emily Dickinson
> No. 254 (c. 1861)

THE FEARS THAT haunt me at four in the morning have changed in the last two months. So, in fact, has my whole life. I have a new daughter, Lara Catrina Seligman. She is a beauty. Now, as I type, she is suckling at her mother's breast, and every minute or so she stops, stares penetratingly at me (deep blue eyes on amazingly azure-tinted whites) and breaks into a smile. Smiling is her latest accomplishment. Her smiles take up her whole face. I think of the baby humpback whale I saw last winter in Hawaii, far off the Kona coast of the Big Island, so happy just to be alive, breaching joyously over and over, with her more sedate parents standing guard. Lara's smile is overwhelming, and it comes back to me at four in the morning.

What does the future hold for her? What will become of all that affirmation? A huge new generation is just being born. The *New York Times* reports that married American women are now, suddenly, almost twice as likely to plan to have children as they were ten years ago. This new generation is our affirmation of the future. But it will be a generation in peril— the usual atomic and political and environmental peril, of course, but also a spiritual and psychological peril.

The peril, though, may have a cure, and learned optimism may have a role in that cure.

Depression Revisited

AS WE SAW in chapter four, depression has been on the rise since World War II. Young people today are ten times likelier to suffer severe depression than their grandparents were, and depression takes a particularly heavy toll among women and among the young. There is no sign that the epidemic of depression is easing, and my four A.M. fears tell me that for Lara and her generation, this is the real peril.

To explain why depression is so much more common now and why modern life in developed countries makes its children so vulnerable to crippling depression, I want to look first at two other alarming trends, the waxing of the self and the waning of the commons.

The Waxing of the Self

THE SOCIETY we live in exalts the self. It takes the pleasures and pains, the successes and failures of the individual with unprecedented seriousness. Our economy increasingly thrives on individual whim. Our society grants power to the self that selves have never had before: to change the self and even to change the way the self thinks. For this is the age of personal control. The self has expanded to such a point that individual helplessness is deemed something to remedy, rather than our expected and accepted lot in life.

When the assembly line was created at the turn of this century, it at first presented the self with no problems of personal control. We could buy only white refrigerators because the assembly line made it more profitable to paint every refrigerator the same color. In the 1950s, however, with the advent of the transistor and of rudimentary machine intelligence, choice began to be imposed upon us, for it became just as profitable to encrust every hundredth refrigerator with rhinestones, if there had been a market for them. Machine intelligence opened an enormous market for customization, a market that thrived on individual choice. Now blue jeans are no longer all blue; they come in dozens of colors and hundreds of varieties. With the permutations of options available, you are offered tens of millions of models of new cars. There are hundreds of kinds of aspirin and thousands of kinds of beer.

To create the market for all this, advertising whipped up a great enthusiasm for personal control. The deciding, choosing, hedonistically preoccupied individual became big business. When the individual has a lot of money to spend, individualism becomes a powerful, and profitable, worldview.

During this same period, America was becoming a Croesus-rich country. Although millions of people are left out of the prosperity, Americans on the average now have more buying power than any other people in history. Wealth today means something different from what it did in centuries past. Consider the medieval prince: He was wealthy, but most of what he owned was inalienable. He could no more sell his land and go out and buy horses than he could sell his title. His wealth, unlike ours, could not be translated directly into purchasing power. Our wealth, in contrast, is tied to the bewildering array of choices opened to us by the process that produced the rhinestone refrigerator. We have more food, more clothes, more education, more concerts and books, more knowledge, some even say more love to choose from, than any other people ever had.

Along with this escalation in material expectations has come an escalation in what counts as acceptable in work and in love. Our job used to be counted satisfactory if it brought home the bacon. Not so today. It must also be meaningful. There must be room to move up. It must provide for a comfortable retirement. Coworkers must be congenial and the endeavor ecologically sound.

Marriage also now requires more than it used to. It's no longer just a matter of raising children. Our mate must be eternally sexy, and thin, and interesting to talk to, and good at tennis. These inflated expectations are rooted in the expansion of choice.

Who chooses? The individual. The modern individual is not the peasant of yore with a fixed future yawning ahead. He (and now she, effectively doubling the market) is a frantic trading floor of options, decisions, and preferences. And the result is a new kind of self, a "maximal" self.

The self has a history. In one form or another, it has been around for a long time, its properties varying with the time and with the culture. From the Middle Ages until the late Renaissance the self was minimal; in a painting by Giotto, everyone but Jesus looks like everyone else. Toward the end of the Renaissance the self expanded, and in Rembrandts and El Grecos the bystanders no longer all look like members of a chorus.

The expansion of the self has continued into our times. Our wealth and our technology have culminated in a self that chooses, that feels pleasure and pain, that dictates action, that optimizes or satisfices, and that even has rarefied attributes—like esteem and efficacy and confidence and control. I call this new self, with its absorbing concern for its gratifications and losses, the maximal self to distinguish it from what it has replaced, the minimal, or Yankee, self, the self our grandparents had. The Yankee self, like the medieval self, did little more than just behave; it was certainly less preoccupied with how it felt. It was less concerned with feelings and more concerned with duty.

For better or for worse, we are now a culture of maximal selves. We freely choose among an abundance of customized goods and services and reach beyond them to grasp more exquisite freedoms. Along with the freedoms the expanded self brings some dangers. Chief among them is massive depression. I believe that our epidemic of depression is a creature of the maximal self.

If it had happened in isolation, exalting the self might have had a positive effect, leading to more fully lived lives. But it was not to work out that way. The waxing of the self in our time coincided with a diminished sense of community and loss of higher purpose. These together proved rich soil for depression to grow in.

The Waning of the Commons

THE LIFE COMMITTED to nothing larger than itself is a meager life indeed. Human beings require a context of meaning and hope. We used to have ample context, and when we encountered failure, we could pause and take our rest in that setting—our spiritual furniture—and revive our sense of who we were. I call the larger setting the commons. It consists of a belief in the nation, in God, in one's family, or in a purpose that transcends our lives.

In the past quarter-century, events occurred that so weakened our commitment to larger entities as to leave us almost naked before the ordinary assaults of life. As has often been observed, the assassinations, the Vietnam War, and Watergate combined to destroy for many the idea that our nation was a means through which we could accomplish lofty goals. Those of you who grew up in the early 1960s probably sensed this, as I did, on November 22, 1963, as we watched our vision of the future wiped out. We lost hope that our society could cure human ills. It's a commonplace, perhaps, but an accurate observation, that many in my generation shifted their commitment, out of fear and out of despair, from careers in public service to careers in which we could at least make ourselves happy.

This shift from the public good to private goods was reinforced by the assassinations of Martin Luther King, Jr., Malcolm X, and Robert Kennedy. The Vietnam War taught those a bit younger the same lesson. The futility and cruelty of a decade of war eroded youth's commitment to patriotism and America. And for those who missed the lesson of Vietnam, Watergate was hard to ignore.

So commitment to the nation lost its ability to provide us with hope. This erosion of commitment, in turn, caused people to look inward for satisfaction, to focus upon their own lives. While political events were nullifying the old idea of the nation, social trends were nullifying God and the family, as scholars have noted. Religion or the family might have replaced the nation as a source of hope and purpose, keeping us from turning inward. But, by unfortunate coincidence, the erosion of belief in the nation coincided with a breakdown of the family and a decline of belief in God.

A high divorce rate, increased mobility, and twenty years of low birthrate are the culprits in the erosion of family. Because of frequent divorce, the family is no longer the abiding institution it once was, a sanctuary that would always be there unchanged when we needed balm on our wounds. Easy mobility—the ability to pick up and move great distances—tends to shatter family cohesion. Finally, having no siblings or just one—which is the case in so many American families—isolates a person. The extra attention that results when parents are centered on just one or two children, although gratifying to the kids in the short run (it actually ups their mean IQ about half a point), in the long run gives them the illusion that their pleasures and pains are rather more momentous than they are.

So put together the lack of belief that your relationship to God matters, the breakdown of your belief in the benevolent power of your country, and the breakdown of the family. Where can one now turn for identity, for purpose, and for hope? When we need spiritual furniture, we look around and see that all the comfortable leather sofas and stuffed chairs have been removed and all that's left to sit on is a small, frail folding chair: the self. And the maximal self, stripped of the buffering of any commitment to what is larger in life, is a setup for depression.

Either growing individualism alone or a declining commons alone would increase vulnerability to depression. That the two have coincided in America's recent history is, in my analysis, why we now have an epidemic of depression. The mechanism through which it works is learned helplessness.

In chapters four and five we saw that when individuals face failures they cannot control, they become helpless. And as this book has shown, helplessness becomes hopelessness and escalates into full-blown depression when a person explains his failures with permanent, pervasive, and personal causes.

Life is inevitably full of personal failures. We rarely get all we aspire to. Frustration, defeat, and rejection are daily experiences. In an individualistic culture such as ours, which places little importance on anything beyond the self, a person gets scant comfort from society when personal loss occurs. More "primitive" societies go out of their way to nurture the individual when loss occurs, and thus prevent helplessness from becoming hopelessness. A psychological anthropologist, Buck Schieffelin, has tried, without success, to find an equivalent of depression among the Stone Age Kaluli tribesmen of New Guinea. Schieffelin suggests that the reciprocity between the individual and the Kaluli tribe prevents depression. When a Kaluli's pig runs away and he displays his grief over the loss, the tribe will give him another pig. Loss is recompensed by the group, and helplessness does not escalate into hopelessness, loss does not escalate into despair.

But our epidemic of depression is not merely a matter of the paltry comfort we get from society at large. In many ways extreme individualism tends to maximize pessimistic explanatory style, prompting people to explain commonplace failures with permanent, pervasive, and personal causes. The growth of the individual, for example, means that failure is probably my fault—because who else is there but me? The decline of the commons means that failure is permanent and pervasive. To the extent that larger, benevolent institutions (God, nation, family) no longer matter, personal failures seem catastrophic. Because time in an individualistic society seems to end with our own death, individual failure seems permanent. There is no consolation for personal failure. It contaminates all of life. To the extent that larger institutions command belief, any personal failure seems less eternal and less pervasively undermining.

Changing the Balance

SO THAT IS my diagnosis: The epidemic of depression stems from the much-noted rise in individualism and the decline in the commitment to the common good. This means there are two ways out: First, changing the balance of individualism and the commons; second, exploiting the strengths of the maximal self.

The Limits of Individualism

DO THE MAXIMAL SELF and its traps tell us anything about the long-term future of individualism? I believe unbridled individualism has such negative consequences that, as it destroys us, it may destroy itself.

For one thing, a society that exalts the individual to the extent ours now does will be riddled with depression. And as it becomes apparent that individualism produces a tenfold increase in depression, individualism will become a less appealing creed to live by.

A second and perhaps more important factor is meaninglessness. I am not going to be foolish enough to attempt to define *meaning* for you, but one necessary condition for meaning is the attachment to something larger than you are. The larger the entity you can attach yourself to, the more meaning you can derive. To the extent that it is now difficult for young people to take seriously their relationship to God, to care about their duties to the country, or to be part of a large and abiding family, meaning in life will be very difficult to find.

The self, to put it another way, is a very poor site for meaning.

If an individualism without commitment to the commons produces depression and meaninglessness on a massive scale, then something has to give. What? One possibility is that exaggerated individualism will fade away, that the maximal self will change back into the Yankee self. Another, frightening possibility is that, in order to shed depression and attain meaning, we will rashly surrender the newly won freedoms that individualism brings, giving up personal control and concern for the individual. The twentieth century is riddled with disastrous examples of societies that have done just this to cure their ills. The current yearning for fundamentalist religion throughout the world appears to be such a response.

The Strengths of the Maximal Self

THERE ARE TWO other possibilities, both more hopeful. Both exploit the strengths of the maximal self. The first changes the balance between the self and the commons by choosing to expand its commitment to the commons. The second uses learned optimism.

Moral Jogging

ALTHOUGH ITS DEFENSES have been unknown and untapped until recently, the maximal self is not defenseless: It is self-improving. Perhaps, through the very process of improvement, it can come to see that its inordinate preoccupation with itself, while gratifying in the short run, is bad for its well-being in the long run.

Among the choices the maximal self might make is a paradoxical one. Selfishly, as a tactic of self-improvement, it might actually choose to scale down its own importance, in the knowledge that depression and meaninglessness follow from self-preoccupation. Perhaps we could retain our belief in the importance of the individual but diminish our preoccupation with our own comfort and discomfort. This would allow room for a new attachment to larger things.

Even if we want it, a commitment to the commons is not going to spring up overnight in a culture as individualistic as our own. There is still too much self. A new tactic is in order.

Consider jogging. Many of us now choose to jog. We slog along in all sorts of weather, waking up at ungodly hours to do so. The activity in itself gives most of us little or no pleasure. It is sometimes annoying and not infrequently painful. We do it because it appeals to our long-term self-interest. We believe that in the long run we will be better off, that we will live longer and healthier lives and be more attractive if we engage in this daily flagellation. A little daily self-denial is exchanged for long-term self-enhancement. Once we became convinced that lack of exercise would likely be costly to our health and well-being, the alternative of jogging became attractive.

Individualism and selfishness present a wholly parallel situation. Depression, I have argued, stems partly from an overcommitment to the self and an undercommitment to the common good. This state of affairs is hazardous to our health and well-being just as lack of exercise and certain cholesterols are. The consequence of preoccupation with our own successes and failures and lack of serious commitment to the commons is increased depression, poor health, and lives without meaning.

How do we—in our own self-interest—lessen our investment in ourselves and heighten our investment in the commons? The answer may be "moral jogging."

The sacrifice involved in giving to others and spending serious time, money, and effort enhancing the common good does not come naturally to the present generation. Looking out for number one is what seems to come naturally these days. A generation ago it was rest and feasting that came naturally—the ideal Sunday; yet we have become convinced it is better for us to forgo these pleasures, and we now spend Sundays doing the opposite: exercising and dieting. Big changes, then, are at least possible.

How can we break the strong habits of selfishness in ourselves and our children? Exercise—not physical but moral—may be the antidepressant tactic we need. Consider adopting one of the following for yourself:

- Put aside 5 percent of last year's taxable income to give away, not to charities like United Way, which do the work for you; you must give the money away yourself, personally. Among potential recipients in the charitable field you are interested in, you must advertise that you are giving away $3,000 (or whatever) and for what general purposes. You must interview prospective grantees and decide among requests. You give out the money and follow its use to a successful conclusion.

- Give up some activity which you do regularly for your own pleasure—eating out once a week, watching a rented movie on Tuesday night, hunting on fall weekends, playing video games when you come home from work, shopping for new shoes. Spend this time (the equivalent of an evening a week) in an activity devoted to the well-being of others or of the community at large: helping in a soup kitchen or a school-board campaign, visiting AIDS patients, cleaning the public park, fund-raising for your alma mater. Use the money you saved by canceling the pleasurable activity to further that cause.

- When asked by a homeless person for money, talk to him. Judge as well as you can if he will use the money for nondestructive purposes. If you think he will, give it to him (give no less than five dollars). Frequent areas where you will find beggars, talking to the homeless and giving money to the ones in true need. Spend three hours per week doing this.

- When you read of particularly heroic or despicable acts, write letters: fan letters to people who could use your praise and mend-your-ways letters to people and organizations you detest. Follow up with letters to politicians and others who can act directly. Spend three hours per week at this. Do it slowly. Compose the letters every bit as carefully as you would a crucial report for your company.

- Teach your children how to give things away. Have them set aside one-fourth of their allowance to give away. They should discover a needy person or project to give this money to, personally.

It is not necessary to undertake this in a selfless spirit. It is perfectly all right for you to do this because it is good for you, regardless of its effect on the common good.

It might be argued that increased contact with the commons can be depressing, and that if it's depression you want to escape, better to mingle with the rich and beautiful in Acapulco than spent a night proctoring a homeless shelter. One might assume that visiting mortally ill AIDS patients once a week would be a surefire recipe for weekly depression. And there's no denying that for some people, that might be the case. But I would suggest that exposure to human suffering, while saddening, is not "depressing" as we have used the term in this book. What is authentically depressing is to *imagine* oneself trapped in a world full of monsters—the uncouth, unkempt poor, the emaciated sufferers from terminal AIDS, and so on. Experienced volunteers, however, report that a major surprise for them has been the lift they derive from their work. They discover, through contact, that the poor and the sick are not monsters but very human beings; that modest heroism among the afflicted is the rule rather than the exception; that while what they see as volunteers may sadden them it does not depress them; and that quite often they are deeply moved. It is liberating to see firsthand that among the theoretically helpless there is frequently an amazing degree of mastery, spiritual and psychological.

If you engage in activity in service of the commons long enough, it will gain meaning for you. You may find that you get depressed less easily, that you get sick less often, and that you feel better acting for the common good than indulging in solitary pleasures. Most important, an emptiness inside you, the meaninglessness that rampant individualism nurtures, will begin to fill.

Surely in this age of choice, this choice is ours.

Learned Optimism

THE SECOND WAY of exploiting the strengths of the maximal self has been the topic of this book. We have seen throughout how depression follows from a pessimistic way of thinking about failure and loss. Learning how to think more optimistically when we fail gives us a permanent skill for warding off depression. It also can help us achieve more and have better health.

Advocating that we can learn optimism would have made little sense, however, before the rise of the maximal self. A society that viewed depression as stemming from bad genes or bad biology would see little point in trying to change what we think when we fail. A society that views the self as minimal would not be much interested in psychology in the first place. But when a society exalts the self, as ours does, the self, its thoughts and their consequences become subjects of careful science, and of therapy and self-improvement. This improved self is not a chimera. As we have seen, its own level of optimism can profoundly change what will happen to it, and its optimism can itself be changed.

My daughter Lara's generation, if fortune holds, may view depression as stemming from how we think, and more important, it may view how we think as changeable. One of the great bulwarks of the maximal self is that it believes the self can change the way it thinks. And this belief allows change to take place.

I do not believe learned optimism alone will stem the tide of depression on a society-wide basis. Optimism is just a useful adjunct to wisdom. By itself it cannot provide meaning. Optimism is a tool to help the individual achieve the goals he has set for himself. It is in the choice of the goals themselves that meaning—or emptiness—resides. When learned optimism is coupled with a renewed commitment to the commons, our epidemic of depression and meaninglessness may end.

Flexible Optimism

THERE CAN BE little doubt about it: Optimism is good for us. It is also more fun: What goes on in our head from minute to minute is more pleasant. But optimism and optimism alone cannot remedy the depression, the failure, and the ill health that have been the topic of this book. Optimism is no panacea. As we have seen above and in earlier chapters, it has its limits. For one thing, it may work better in some cultures than in others. For another, it may sometimes keep us from seeing reality with the necessary clarity. Finally, it may help some to evade responsibility for their failures. But these limits are just that: limits. They do not nullify the benefits of optimism; rather they put it in perspective.

In the first chapter we talked about two ways of looking at the world, the optimistic and the pessimistic. Until now, if you were a pessimist you had no choice but to live in pessimism. You would endure frequent depressions. Your work and your health would suffer. It would always be wet weather in your soul. In exchange for this you might have gained a keener sense of reality and a stronger sense of responsibility.

You now have a choice. If you learn optimism, you can choose to use its techniques whenever you need them—without becoming a slave to them.

For example, let's say you have learned the techniques well. When you face defeats and setbacks, you are now able to curtail depression by disputing the catastrophic thoughts that used to plague you. Along comes a new setback. Your child, let's call her May, is in kindergarten. May is the youngest and the smallest kindergartner. She faces the prospect of being less mature than her classmates year after year. Her teacher wants to hold her back and have her repeat the year. And you are now worrying about this. Holding her back a year—a depressing prospect.

You might, if you choose, launch into all the disputations that would let you think that she should go on to the first grade: She has such a high IQ, her musical talents are way above kindergarten level, she's very pretty. But you can also choose not to dispute. You can say to yourself that this is one of those moments that call for seeing reality with merciless clarity, not one of those moments that call for warding off your own depression. Your daughter's future is at stake. The cost of being wrong here outweighs the importance of fighting off your own demoralization. So this is the time to take stock. You can choose *not* to dispute the pessimistic thoughts.

What you now have is more freedom—an additional choice. You can choose to use optimism when you judge that less depression, or more achievement, or better health is the issue. But you can also choose not to use it, when you judge that clear sight or owning up is called for. Learning optimism does not erode your sense of values or your judgment. Rather it frees you to use a tool to better achieve the goals you set. It allows you to use to better effect the wisdom you have won by a lifetime of trials.

And what of the born optimist? Until now, he was as much a slave to the tyrannies of optimism as the pessimist was to the tyrannies of pessimism. He got great benefits: less depression, better health, higher achievement. He was even more likely to be elected to high office. But he paid a price: benign illusions, a weaker sense of responsibility. Until now.

The optimist is also set free by the knowledge of what optimism does and how it works. He too can invoke his values and his judgment and say to himself that the present moment does not call for his very effective habits of disputing dire thoughts. This moment is a time for heeding their call. Now he can choose whether to use his disputing tactics, since he knows their benefits and their cost.

So optimism's benefits are not unbounded. Pessimism has a role to play, both in society at large and in our own lives; we must have the courage to endure pessimism when its perspective is valuable. What we want is not blind optimism but flexible optimism—optimism with its eyes open. We must be able to use pessimism's keen sense of reality when we need it, but without having to dwell in its dark shadows.

The benefits of this kind of optimism are, I believe, without limit.

Notes

Chapter One

page   9 *In 1959, Noam Chomsky*: N. Chomsky, Review of *Verbal Behavior* by B.F. Skinner, *Language*, 35 (1959), 26–58.

10 *With these freedoms*: Gerald Klerman, during his tenure as administrator of the federal Alcohol, Drug Abuse, and Mental Health Administration (ADAMHA), sponsored several large-scale studies to find out how much mental illness existed in America. In "The Age of Melancholy?", *Psychology Today*, April 1979, pp. 37–42. Klerman presents some of the alarming statistics on the prevalence of depression today.

Until recently: Sigmund Freud presents the psychoanalytic theory in the speculative but spellbinding paper "Mourning and Melancholia," in *Standard Edition of the Complete Psychological Works of Sigmund Freud*, ed. and trans. J. Strachey, Vol. 14 (London: Hogarth Press, 1957; originally published 1917), 237–58. Freud distinguishes mourning, a normal condition, from melancholia, a mental disorder. Modern psychological research, in contrast, highlights the continuity of the two conditions.

11 *The other, more acceptable*: Two useful works by partisans of the biomedical position are R.R. Fieve, *Moodswing* (New York: William Morrow, 1975) and, more technically, D.F. Klein and J.M. Davis, *Diagnosis and Drug Treatment of Psychiatric Disorders* (Baltimore: Williams and Wilkins, 1969).

16 *Each of us carries*: I am indebted to Robertson Davies's marvelous essay "What Every Girl Should Know," in *One Half of Robertson Davies* (New York: Viking, 1977) for the apt phrase "the word in heart." I am indebted to him for much else besides.

Chapter Two

19 *It's the dogs*: The transfer experiments ultimately demonstrated that Pavlovian conditioning could energize or inhibit instrumental learning (see R.A. Rescorla

and R.L. Solomon, "Two-Process Learning Theory: Relationship Between Pavlovian Conditioning and Instrumental Learning," *Psychological Review*, 74 [1967], 151–82).

22–8 *I returned to the lab*: A fuller account, and complete bibliography, of the helplessness experiments in animals is found in M. Seligman, *Helplessness: On Depression, Development, and Death* (San Francisco: Freeman, 1975). See also S.F. Maier and M. Seligman, "Learned Helplessness: Theory and Evidence," *Journal of Experimental Psychology: General*, 105 (1976), 3–46.

27 *When worldviews clash*: An account of a several-day debate between the behaviorist and cognitive views on learned helplessness was published in *Behavior Research and Therapy* 18 (1980), 459–512. You can decide for yourself who won.

The behaviorists' acrobatic: An account of the role of epicycles can be found in T. Kuhn, *The Copernican Revolution: Planetary Astronomy in the Development of Western Thought* (Cambridge, Mass.: Harvard University Press, 1957), 59–64.

29 *According to Hiroto's*: See D.S. Hiroto, "Locus of Control and Learned Helplessness," *Journal of Experimental Psychology*, 102 (1974), 187–93.

Chapter Three

40 *This view ran*: For an account of the role attribution theory plays in achievement situations see B. Weiner, I. Frieze, A. Kukla, L. Reed, S. Rest, and R.M. Rosenbaum, *Perceiving the Causes of Success and Failure* (Morristown, N.J.: General Learning Press, 1971) and Julian Rotter's classic monograph "Generalized Expectancies for Internal Versus External Control of Reinforcement," *Psychological Monographs*, 80 (1966) (1, Whole No. 609).

43 *At that moment*: The special issue of the *Journal of Abnormal Psychology*, 87 (1978), contained the Abramson, Seligman, and Teasdale reformulation, about a dozen other articles, mostly critical of original helplessness theory, and some heated replies and rebuttals.

Since that time there have been hundreds of journal articles and scores of doctoral dissertations about explanatory style, learned helplessness, and depression. This massive literature has been controversial, but consensus has emerged that pessimistic explanatory style and depression are robustly related, as the theory predicts. P. Sweeney, K. Anderson, and S. Bailey, "Attributional Style in Depression: A Meta-analytic Review," *Journal of Personality and Social Psychology*, 50 (1986), 974–91, review 104 studies excluding all those from my own laboratory. C. Robins, "Attributions and Depression: Why Is the Literature So Inconsistent?" *Journal of Personality and Social Psychology*, 54 (1988), 880–9, concludes that studies that have not found the predicted pessimism-depression relationship consistently used inappropriately small samples.

H. Tenen, and S. Herzberger, "Attributional Style Questionnaires," in J. Keyser and R.C. Sweetland, eds., *Test Critiques*, Vol. 4 (1986), 20–30, review the history and use of the questionnaire.

48 *Whether or not*: The most up-to-date variant of hope theory is L.Y. Abramson, G.I. Metalsky, and L.B. Alloy, "Hopelessness Depression: A Theory-Based

Process-Oriented Sub-type of Depression," *Psychological Review*, 96 (1989), 358–72.

52 *There is a . . .* : The conflict between self-blame and responsibility, on the one hand, and helplessness on the other was first discussed in a lucid paper about depression by L.Y. Abramson and H. Sackeim, "A Paradox in Depression: Uncontrollability and Self-blame," *Psychological Bulletin*, 84 (1977), 838–51. How, they ask, is it possible for a depressed person both to believe he is to blame for the tragedies in his life *and* to believe he is helpless?

Chapter Four

The most illuminating general reference I know on the psychology of depression is still Aaron T. Beck's 1967 classic *Depression* (New York: Hoeber). Two excellent guides to treatment are Albert Ellis, *Reason and Emotion in Psychotherapy* (New York: Stuart, 1962), and A.T. Beck, A.J. Rush, B.F. Shaw, and G. Emery, *Cognitive Therapy of Depression: A Treatment Manual* (New York: Guilford, 1979).

54 *When in a pessimistic*: For unpacking the functions of complicated everyday objects, see David Macaulay, *The Way Things Work* (Dorling Kindersley, 1988).

55 *Bipolar depression always*: M.G. Allen, "Twin Studies of Affective Illness," *Archives of General Psychiatry*, 33 (1976), 1476–8.

57 *Aaron Beck*: The dialogue about wallpaper comes from Beck, et al., *Cognitive Therapy of Depression*, 130–1.

59 *How depressed are you*: The CES-D (Center for Epidemiological Studies–Depression) Test is a widely used inventory of the symptoms of depression. The CES-D scale: a self-report depression scale for research in the general population. L. Radloff, *Applied Psychological Measurement*, 1 (1977), 385–401.

63–5 *As you took the test*: In "The Age of Melancholy?" (*Psychology Today*, April 1979, 37–42), Gerald Klerman presents some of the alarming statistics on the prevalence of depression and coins the term "Age of Melancholy." The two major studies that found the epidemic of depression are L. Robins, J. Helzer, M. Weissman, H. Orvaschel, E. Gruenberg, J. Burke and D. Regier, "Lifetime Prevalence of Specific Psychiatric Disorders in Three Sites," *Archives of General Psychiatry*, 41 (1984), 949–58, and G. Klerman, P. Lavori, J. Rice, T. Reich, J. Endicott, N. Andreasen, M. Keller and R. Hirschfeld, "Birth Cohort Trends in Rates of Major Depressive Disorder Among Relatives of Patients with Affective Disorder," *Archives of General Psychiatry*, 42 (1985), 689–93. Both these studies are gold mines for the serious student of abnormality.

My one dissent from these important studies is that the biomedically inclined authors speak of them as indicating a "gene-environment interaction over time" in the production of so much depression today. I see no evidence at all in their data for an interaction; rather, the effect appears to be purely environmental. *Both* those who are genetically vulnerable (the relatives) and the public in general (the ECA population) seem to be getting depressed at much higher rates recently.

65 *Not only is severe depression*: The finding that depression now starts younger

comes from the elegant mathematization of the data from T. Reich, P. Van Eerdewegh, J. Rice, J. Mullaney, G. Klerman and J. Endicott, "The Family Transmission of Primary Depressive Disorder," *Journal of Psychiatric Research*, 21 (1987), 613–24.

page 66 *Wilbur and Orville*: I am grateful to Seymour Papert, who made this clever observation about modeling intelligence in about 1970 to the members of a group that is not supposed to exist (Psychological Round Table).

67–70 *Thus was the learned-helplessness*: The criteria for adequacy in a model of psychopathology have been enumerated by L.Y. Abramson and M. Seligman, "Modeling Psychopathology in the Laboratory: History and Rationale," in J. Maser and M. Seligman, eds., *Psychopathology: Experimental Models* (San Francisco: Freeman, 1977), 1–27. The major criterion is the mapping of symptoms from model to pathology. As the reader can see, this criterion is met extraordinarily well in this case.

The most detailed argument for the close symptom correspondence of learned helplessness and DSM-III-R–diagnosed depression is made by J.M. Weiss, P.G. Simson, M.J. Ambrose, A. Webster, and L.J. Hoffman, "Neurochemical Basis of Behavioral Depression," *Advances in Behavioral Medicine*, 1 (1985), 253–75. This paper and the important work of Sherman and Petty also lay out the powerful brain-chemistry and pharmacological similarities between learned helplessness and depression (see, for example, A.D. Sherman and F. Petty, "Neurochemical Basis of Antidepressants on Learned Helplessness," *Behavioral and Neurological Biology*, 30 [1982], 119–34).

Chapter Five

73 *"The troubled person"*: Beck's quote is from A.T. Beck, *Cognitive Therapy and the Emotional Disorders* (New York: New American Library, 1976).

A progenitor: Wolpe's revolutionary findings were published in J. Wolpe, *Psychotherapy by Reciprocal Inhibition* (Stanford: Stanford University Press, 1958). Freud's theory of phobia is laid down in the famous 1909 Little Hans case (S. Freud, "The Analysis of a Phobia in a Five-year-old Boy" in *Collected Papers of Freud*, Vol. III [London: Hogarth Press, 1950], 149–289).

Wolpe's therapy has generated a great deal of outcome research, mostly showing that it works very effectively on phobias, without the symptom substitution that Freudian theory predicts. There is still dispute, however, about what its active ingredients are. For a review, see A.E. Kazdin and L.A. Wilcoxon, "Systematic Desensitization and Nonspecific Treatment Effects: A Methodological Evaluation," *Psychological Bulletin*, 83 (1976), 729–58.

75 *Our reasoning*: The NIMH collaborative study was recently published (I. Elkin, P. Pilkonis, J.P. Docherty, and S. Sotsky, "Conceptual and Methodological Issues in Comparative Studies of Psychotherapy and Pharmacotherapy," *American Journal of Psychiatry*, 145 (1988), 909–17.

Perhaps even more important, because it also tracked *how* therapy worked as well as documenting that cognitive therapy worked as well as tricyclic drugs, is S.D. Hollon, R.J. DeRubeis, and M.D. Evans, "Combined Cognitive Therapy and Pharmacotherapy in the Treatment of Depression," in D. Manning and A. Frances, eds., *Combination Drug and Psychotherapy in Depression*

(Washington, D.C.: American Psychiatric Press, 1990). This study will, I predict, become the classic in the field.

76–80 *The difference between*: Detailed reviews of explanatory style and depression, and extensive bibiliographies, can be found in C. Peterson and M. Seligman, "Causal Explanations as a Risk Factor for Depression: Theory and Evidence," *Psychological Review*, 91 (1984), 347–74; in P. Sweeney, K. Anderson, and S. Bailey, "Attributional Style in Depression: A Meta-Analytic Review," *Journal of Personality and Social Psychology*, 50 (1986), 974–91; and in L.Y. Abramson, G.I. Metalsky, and L.B. Alloy, "Hopelessness Depression: A Theory-Based Process-Oriented Sub-type of Depression," *Psychological Review*, 96 (1989), 358–72.

81–2 *First, both treatments*: The basic findings that cognitive therapy breaks up depression as well as tricyclic antidepressants do, that cognitive therapy works by changing explanatory style, and that explanatory style at the end of therapy predicts relapse come from a series of three major forthcoming papers primarily authored by Steve Hollon, Rob DeRubeis, and Mark Evans. The "Tanya" quotes are from transcripts from this study. As in the other quotes from patients in this book names and identifying facts have been changed to preserve anonymity.

82–3 *People who mull over*: Three psychologists have made the major contributions to the recent study of rumination: Julius Kuhl, Susan Nolen-Hoeksema, and Harold Zullow. See J. Kuhl, "Motivational and Functional Helplessness: The Moderating Effect of State Versus Action-Orientation," *Journal of Personality and Social Psychology*, 40 (1981), 155–70; H.M. Zullow, "The Interaction of Rumination and Explanatory Style in Depression," Master's Thesis, University of Pennsylvania, 1984; and S. Nolen-Hoeksema, *Sex Differences in Depression* (Stanford: Stanford University Press, 1990).

83–7 *Depression is primarily*: That women suffer more depression than men do is incontrovertible. *Why* is a heated question. Perhaps the best recent reviews of the topic are S. Nolen-Hoeksema, "Sex Differences in Depression: Theory and Evidence," *Psychological Bulletin*, 101 (1987), 259–82, and her important book *Sex Differences in Depression*.

89–91 *Cognitive therapy uses*: Four of the five basic moves of cognitive therapy are taken from A.T. Beck, A. J. Rush, B. F. Shaw, and G. Emery, *Cognitive Therapy of Depression: A Treatment Manual* (New York: Guilford, 1979). The fifth move, assumption challenging, is unique to Ellis (A. Ellis, *Reason and Emotion in Psychotherapy*, [New York: Stuart, 1979]). The therapies of Beck and Ellis are now very similar and one of the only distinctions concerns assumption challenging. Assumption challenging is typically not much used in the Socratic therapy of Beck, but is a large part of the more counterpropagandistic therapy of Ellis.

93 *"Meanwhile, the Ice Kings"*: I have for years collected poems, jokes, sayings, and anecdotes about optimism and pessimism. Wagoner's poem, "The Labors of Thor," in David Wagoner, *Collected Poems (1956–76)* (Bloomington: Indiana University Press, 1976), is at the top of my list. The two stanzas quoted are the closing stanzas of what I think is one of the great pieces of modern American verse. I am grateful to Bert Brim for having shown me it.

Chapter Six

page   99–106 *Even before I walked*: Most of the data on sales and explanatory style lie
        in internal reports of Foresight, Inc., of Falls Church, Va., and its business
        clients. Two papers are available, however: M. Seligman and P. Schulman,
        "Explanatory Style as a Predictor of Performance as a Life Insurance Agent,"
        Journal of Personality and Social Psychology, 50 (1986), 832–8; and P. Schul-
        man, M. Seligman, and D. Oran, "Explanatory Style Predicts Productivity
        Among Life Insurance Agents: The Special Force Study" (unpublished manu-
        script available from Foresight, Inc., 3516 Duff Drive, Falls Church, Va. 22041
        [703-820-8170]).

    104 *Success Magazine heard*: Jill Neimark, "The Power of Positive Thinkers,"
        Success Magazine, September 1987, 38–41.

    108 *That evening*: Lionel Tiger, *Optimism: The Biology of Hope* (N.Y.: Simon
        and Schuster, 1979).

    109 *Ten years ago*: Already a classic, L.B. Alloy and L.Y. Abramson, "Judgment
        of Contingency in Depressed and Nondepressed Students: Sadder but Wiser,"
        Journal of Experimental Psychology: General, 108 (1979), 441–85, was the first
        study to demonstrate depressive realism.
        Another kind of evidence: P. Lewinsohn, W. Mischel, W. Chaplin, and
        R. Barton, "Social Competence and Depression: The Role of Illusory Self-
        perceptions," *Journal of Abnormal Psychology*, 89 (1980), 203–12, demon-
        strated depressive realism in the judgment of social skill.

    110 *Still another variety*: Depressive realism seems to hold for memory as well,
        but the evidence conflicts. See, for example, R. DeMonbreun and E. Craig-
        head, "Distortion of Perception and Recall of Positive and Neutral Feedback
        in Depression," *Cognitive Therapy and Research*, 1 (1977), 311–29.
        This pattern: Lopsidedness in nondepressed people is reviewed by C. Peterson
        and M. Seligman, "Causal Explanations as a Risk Factor for Depression:
        Theory and Evidence," *Psychological Review*, 91 (1984), 347–74.

    111 *Pessimists "see the world aright"*: Ambrose Bierce, *The Devil's Dictionary*
        (N.Y.: Dover, 1958 [original edition 1911]).

Chapter Seven

    116–25 *You can measure*: The Children's Attributional Style Questionnaire
        (CASQ) is the most widely used measure of explanatory style in children
        between the ages of eight and twelve. See M. Seligman, N.J. Kaslow, L.B.
        Alloy, C. Peterson, R. Tannenbaum, and L.Y. Abramson, "Attributional
        Style and Depressive Symptoms Among Children," *Journal of Abnormal Psy-
        chology*, 93 (1984), 235–8.

    126 *Children do get*: See, for example, J. Puig-Antich, E. Lukens, M. Davies,
        D. Goetz, J. Brennan-Quattrock, and G. Todak, "Psychosocial Functioning
        in Prepubertal Major Depressive Disorders: I. Interpersonal Relationships
        During the Depressive Episode," *Archives of General Psychiatry*, 42 (1985),
        500–7. As this book was in production, Kim Puig-Antich, America's leading
        investigator of severe depression in young children, died suddenly at the age

of forty-seven. Psychiatry and psychology are much poorer for the loss of so humane and insightful an investigator.

129–30 *Let's look for a minute*: The leading investigator of helplessness in the classroom is Carol Dweck, and she and her colleagues carried out the work detailed in this section. For a review, see C.S. Dweck and B. Licht, "Learned Helplessness and Intellectual Achievement," in J. Garber and M. Seligman, eds., *Human Helplessness: Theory and Applications* (New York: Academic Press, 1980), 197–222.

131–4 *In Heidelberg in 1981*: See M. Seligman and G. Elder, "Learned Helplessness and Life-Span Development," in A. Sorenson, F. Weinert, and L. Sherrod, eds., *Human Development and the Life Course: Multidisciplinary Perspectives* (Hillsdale, N.J.: Erlbaum, 1985), 377–427.

132 *The most creative idea*: If you would like to learn to become a skilled rater of verbatim speech, a manual can be found in the appendix to P. Schulman, C. Castellon, and M. Seligman, "Assessing Explanatory Style: The Content Analysis of Verbatim Explanations and the Attributional Style Questionnaire," *Behavior Research and Therapy*, 27 (1989), 505–12. It takes about half a day to become a reliable rater.

134–5 *In addition to the findings*: This important work on vulnerability factors is found in G.W. Brown and T. Harris, *Social Origins of Depression* (London: Tavistock, 1978).

Chapter Eight

138–41 *How can you tell*: The rating scale for your child's depression is my slightly modified version of the CES–DC (Center for Epidemiological Studies–Depression Child) test. This test was devised by M. Weissman, H. Orvaschell, and N. Padian, "Children's Symptom and Social Functioning: Self-Report Scales," *Journal of Nervous and Mental Disease*, 168 (1980), 736–40.

141 *I elaborated*: For more on Carol Dweck's work, see C.S. Dweck and B. Licht, "Learned Helplessness and Intellectual Achievement," in J. Garber and M. Seligman, eds., *Human Helplessness: Theory and Applications* (New York: Academic Press, 1980), 197–222.

143–9 *In the fall of 1985*: For a representative article from the Princeton-Penn Longitudinal Study, see S. Nolen-Hoeksema, J. Girgus, and M. Seligman, "Learned Helplessness in Children: A Longitudinal Study of Depression, Achievement, and Explanatory Style," *Journal of Personality and Social Psychology*, 51 (1986), 435–42.

145–7 *Because divorce and serious turmoil*: There has been some convergence of research lately on the surprisingly deleterious effects on children of divorce, separation, and most of all, parental fighting. Three important references: J. Wallerstein and S. Blakeslee, *Second Chances: Men, Women, and Children a Decade After Divorce* (New York: Ticknor & Fields, 1989); E.M. Hetherington, M. Cox, and C. Roger, "Effects of Divorce on Parents and Children," in M.E. Lamb, ed., *Non-traditional Families* (Hillsdale, N.J.: Erlbaum, 1982), 233–88; and E.M. Cummings, D. Vogel, J.S. Cummings, and M. El-Sheikh, "Children's Responses to Different Forms of Expression of Anger Between Adults," *Child Development*, 60 (1989), 1392–1404.

page 147 *I am not naïve*: For the experiments on resolution of fights, see E.M. Cummings
       et al., "Children's Responses to Different Forms of Expression of Anger
       Between Adults."
      148 *I believe it is important*: The destructive effects of anger, as well as its (over-
       blown) constructive aspects, are ably reviewed in Carol Tavris's bold book
       Anger: The Misunderstood Emotion (New York: Simon and Schuster, 1982).
      149–50 *As you know*: For an excellent treatment of sex differences in depression,
       see S. Nolen-Hoeksema, "Sex Differences in Depression: Theory and Evi-
       dence," *Psychological Bulletin*, 101 (1987), 259–82, as well as her important
       book *Sex Differences in Depression* (Stanford: Stanford University Press,
       1990).
      151–2 *So the week the class of '87*: This work was carried out in collaboration with
       Leslie Kamen, but we were beaten to publication by Peterson and Barrett,
       who were simultaneously doing essentially the same study at another univer-
       sity. C. Peterson and L. Barrett, "Explanatory Style and Academic Perfor-
       mance Among University Freshmen," *Journal of Personality and Social
       Psychology*, 53 (1987), 603–7.
      152–3 *But at least one*: The West Point work was carried out in collaboration with
       Dick Butler, Bob Priest, and William Burke of West Point, and with Peter
       Schulman. The most important contributors, however, are the twelve hundred
       plebes of the class of 1991 who have now cooperated with this study for three
       years.

Chapter Nine

      158 *We also wanted to know*: The yearly "Elias" compendium of fascinating base-
       ball statistics is our source for batting and pitching under pressure. See
       S. Siwoff, S. Hirdt, and T. Hirdt, *The 1988 Elias Baseball Analyst* (New York:
       Collier, Macmillan Publishing Company, 1988). We also used the 1985, 1986,
       and 1987 volumes.
      165–6 *In October 1988*: See M. Seligman, S. Nolen-Hoeksema, N. Thornton, and
       K.M. Thornton, "Explanatory Style as a Mechanism of Disappointing Athletic
       Performance," *Psychological Science*, 1 (1990), 143–6.

Chapter Ten

      167–8 *Daniel was only nine*: Daniel's story is told in M. Visintainer and M. Selig-
       man, "The Hope Factor," *American Health*, 2 (1983), 58–61.
      169 *She was tremendously excited*: See E. J. Langer and J. Rodin, "Effects of
       Choice and Enhanced Personal Responsibility for the Aged: A Field Exper-
       iment in an Institutional Setting," *Journal of Personality and Social Psychol-
       ogy*, 34 (1976), 191–9.
      169–70 *Madelon Visintainer wanted*: See M. Visintainer, J. Volpicelli, and M. Sel-
       igman, "Tumor Rejection in Rats After Inescapable or Escapable Shock,"
       Science, 216 (1982), 437–9.
      170 *Actually, almost the first*: See L.S. Sklar and H. Anisman, "Stress and Coping
       Factors Influence Tumor Growth," *Science*, 205 (1979), 513–15.
       Another of Madelon's discoveries: M. Seligman, and M. Visintainer, "Tumor

Rejection and Early Experience of Uncontrollable Shock in the Rat," in F.R. Brush and J.B. Overmier, eds., *Affect, Conditioning, and Cognition: Essays on the Determinants of Behavior* (Hillsdale, N.J.: Erlbaum, 1985), 203–10.

172–3 *Researchers looking at the immune systems*: For a useful dip into this highly technical field, see S.F. Maier, M. Laudenslager, and S.M. Ryan, "Stressor Controllability, Immune Function, and Endogenous Opiates," in *Affect, Conditioning, and Cognition*, 203–10.

174 *The first systematic study*: See C. Peterson, "Explanatory Style as a Risk Factor for Illness," *Cognitive Therapy and Research*, 12 (1988), 117–30.

175 *Other studies looked*: See S. Greer, T. Morris, and K.W. Pettingale, "Psychological Response to Breast Cancer: Effect on Outcome," *The Lancet*, II (1979), 785–7.

In a later study: See the unpublished manuscript by S. Levy, M. Seligman, L. Morrow, C. Bagley, and M. Lippman, "Survival Hazards Analysis in First Recurrent Breast Cancer Patients: Seven Year Follow-up."

175–6 *Such results*: B.R. Cassileth, E.G. Lusk, D.S. Miller, L.L. Brown, and C. Miller, "Psychosocial Correlates of Survival in Malignant Disease," *New England Journal of Medicine*, 312 (1985), 1551–5; and M. Angell, "Disease as a Reflection of the Psyche," *New England Journal of Medicine*, 312 (1985), 1570–2.

177 *About a decade ago*: See R. Bartrop, L. Lockhurst, L. Lazarus, L. Kiloh, and R. Penney, "Decreased Lymphocyte Function After Bereavement," *The Lancet*, I (1979), 834–6.

Depression also seems to affect: See M. Irwin, M. Daniels, E.T. Bloom, T.L. Smith, and H. Weiner, "Life Events, Depressive Symptoms, and Immune Function," *American Journal of Psychiatry*, 144 (1987), 437–41.

To test this: see the unpublished manuscript by L. Kamen, J. Rodin, C. Dwyer, and M. Seligman, "Pessimism and Cell-mediated Immunity."

178 *Before we could answer*: See M. Burns and M. Seligman, "Explanatory Style Across the Lifespan: Evidence for Stability over 52 years," *Journal of Personality and Social Psychology*, 56 (1989), 471–7.

179–81 *We needed a large group*: See C. Peterson, M. Seligman, and G. Vaillant, "Pessimistic Explanatory Style as a Risk Factor for Physical Illness: A Thirty-five-year Longitudinal Study," *Journal of Personality and Social Psychology*, 55 (1988), 23–7.

Chapter Eleven

186 *We read*: E. Erikson, *Young Man Luther* (New York: Norton, 1957).

187–98 *What kind of president*: See H.M. Zullow, G. Oettingen, C. Peterson, and M. Seligman, "Pessimistic Explanatory Style in the Historical Record: CAVEing LBJ, Presidential Candidates and East versus West Berlin," *American Psychologist* 43 (1988), 673–82; and H.M. Zullow and M. Seligman, "Pessimistic Rumination Predicts Defeat of Presidential Candidates: 1900–1984," *Psychological Inquiry* 1 (1990).

198–204 *In 1983 I went*: See Zullow, et al., "Pessimistic Explanatory Style in the Historical Record," and G. Oettingen and M. Seligman, "Pessimism and

Behavioural Signs of Depression in East versus West Berlin," *European Journal of Social Psychology* 20 (1990), 207–20.

Chapter Twelve

The exercises in chapters twelve through fourteen originate first in the seminal work of Aaron Beck and Albert Ellis, referred to in chapters four and five. They formulated the first versions of our techniques in order to alleviate depression among those already afflicted. In 1987 Metropolitan Life asked Foresight, Inc., to adapt these techniques for a normal population and in a preventive mode, so that they could use them with their sales force—a very nondepressed group. I called on the considerable talents of Steve Hollon, professor at Vanderbilt University and editor of *Cognitive Research and Therapy*, and Art Freeman, professor at the New Jersey College of Medicine and Dentistry and one of the world's leading teachers of cognitive therapy, to help change basic cognitive therapy techniques in the two ways I have noted. Dan Oran of Foresight, Inc., and Dick Calogero of Metropolitan Life administered the workshop project; Karen Reivich was principal editor of the manuals created.

In these three chapters I draw heavily on what we did and what we learned.

page 221 *Learned optimism works*: I believe that Phillip Kendall, professor of psychology at Temple University, first used the phrase "the power of non-negative thinking" to describe the mechanism by which cognitive therapy works.

Chapter Fourteen

The techniques outlined in this chapter were developed under the auspices of Foresight, Inc. Steve Hollon, Art Freeman, Dan Oran, Karen Reivich, and I systematized the techniques of cognitive therapy for preventive use by nondepressed sales agents. Foresight developed one-, two-, and four-day workshops for businesses, based on this material. Copies can be obtained from Foresight, Inc., 3516 Duff Drive, Falls Church, Va. 22041 [703–820–8170].

Chapter Fifteen

A more detailed exposition of the role of individualism in the modern epidemic of depression can be found in M. Seligman, "Why Is There So Much Depression Today? The Waxing of the Individual and the Waning of the Commons," *The G. Stanley Hall Lecture Series*, 9 (Washington, D.C.: American Psychological Association, 1989). See also M. Seligman, "Boomer Blues," *Psychology Today*, October 1988, 50–5.

283 *Who chooses?*: Christopher Lasch's insightful *The Culture of Narcissism* (New York: Norton, 1979) makes a similar point in a rather different framework. *The self has a history*: One night over poker, Henry Gleitman made this point about background figures in medieval and Renaissance painting. I hope I have not preempted Gleitman's using it in his best-selling introductory psychology text.

The expansion of the self: Harold Zullow first used the phrase "Yankee Self" in one of my graduate seminars about individualism.

285–6 *Life is inevitably full*: The investigation of the Kaluli is found in E. Schieffelin, "The Cultural Analysis of Depressive Affect: An Example from New Guinea," in A. Kleinman and B. Good, eds., *Culture and Depression* (University of California Press, 1985).

286–90 Selfishness may not be as entrenched a habit as we think and therefore more modifiable than generally believed. See B. Schwartz, *The Battle for Human Nature* (New York: Norton, 1988).

Acknowledgments

There are four people without whose help this book would not have come into being.

First and foremost is Tom Congdon. When I finally decided I would write a book that tried to explain the field of personal control to the layman, I knew I needed help. I am vain enough to think my technical writing is pretty good, but writing dialogue, sustaining suspense, characterizing the scientists I've known were all tasks beyond anything I had done before. I met Tom and was able to convince him to work with me. Tom not only rewrote most sentences in the book, but he helped reorganize it. He challenged notions that had eluded the professionals in the field and made me rethink them. But best of all, when spirits flagged, when editors carped, when hard discs crashed, when ideas ran dry, Tom was always there to encourage and support and nurture. And he became a friend.

Dan Oran, the president of Foresight, Inc., urged me to write this book. I balked. Too much else to do: too many experiments on personal control yet undone, too many manuals for preventing depression, low achievement of infectious illness to work on, too many other walks of life in which to test optimism. He made the case more palatable by offering to write it with me. But as he made me take the project more and more seriously, I realized that it was the story of my life's work and since I was responsible for that, I wanted to be the sole author.

Dan also introduced me to Richard Pine, who became my agent. Agents, I read recently in *The New York Times*, are supposed to be the people "who never return your calls." Not Richard. He is an author's dream. He has read every word of this book at least four times. Not a few words, he urged changing. At the end of our first meeting, sensing my balkiness, Richard said, "I pray for this book. This is the sort of stuff religions are made of."

I was taken aback and repeated this extraordinary statement to my new father-in-law, a reserved British industrialist, Dennis McCarthy, the next week. "I don't know about that," he said, "but think about large companies. A successful company has both a research and a development department. You've spent the last twenty-five years doing basic research on personal control and in recent times you've begun your development phase. This book, giving away the basic ideas to the layman who wants to know how to lead a more rational life, is development of a high order." In that moment I decided to do the book. For the next year and a half it was pretty much all I did. Dennis also gave me invaluable suggestions about the business chapters.

A number of other people had very useful advice about the manuscript as a whole or about large swaths of it.

First my editor, Jonathan Segal. Jonathan's tough-minded readings of the manuscript were not only for style ("Always write up"), but about major issues of substance as well ("Emphasize flexible optimism. You no more want people to be prisoners of optimism than prisoners of pessimism. What is pessimism good for? Under what conditions should people deploy pessimism rather than optimism?" And many more). The book is meatier because of Jonathan's help.

Next, Karen Reivich. Karen writes dialogue beautifully, and I asked her to generate lots of it from her experience running and designing seminars for Foresight, Inc., in changing explanatory style. Many of the dialogues between therapist and patient, mother and child, originate in Karen's experience or in her fertile imagination. She also argued with me about the title (and subtitle) at length and helped select the poetry. I hope Karen becomes a psychologist. Tom Congdon wants her to become a writer. Both of us hold her and her talents in high esteem.

Peter Schulman has worked with me for the last eight years as the administrator of my scientific research and the vice-president for operations of Foresight, Inc. At many points in writing this book, I went to Peter and asked him to analyze still more data. "By how much in grade-point average did the West Point optimists beat the West Point pessimists?" "Does Prudential's special force do as well as Met Life's special force?" And many more. Peter's answers were always prompt, careful, and not infrequently brilliant.

My daughter, Amanda Seligman, presently a senior classics major at Princeton, read the first third of the manuscript in early draft and helped me bring it down to earth.

Terry Silver, my secretary, helped in ways too numerous to list.

Finally the twenty undergraduate and eight graduate students who took my seminar in 1989–90 at the University of Pennsylvania read the whole first draft. Many commented usefully.

A large number of other people helped with individual chapters. I am grateful to all of the following people, most of whom have allowed me to collaborate with them or whose work has directly inspired my own:

Chapter one. To get started I asked the help of several skilled writers. Ralph Keyes, Carol Stillman, and Bob Trotter all read the very first draft and each tried to point me in the right direction.

Chapter two narrates the history of learned helplessness. Though their contributions are chronicled there, Steve Maier, Bruce Overmier, Dick Solomon, and Don Hiroto must be singled out as the major forces who helped create and guide this field. The National Institute of Mental Health, the National Science Foundation, the Guggenheim Foundation, and the Woodrow Wilson Foundation all supported my work during this period.

Chapter three discusses explanatory style. This concept had its beginning with Lyn Abramson, Chris Peterson, John Teasdale, and Judy Garber. Their story is told in this chapter. Karen Reivich helped create and validate the questionnaire in this chapter. The National Institute of Mental Health (especially Jack Maser and Bob Hirschfeld), which has supported my work for over twenty years, and the National Science Foundation deserve special thanks. The Center for Advanced Study in the Behavioral Sciences also supported me during this period.

Chapters four and five are about depression. Aaron Beck and Albert Ellis must be singled out for demystifying depression and bringing it from the darkness into the penumbra. Along with Dean Schuyler and Mickey Stunkard, Beck was the mentor who showed me how depression could be cured. Gerry Klerman, Myrna Weissman, Janice Egeland, and Buck Schieffelin have all made fundamental contributions to the understanding of depression as it is found across the world. Lenore Radloff developed the CES–D. Steve Hollon, Rob DeRubeis, and Mark Evans carried out the definitive study of cognitive therapy for depression and I am grateful to them for their collaboration. Susan Nolen-Hoeksema devised and tested the theory of rumination and gender differences in depression. The National Institute of Mental Health supports my work in this area, and it must be said that without this institution's support of the hundreds of scientists in the field of affective disorders, depression would still be a mystery with no cure. Humanity should be grateful to this great American institution.

Chapter six is about success at work, and Metropolitan Life has been the inspiration for it. Met Life is also the organization in which many of the ideas were tested and validated. I am particularly grateful to Dick Calogero, who was my patient collaborator for seven years, to John Creedon, who got everything started, to Howard Mase and Bob Crimmins, who led the charge, to Al Oberlander, Joyce Jiggetts, Yvonne Miesse and the nearly 200,000 applicants and agents who have taken the Attributional Style Questionnaire. I would like to acknowledge the significant contribution of Dr. Mary Anne Layden to the authorship of this questionnaire. Numerous meetings with Amy Semmel, Lyn Abramson, Lauren Alloy, and Nadine Kaslow then refined it.

John Riley introduced me to the leaders of the insurance industry, and Dan Oran and Peter Schulman of Foresight, Inc., ran the studies and analyzed the findings. Robert Dell exemplifies what it is to be a fine "special agent," and I am grateful to him for letting me tell his intimate story. I also thank the many applicants and agents of Mutual of Omaha, Prudential, and Reliance who have taken the ASQ.

Dennis McCarthy provided insights into optimism and industry. Lauren Alloy and Lyn Abramson are the psychologists who have most shaped the field of depressive realism.

Chapters seven and eight are about parents and children. Nadine Kaslow and Richard Tanenbaum led the way in creating the CASQ. Carol Dweck's research on schoolchildren and helplessness opened up the field of achievement and explanatory style. Chris Peterson devised the CAVE technique and Glen Elder inspired its first use with historical data. The Social Science Research Council Committee on Life Span Development, led by Matilda Riley, Bert Brim, Paul

Baltes, Dave Featherman, and Judy Dunn, nurtured and inspired our longitudinal studies of children. The National Institute of Mental Health funded it.

Joan Girgus and Susan Nolen-Hoeksema have been the central contributors to the field of explanatory style and depression in children. Both read and made major changes in chapter eight. The school systems of Princeton, Trenton, and East Windsor townships in New Jersey have patiently allowed us to test their wards for the last five years. We are very grateful to the teachers, parents, and administrators, and mostly to the kids, from these schools. Cindy Fruchtman and Gilda Paul ran these studies. Willis Stetson and the admissions officials at the University of Pennsylvania, and Dick Butler, Bob Priest, and William Burke at West Point were generous collaborators. My son, David Seligman, helped me give the test at West Point.

Several of my graduate students gave me good advice about the naïveté of advising warring couples not to fight. Lisa Jaycox, Deborah Stearns, Jane Eisner, Greg Buchanan, Nicholas Maxwell, Karen Reivich, and Jane Gillham all read this chapter carefully and changed my thinking about how to present the issue.

Chapter nine is about sports. Chris Peterson did the first work on explanatory style and sports. David Rettew, Karen Reivich, and David Seligman worked long and hard on these studies. David Rettew originated the National League study. The Elias Sports Bureau's compilations of baseball statistics are a marvel. Susan Nolen-Hoeksema carried out the studies of the Berkeley swimmers; special thanks must go to Nort and Karen Moe Thornton, the Berkeley swimming coaches, and most of all to the men and women of the Berkeley varsity swim teams.

Chapter ten is about health. Madelon Visintainer, Joe Volpicelli, Steve Maier, Leslie Kamen, and Judy Rodin did the seminal work in learned helplessness, explanatory style, and health. Chris Peterson and George Vaillant led the study of explanatory style and health over the life span. Judy Rodin and Sandy Levy are the leaders and inspiration of the MacArthur studies of health, the immune system, and personality. T George Harris kept reminding me how important this work was and let the world know about it. The MacArthur Foundation, generous and adventurous souls, and the National Institute on Aging have funded this work.

Chapter eleven is about politics, culture, and religion. Harold Zullow spearheaded the work on American politics. I cheered him on. Gabriele Oettingen, likewise, spearheaded the work on explanatory style across cultures. I cheered her on. Eva Morawska and Gabriele carried out the studies of Judaism and Russian Orthodoxy. Dan Goleman suggested predicting the 1988 primaries and Alan Kors, almost twenty years ago, insisted that a rigorous and predictive psychohistory was possible. (It was also Alan who, when my book *Helplessness* came out fifteen years ago, remarked that he hoped that my next one would be about the opposite. It is.) Jack Rachman took me to the betting shops of Edinburgh. Poor man, he too bet on Dukakis.

Chapters twelve, thirteen, and fourteen are about how to change explanatory style. Art Freeman and Steve Hollon led the work which transformed Beck's principles of cognitive therapy with depressed people to workshops and exercises which nondepressed people could usefully carry out—and carry out preventively. Dan Oran and Karen Reivich administered these projects and also made major intellectual contributions to the content. Tim Beck and Albert Ellis founded this whole field and many of their ideas and schemae are incorporated.

Ed Craighead and Robert DeMonbreun wrote the first prevention program for children almost fifteen years ago, when its time had not yet come. Susan Nolen-Hoeksema and Judy Garber have also played a major role in the understanding of how to prevent depression in kids, and made useful suggestions for chapter thirteen.

Metropolitan Life in general, and Dick Calogero, Howard Mase, Bob Crimmins, Yvonne Miesse, Joyce Jiggetts, and John Creedon in particular played important roles in our studies of how to change explanatory style in industry. I am especially grateful to the agents of Metropolitan Life who have taken Foresight, Inc.'s seminars.

Chapter fifteen is about the future and I am grateful to Lara Catrina Seligman just for being part of it. T George Harris twisted my arm to write about depression and individualism, and the American Psychological Association's invitation to deliver the 1988 G. Stanley Hall Lecture provided the first occasion for these thoughts. Knopf's anonymous proofreader should be singled out for praise. She made a special trip to the Cloister's collection to check out the accuracy of the remark about Renaissance painting. Proofreading at its best. Barry Schwartz, my bridge partner and source of intellectual stimulation for over twenty years, has been a major force in getting me to rethink the questions of selfishness and individualism and the weak no trump.

Finally there have been two global influences on my life and this book. The psychology department at the University of Pennsylvania has been the home and support of all this work for twenty-five years. I owe a debt of gratitude I can never repay to my teachers, my students, and my colleagues there.

Most of all, I wish to thank Mandy McCarthy, Lara's mother, my wife. Her love, her intellectual insight, and her unflagging support allowed this book to happen.

January 24, 1990

Index